Kazan
REVISITED

Kazan REVISITED

Edited by
LISA DOMBROWSKI

WESLEYAN UNIVERSITY PRESS
MIDDLETOWN, CONNECTICUT

Wesleyan University Press
Middletown CT 06459
www.wesleyan.edu/wespress
© 2011 Wesleyan University Press
All rights reserved
Manufactured in the United States of America

Wesleyan University Press is a member of the Green Press
Initiative. The paper used in this book meets their minimum
requirement for recycled paper.

An earlier version of Jonathan Rosenbaum's "Elia Kazan,
Seen from 1973" appeared in *Cinema: A Critical Dictionary:
The Major Filmmakers Volume One*, ed. Richard Roud
(New York: Viking Press, 1980) and is hereby reprinted
with the permission of the author.

Photo on page ii courtesy of the
Wesleyan Cinema Archives.

Library of Congress Cataloging-in-Publication Data
Kaza revisited / edited by Lisa Dombrowski.
    p. cm.
ISBN 978-0-8195-7084-0 (cloth: alk. paper)
1. Kazan, Elia — Criticism and interpretation.
I. Dombrowski, Lisa.
PN1998.3.K39K39   2011
791.4302'33092 — dc22   2010033336

5 4 3 2 1

CONTENTS

ACKNOWLEDGMENTS

This book originated as part of Wesleyan University's celebration of Elia Kazan's centennial, including a partial film retrospective and an exhibition of materials from the Kazan Collection held at the Wesleyan Cinema Archives. The Kazan Collection includes correspondence, scripts, notebooks, production documents, photographs, clippings, awards, writings, and other materials associated with Kazan's life and career. Jeanine Basinger, the Curator of the Archives, and I would like to thank Michael Roth, Wesleyan's president, for his support of the centennial.

Kazan Revisited has benefited from the contributions of many here at Wesleyan. Jeanine provided the inspiration for the book, and as ever has my gratitude, love, and admiration. Joan Miller, our film archivist, assisted almost half of the writers with archival research, steered me through the photo selection, and generally served as a font of Kazan information. I greatly appreciate her patience, dedication, and encyclopedic memory. Marc Longenecker, Thaddeus Ruzicka, and Sal Privitera provided key help with film prints and frame enlargements, while Marc and Thad joined me and Steve Collins, Scott Higgins, David Laub, Katja Straub, and Jacob Bricca in discussions about Kazan's work. I am fortunate to have such creative colleagues with whom to analyze movies, laugh, and share good food. Finally, my ever-abundant hurrahs go to Lea Carlson and Joyce Heidorn, the pillars of the department, without whom Film Studies — and I — could not stand.

The editors and staff at Wesleyan University Press generously provided a home for this project and patient guidance during its production. I much appreciate the editorial and marketing suggestions of Suzanna Tamminen, Parker Smathers, Leslie Starr, and Stephanie Elliott, from whom I continue to learn about publishing.

Last in my list but always first in my heart is my family — Helen, Carol, Chuck, Eleanor, and Michael — and my partner in dance and life, Brett. The next one checking page proofs will be you!

LISA DOMBROWSKI

Introduction

What do we talk about when we talk about Elia Kazan?

We talk about his work. As an actor, director, and writer, Kazan's groundbreaking contributions to American art and culture span over five decades and continue to permeate our popular consciousness. His participation in the activism of the Group Theatre, promulgation of the Method via the Actors Studio, and acclaimed direction of Broadway milestones such as *The Skin of Our Teeth*, *A Streetcar Named Desire*, *Death of a Salesman*, and *Cat on a Hot Tin Roof* situate him as the most influential director of midcentury American theater. With films such as the adaptation of *A Streetcar Named Desire* (1951), *On the Waterfront* (1954), *East of Eden* (1955), and *Splendor in the Grass* (1961), Kazan made an equally indelible mark on cinema. Between 1948 and 1964 he was nominated for a Best Director Academy Award five times and won twice. His name is repeatedly linked with those of his many collaborators, including the era's defining writers (Tennessee Williams, Arthur Miller, John Steinbeck, Budd Schulberg) and stars (Marlon Brando, James Dean, Montgomery Clift, Warren Beatty).

Kazan's films engage seriously with the social problems and conflicts of their day, but their timeless appeals to feelings of alienation, longing, and rebellion return them to us again and again — so frequently, in fact, that their oft-quoted scenes have become ripe for parody. While my undergraduate students — all born over a decade after Kazan's last film was made — still root for Dean's misjudged, mopey Cal in *East of Eden*, they are also quick to laugh when they catch Peter Boyle and John Belushi trading lines from *On the Waterfront* as "Dueling Brandos" on an old *Saturday Night Live* rerun, or when Homer Simpson embodies the boorishness of Stanley Kowalski in the much-loved 1992 *The Simpsons* episode "A Streetcar Named Marge." They may never have seen *A Streetcar Named Desire*, but at the drop of a dime they will all yell "Stellllaaaaaaa!"

We also talk about Kazan's life — in particular, his appearance before the House Un-American Activities Committee (HUAC) in 1952. Kazan was a member of the Communist Party for about eighteen months in the early 1930s while working with the Group Theatre, but he came to view Communism with suspicion and disgust after the Party began dictating artistic terms to its Group members and subjected him to a show trial. When Kazan was called to testify before HUAC during its investigation into the alleged Communist infiltration of Hollywood, he initially balked at providing the names of former associates who were Party members but then changed his mind. Although Kazan remained a committed liberal, his testimony and the subsequent advertisement he published in the *New York Times* defending his decision to name names marked him as a traitor in the eyes of many on the Left, guilty of complicity and betrayal, careerism and pride.

Decades later, Kazan reflected on his decision to testify in interviews and his startlingly frank 1988 autobiography *Elia Kazan: A Life*, revealing his evolving and frequently mixed feelings about HUAC. *A Life* did little to satisfy Kazan's critics — as evidenced by the controversy surrounding his receipt of an honorary Lifetime Achievement Academy Award in 1999 — while also exposing him to additional charges of disloyalty — of a marital sort this time. From adulterous escapades in alleyways, described pages into the first chapter, through the tale of bedding Marilyn Monroe on the night after she decided to marry Joe DiMaggio, *A Life* opened all aspects of Kazan's private life to scrutiny. The man was an obsessive observer, analyzer, and recorder of human behavior — especially his own. Was his autobiography an attempt to honestly and bravely account for his thoughts and actions — however flawed they sometimes were — or to preempt and thus deflect the criticism of others, so as to appear above it all?

All too often, what we talk about when we talk about Kazan comes down simply to the question one film scholar asked me: "Are you for or against?"

We've been talking about Kazan for over half a century now. Is there anything left to say?

Plenty.

In the wake of the opening of Kazan's personal archive to researchers, the centenary of his birth, the accompanying film retrospectives, and recent books, now is the time to revisit Kazan, and in particular his cinematic legacy. The topics of conversation thus far have been meaty, and they deserve to be chewed over: his status as author, collaborator, and artist; his accomplished work with actors; his psychological approach to realism; his interest in social problems and family dynamics; and the stain of HUAC on our national, and in Kazan's case personal, character. This book engages these subjects in new ways and expands the conversation, providing a survey of what a select group of film critics and scholars — some with prior publications on Kazan, others writing on him for the first time — find significant about his life and movies today. The authors chose their own themes and adopted a range of approaches, examining Kazan's importance to American cinema from historical, industrial, aesthetic, and social perspectives. Not all of the authors are "for" Kazan — and they don't always agree.

The book groups the essays together into a series of conversations about a shared topic or film and proceeds roughly chronologically through Kazan's career. Some films are noticeably absent — nobody wants to spend time on *The Sea of Grass* (1947), it seems, and there appears to be a consensus that enough has been said about *On the Waterfront*. Other films emerge as worthy of expanded critical consideration, in particular *Panic in the Streets* (1950), *A Face in the Crowd* (1957), *Wild River* (1960), and *America America* (1963). Authors draw attention to Kazan's visual style with unprecedented depth, emphasizing his use of staging and the environment to shape mood and express character psychology. And the relationship between Kazan's life, politics, and art is plumbed in new ways, revealing fresh viewpoints on his approach to character, story, and aesthetics.

The initial essays provide an overview of Kazan and his films, raising key issues and questions that will be explored throughout. Jeanine Basinger, the curator of Kazan's papers at the Wesleyan Cinema Archives, offers a personal reflection on his character, interests, and working methods. She discusses the life experiences that defined Kazan's identity and shaped his worldview, including what drove a man in his sixties to archive a dance card from high school. Kent Jones initiates a discussion of Kazan's aesthetics, highlighting the "luminous pockets of serenity" that alternate with the director's more frequently noted scenes of impassioned fervor. Comparing and contrasting Kazan's strategies for harnessing the specificity of time and place with those of Joseph Mankiewicz, Douglas Sirk, William Wyler, and Nicholas Ray, Jones argues for renewed attention to how Kazan articulates the relationship between character and environment through staging and mise-en-scène. Jonathan Rosenbaum reconsiders a survey of Kazan's career that he wrote in 1973, when he found the director's films "uneven, varied, and unsystematic." While Rosenbaum champions Kazan's work with actors and location, he finds his approach to storytelling frequently overwrought. Jones and Rosenbaum come closest to agreeing on *Wild River*, which both embrace for its quiet visual power and depth of feeling. Leo Braudy concludes the section with a focused consideration of Kazan as auteur and collaborator, using *Viva Zapata!* (1952) as a window into the director's conflicted views on authority and power.

Braudy's exploration of the relationship between Kazan's politics and his aesthetics leads into the next set of essays — about Kazan's decision to testify before HUAC and how it shaped his subsequent work. Victor Navasky reviews the controversy surrounding Kazan's cooperation with HUAC in the context of recent revelations regarding the depth of Soviet spy infiltration in the United States during the Cold War. Navasky considers whether Kazan's negative reputation as an informer should be reassessed — or, if he was guilty of betrayal, exactly what or who did he betray? Brenda Murphy continues the thread in her analysis of the first film Kazan made following his testimony, *Man on a Tightrope* (1953), about a Czechoslovakian circus troupe that escapes across the Iron Curtain. Murphy situates the film in relation to *Boomerang!* (1947), *Panic in the Streets*, *Viva Zapata!*, and *On the Waterfront* as a paean to the "man of individual conscience" battling authority, foregrounding its concern with threats to the artist's right to self-definition and creative freedom. As such, she links the film to Kazan's defense of his HUAC testimony and considers it a marker of his liberal anticommunism.

The critical and commercial success of *On the Waterfront* enabled Kazan to begin to break away from Twentieth Century-Fox, the studio where he had been under long-term contract, and venture into independent filmmaking with Newtown Productions. His two initial independent entries, *Baby Doll* (1956) and *A Face in the Crowd*, are the subject of the next essays. Brian Neve reveals the impetus of Kazan's desire to produce and makes a case for *Baby Doll* as the harbinger of a new direction in his filmmaking. With its location shooting, extended takes, tonal shifts, adult-oriented themes, moral ambivalence, and lack of a clear resolution, *Baby Doll* finds Kazan experimenting with art cinema techniques rooted in an objective form of realism. Sam Wasson also considers the Newtown films, but argues that the partisan nature of Kazan's approach to character undermines his humanist impulse. In his search for humor and humanism in Kazan's films, Wasson champions the satirical *A Face in the Crowd* as the director's most effective union of argument, complex character psychology, and comedy.

Mark Harris and Savannah Lee discuss several of the iconic characters and performances in Kazan's films, digging below the surface to reveal hidden meanings. Harris explores the (homo)eroticization of the male movie star in Kazan's films and the formal means that allow gay male moviegoers to construct parallel narratives of identification and desire in *A Streetcar Named Desire*, *Splendor in the Grass*, *East of Eden*, and *Wild River*. Harris considers the films' "generosity of spirit and complicated empathy" in relation to Kazan's own attitudes toward sex and gender, an approach also adopted by Lee in her exploration of the director's presentation of female pain. Seeking to balance previous accounts of Kazan's work that privilege his male protagonists, Lee tackles his interest in the inner lives of women, highlighting the stories of female suffering and strength found in *Pinky* (1949), *A Streetcar Named Desire*, and *Splendor in the Grass*. Together Harris and Lee find Kazan's depiction of sexual desire and gender roles in his middle-period melodramas to be unusually sensitive, modern, and rare for the era.

Three essays return to the topic of location and staging initially considered by Jones, combating the lack of sustained attention historically granted to Kazan's visual style. Andrew Tracy and Patrick Keating explore *Boomerang!* and *Panic in the Streets* as examples of the semidocumentary production cycle that swept Hollywood in the late 1940s. Tracy considers the two films in the context of the progressive goals that underlay the adoption of documentary realism in midcentury American film and Kazan's own didactic inclinations. He suggests that Kazan's semidocs are transitional works in the director's formulation of a hybrid approach to realism that emphasizes both the physical world and inner subjectivity. Keating's detailed analysis of *Boomerang!* and *Panic in the Streets* illustrates how they challenged genre conventions and visually suggested the unpredictability of contemporary urban space. Through the use of long takes and deep, multiplanar staging, Kazan locates narrative information throughout the frame and highlights random connections, anonymous meetings, and surprise appearances in a complex and pioneering way. My own essay continues in this vein by addressing Kazan's employment of depth staging in *East of Eden* and *Wild River*. I argue that the arrangement and movement of characters within a defined environment is an aesthetic tool that is just as important to Kazan's films as his actors' performances. The staging strategies he adopts for his two CinemaScope movies situate him in the company of visual storytellers ranging from D. W. Griffith to Hou Hsiao-hsien and widescreen innovators such as Vincente Minnelli and Otto Preminger.

The final contributions to the book focus on Kazan's late works, including *Wild River* and *America America*, two of his personal favorites. Richard

Schickel examines the inspiration for *Wild River* and its production history, highlighting in particular Kazan's changing conception of the film's central protagonist, played by Montgomery Clift, during script development and shooting. Schickel finds a central theme of the film to be "the hidden price we pay for our choices," a theme that Hayden Guest picks up on in his examination of the narrative and stylistic threads that interweave the director's last four films, *America America*, *The Arrangement* (1969), *The Visitors* (1972), and *The Last Tycoon* (1976). All four films concern male protagonists who are "unmoored and unstable," struggling with personal and professional decisions that frequently reflect Kazan's own. While Guest finds the themes and structures of the final films in keeping with Kazan's recurring narrative interests, he considers how their stylistic experimentation sharply foreground the ambiguity previously entwined with classical conventions in his earlier work.

Taken as a group, these essays reveal Kazan to be a flawed man and an uneven artist, but one who nevertheless created transformative films that shaped the terrain of postwar American cinema. His close attention to human behavior — including strengths and weaknesses — drove him to represent truth both didactic and ambiguous in all its ambiguity and to craft new strategies for communicating physical and psychological realism. His work continues to speak to us, and the discussions and disagreements contained in this book are but a fraction of what we might say in response. Hopefully they'll expand our conversation about Kazan.

Kazan
REVISITED

On Kazan the Man

I first met Elia Kazan in the fall of 1969. He had given his personal and professional papers to Wesleyan University, due to the efforts of Wyman Parker, who was at that time the head of the University's Olin Library. In return for his gift, Kazan was provided with a working office on campus, a convenience he often took advantage of, since he owned a country home in nearby Newtown, Connecticut. Because he was curious about the University's efforts to begin teaching film to undergraduates, he began to visit our classes to talk informally with film students and faculty. Eventually, it was decided that the Kazan archive would be moved into the new Wesleyan Cinema Archives, at that time home to the papers of such Hollywood luminaries as Frank Capra, Ingrid Bergman, Raoul Walsh, and Kay Francis. (Later would be added Clint Eastwood, John Waters, Jonathan Demme, and Martin Scorsese, among others.) I became curator of Kazan's papers, and he and I began going through them together. He gave me very specific instructions about how he wanted things to be handled. (At first, he wanted me to type while he dictated, but my typing wasn't fast enough for him. He decided I should just "remember what I tell you.") The main thing he wanted done was simple: save everything. I once pointed out to him, as we plowed through a box, that he still had a dance card from his high school days, even though it had no names filled in. Could we throw this out, I asked, since he obviously hadn't danced with anyone. Very definitely not, he replied. The fact that it was empty of names was what made it important to him. "I don't ever want to lose that memory."

The dance card was emblematic of Kazan's archive. Small, seemingly irrelevant items — a handful of stones picked up on a Greek isle — represented a personal memory of his past and his emotions. These little mementos were mixed in with his professional working notebooks. All of this archive material is, of course, an explanation of both his personality and his work in film and theater. He was a holder of memories, a detailed observer and recorder of his times, and a believer that small things revealed big things.

Eventually, Kazan and I began a friendship of the everyday sort, the kind where he would turn up unexpectedly, stick his head in my door, and ask if he could sit down and gab for a while. "Don't tell anyone I'm here," he would say, as if they hadn't noticed. Elia Kazan was a powerful presence, but in the most offhand way. He dressed casually, even carelessly, but with a certain jaunty touch that marked him out as a man who understood the meaning of costume and visual nuance. He was down-to-earth, unpretentious, and he liked nothing more than to collect me for a trip to his favorite eatery in nearby Middletown: the Pizza Palace. The Palace was at that time owned by two Greek brothers, and Kazan always plopped down into a booth as if he'd been born there. He liked the food, he liked the camaraderie, and he liked the prices. He enjoyed sitting and talking — with me, with the brothers, with the staff, and with anyone else who happened by. He liked to know what people were doing and what they had on their minds. ("Where are you going later?" and "What are you up to today?") He also liked to quiz me about everything — why I had come to Connecticut, what my parents were like, who I respected on the faculty, what books I had read, what movies were my favorites — anything and everything. He had all kinds of pointers with which to advance my education. "See that man over there? He's worried about something but is trying not to show it" would be offered right alongside "Buy okra today. It's in season." He especially liked giving me advice about who I shouldn't trust. ("Watch out for that guy. He locks his door when there's no need to. He has something to hide.")

Kazan also liked to take walks, rain or shine, hot or cold, and he liked to climb up to the top of what was then the student union building, because it afforded a superb view of the Connecticut River. He liked to stand up there, looking out, thinking, and talking about things. Most of all, I think, he liked to be around the Wesleyan film students.

Whenever I invited students to my house, he liked to sit at the head of the big dining table and ask the young people to tell him about themselves. Where did they come from? Who would they vote for and why? Were their teachers any good? Were they learning anything? Kazan's idea of conversation was to grill someone to extract a sense of who they were, to find the truth about what they thought and felt. Although he seemed comfortable in his own skin, there was nevertheless a wariness about him, an edge. He listened with great intensity, and I often thought of two words as I watched him: *tension* and *truth*, and tension and truth were two hallmarks of his movies. Kazan deflected questions about himself very handily,

Elia Kazan at Wesleyan University in 1955 after receiving an honorary doctorate. Kazan's personal and professional papers are housed at the Wesleyan Cinema Archives. Photograph by the *Hartford Courant*. Photo courtesy of the Wesleyan Cinema Archives.

but if a student asked him something serious about directing or acting, he appreciated it and would give a detailed answer. (Once in a while, he would become anecdotal, and drop little nuggets about Brando or Dean, thrilling the students with his insider's thoughts.)

This dinner table questioning process utterly defines Elia Kazan. He was an observer. He watched people and he listened to people and he queried people, and he used what he learned in his work. After dinner, he could describe each student very clearly to me, speculating on their private feelings and creating imaginary futures for them. He told me how he might cast them, based on their physical characteristics, vocal intonations, accents, physical carriage, and reaction to others. He looked at real people as potential characters, and concurrently, he thought of all his movie characters as real people.

For instance, he wrote interior lives for the major characters in his films. In his intelligent and insightful working journals (both for film and theater), he "talked" to himself, typing out his ideas for any planned project. Even on his lesser-known films, this process was detailed and complete. In *Boomerang!* (1947), one of his earliest efforts, he undertook a true story about the murder of a priest in Bridgeport, Connecticut. On the character of the murderer (Crossman), Kazan wrote: "He is suspicious of everybody in his heart, but feels that people mustn't notice that he is suspicious. He is anxious that people might discover that he really hates them, and therefore, he puts on a supersanct manner. The result is that he seems constantly to be searching for reassurance that people like him; seems constantly to be hoping that people forgive him for something that no one knows he's done." He described Father Lambert, the murdered priest, as "a little old mouse of a man." Lesser characters were also colorfully defined as someone who "falls asleep while he is talking to you" or "the kind of guy that goes to Florida in the winter, and doesn't go alone either." For a young suspect, he wrote: "the audience must love this kid. They should feel his typicality. He should have every boyish kind of stunt possible; like shooting little paper pellets off rubber bands." For a waitress, Irene, he imagined "a little mongrel." She "chews her fingernails . . . worries about getting fat . . . and always has a cigarette going on the edge of a saucer, parks it while she takes your order, then picks it right up again." Since *Boomerang!* was based in fact, Kazan wrote these words as a reminder to himself about keeping truth on the screen: "A town like Bridgeport has a . . . business-man-like front. Everything is traditional, American, pious, industrious. . . . This murder strips off the skin of dignity. . . . The only chance you have to make this story interesting is to really go into the environment. Present the settings and furniture and props . . . but more important . . . the fake activities, the fake love, the emptiness and the griminess and the dullness of bourgeois life . . . the desperate scramble for money."[1]

His visits to the real-life Connecticut setting of *Boomerang!* inspired him to shoot on location as much as he could. He knew if he himself had absorbed a subtext from being in the places the murder had happened, the audience could do the same. He wrote: "This is a story of desperate people. People in a tough spot in one way or another; all at some kind of a crisis in their lives. Every one has a desperate, secret, inner life. . . . Your problem is to show evidence of it all along in such a fashion that the audience anticipates something breaking loose, looks forward to it, and, when it does happen, recognizes the particular desperation at the bottom of it."[2]

Since I inherited the Elia Kazan archive, I have often been asked if I can explain the relationship between art and politics that existed for Kazan.

Elia Kazan enjoys a quiet moment during the production of *Panic in the Streets*. Photo courtesy of the Wesleyan Cinema Archives.

No. I cannot. Can I justify his House Un-American Activities Committee (HUAC) testimony? No. I cannot. Do I reject him as an artist because of it? No. I do not. All I can do is attempt to unite the various elements I know of him. Having read the papers in his archive, studied his working notebooks, seen all his movies, and spent time with him in personal conversations, I can only say that I feel his art is his politics because his politics were his art. I heard him say more than once that movies were "the great art form where you're saying something about yourself by another means." On the basis of our conversations and his papers, I have come to believe that three key things shaped both his personality and his political life:

First: The immigrant experience. Kazan was an immigrant, born an Anatolian Greek in Turkey. His family brought him to the United States when he was four years old.

Second: His years as an outsider at the elite institutions of Williams College and Yale University School of Drama. Kazan was a have-not among the haves, working as a waiter, a nerd without a wardrobe. He lived the outsider experience on a daily basis.

Third: His young years of passion and excitement with the Group Theatre, where he learned to take art seriously and to define his work as art. During these years, two influences found Kazan: Marx, with the concept that art should be a force for social change, and Stanislavsky, with the concept that psychology could be turned into behavior through the art of performance. These were his years of influence and growth — and acceptance — out of which he went on to help found the Actors Studio in the 1940s.

In my opinion, these three aspects of his youth — the immigrant experience, the outsider years in school, and his Group Theatre experiences — were his political and artistic foundation. They help explain his years as a Hollywood filmmaker because, in a sense, Kazan "immigrated" from Broadway to Hollywood, arriving in the immediate postwar period as an outsider, albeit as a man who took art seriously as a political force.

In Hollywood, he found the opportunity of a lifetime to reach a mass audience with his ideas about performance and his goals for social change, but as the new kid on the block (the theater "immigrant"), he had to learn the ways of the town. He was once again the ultimate outsider, this time in an even richer and more elitist world than Williams or Yale. What he found in Hollywood was an encapsulation of his lifetime experience . . . and it energized him. It motivated him. Elia Kazan found himself in the right place at the right time.

The three decades Kazan worked in Hollywood — the 1940s, 1950s, and into the 1960s — were times of change and upheaval in that town. Each decade was different, so each one both presented him with new challenges and gave him new opportunities to succeed. When he arrived, the studio system was intact and fully functioning. Box office returns had been greater than ever in the years of World War II, and Hollywood appeared to be on top of its game. Kazan learned filmmaking inside that thriving system. However, the war years had changed the entertainment appetites of American audiences, and the threat of television was on the horizon. Independent filmmakers began to emerge in a stronger position. More foreign films were being seen and distributed than ever before, so the older Hollywood genres needed an infusion of new attitudes and new issues, such as racism, anti-Semitism, and labor problems.[3]

Kazan was a director who could face these issues. He brought with him solid theater experience and a political background that made him perfect for the new look of movies, the new social attitudes, the seriousness and performance styles that were called for. Being an outsider with a political

Elia Kazan flanked by extras in Greece during the production of *America America*.
Photo courtesy of the Wesleyan Cinema Archives.

and social bias positioned him perfectly for success. And when Hollywood, feeling the pressure, began to experiment with widescreen, color, story structure, and imaginative uses of location, Kazan again had something to give. His work with the Group Theatre contained an open-mindedness to experimentation. In particular, he was master of a style of acting that gave America a new kind of male hero, a new kind of passion and honesty, a new definition of stardom. It made him a dominant force in movies.

Elia Kazan's career in movies is a record of amazing achievement. For thirty years, he remained ahead of the system or on top of it, always adapting himself and his work to the necessary changes, reinventing himself and his filmmaking style. His filmography demonstrates this. In early films such as *Gentleman's Agreement* (1947), which for all its reputation as "groundbreaking" is essentially a studio product, Kazan's leading character faces a social problem outside his daily life, finds it a clear issue, and deals with it. By the time Kazan is making *Wild River* (1960), he presents a hero who finds a social problem that is too complex for an easy wrap-up and who is torn about which way to go, finding no easy solution. This new hero learns that social progress often brings personal sacrifice. From one film to the other, Kazan has shifted his presentation of politics, changing it from an externalized system of beliefs into a personal and emotional problem — a lesson he had presumably encountered himself along the way. Regarding his controversial political actions, Kazan wrote in his autobiography (and in his personal notes to himself), "What I'd done was correct, but was it right? . . . [I'm] still worrying over it";[4] and "That's what a difficult decision means: Either way you go, you lose."[5]

When the studio system collapsed (between 1960 and 1964), leaving many Hollywood big names on the streets, Kazan, who was still a theater man, returned east to the world that had originally nourished him. Kazan could always "immigrate," be comfortable as an outsider, and adapt his politics to his art.

Kazan spoke through the movie screen to audiences about issues that were both personal *and* political. His world was a serious one. In it, women could be pushed into madness by an uncaring society. Fathers could fail their children badly. Being young was a time of confusion and unpredictability. Social progress sometimes ruined the lives of individuals. The media was a dangerous force growing stronger and stronger and creating celebrity politicians for all the wrong reasons. Men did not have to be strong and silent but could scream and shout and smash their hands into glass. In fact, Kazan's major contribution to movies is probably his influence on the concept of the American male hero. He presents a man who can be confused by his world and tortured by self-doubt, and yet still be heroic in his journey toward self-awareness. To delineate this American man, Kazan developed actors such as Brando and Dean and Warren Beatty as movie stars, and showcased actors like Montgomery Clift and James Dunn in new ways.[6]

More than once, in conversations, in classes, and in interviews, I heard Kazan define himself as a filmmaker who wanted to "get the poetry out of the common things in life." In a famous speech Kazan delivered at Wesleyan University in 1972, he described the characteristics needed to become a successful film director. It was a funny, wise, charming, and even shocking list of contradictory qualities, and he had them all. In my experience of him, he was judgmental but tolerant; cooperative but stubborn; stern but humorous. He was both open and devious, trusting and wary. Above all, he was blazingly intelligent, and charming and generous to me. When the time came for us to discuss his HUAC testimony, as it inevitably did, our private conversation was our private conversation, and will remain so. Although I did not see Kazan much after he gave up his Connecticut home, he does not fade in my memory. I picture him clearly, standing on the top floor of our old student union, turning to look at me as he made his concluding remark: "Everyone has his reasons."

NOTES

1. *Boomerang!* script notes, Elia Kazan Collection, Wesleyan Cinema Archives, Wesleyan University.

2. Ibid.

3. Less visible to the general public were legal struggles in which the studios were being forced to divest themselves of their movie theater chains and stop their lucrative practice of block-booking.

4. Elia Kazan, *Elia Kazan: A Life* (New York: Knopf, 1988), 465.

5. Ibid., 462.

6. Throughout his movie career, Kazan directed twenty-one actors and actresses to Academy Award nominations, with nine of them becoming winners.

There is only one way of looking at this trade:
The filmmaker is responsible for everything. To
rephrase that thought: Everything is your fault,
and only rarely will you be praised for anything.

ELIA KAZAN

Opposite page:
Photo courtesy of the Wesleyan Cinema Archives.

The Quiet Side of Kazan

Red Scare politics aside, most of the attention paid to Elia Kazan and his films, positive and negative, has been given over to acting and a laundry list of related issues such as hysteria (*Splendor in the Grass*, 1961), Oedipal entanglements (*East of Eden*, 1955; *The Arrangement*, 1969), real-life conflicts put to dramatic and cinematic use (James Dean and Raymond Massey's mutual antipathy, Lee Remick's overwhelming of Montgomery Clift in *Wild River*, 1960), and such famously inventive pieces of business as Marlon Brando's hand finding its way into Eva Marie Saint's glove or James Dean's animal gesticulations. The less frequently selected Door Number Two opens onto Kazan's themes, which are invariably linked to his appearance before the House Un-American Activities Committee (HUAC): *On the Waterfront* (1954) thus becomes a pro–"friendly testimony" movie, and the frequent instances of betrayal (in *On the Waterfront* as well as *East of Eden*; *A Face in the Crowd*, 1957; *Wild River*; *America America*, 1963; and beyond) are scrupulously noted. These subjects are obviously important, but it's possible that they've been overdiscussed. Appreciations of Kazan have tended to remain stuck in first gear, perhaps due to an unconscious fear of sidelining the importance of the HUAC affair. Kazan's universally acknowledged talent has kept him away from hell, but he has been consigned to a strange, grey-on-grey purgatory as punishment for his sin.

One area of his filmmaking that has never received the attention it deserves is his meticulous sense of environment. So much time has been spent on the brilliance of the acting in Kazan's work that one might conclude it occurred in a void, or on a Broadway stage. There's been precious little said about the locations, rooms, and houses to which the acting is so deeply cathected, and the light under which it is realized. Kazan's films have a consistency of passionate attention to environment, so vividly realized that it can be as commanding of our attention and perception as the faces of Marlon Brando or Andy Griffith. Like Howard Hawks and his friend Nick Ray but to vastly different effect, Kazan unconsciously anticipated many of the aesthetic preoccupations that dot the current filmmaking landscape, from a syntax that is intimately tied and responsive to the behavioral nuances of the actors to the odd blending of foreground and background in a manner that foreshadows Hou Hsiao-hsien and Apichatpong Weerasethakul.

At this point, eyebrows are doubtlessly being raised. How can a high-powered king of stage and screen like Elia Kazan, rooted as he was in conventional dramaturgy, be compared to the current urge toward the diffusion of drama into light, wind, mood, and climate? From a temperamental standpoint, he can't. But if you look closely at where his instincts and fancies took him, the link seems a little less implausible. Take the final stretch of *Splendor in the Grass*, which Kazan himself reckoned to be one of his peak moments. General descriptions of Kazan's work as a parade of cranked-up hysteria tend to be culled from certain standout scenes and performances — Andy Griffith's megalomaniac in *A Face in the Crowd*, Lee J. Cobb and Karl Malden's ripe-to-bursting performances in *On the Waterfront*, James Dean's spastic pantomiming of contentment in *East of Eden*, the hothouse stylizations of *A Streetcar Named Desire* (1951). Pegging Kazan as a barnstorming psychodramatist just doesn't jibe with this extended passage of regret and contentment quietly commingled with summer heat, delicate body language, rustling breezes, and a perfectly realized Kansas farm (shot somewhere in deepest New York state). Zohra Lampert's rangy, pungent acting is a boost to any movie, but she reaches perfection in this scene, and it's partly due to the sense of place (a vibrant Italian-American woman stuck in a grimy country kitchen) and a frumpy housedress that looks like it was whisked out of the donations bin at the nearest Salvation Army. After Natalie Wood, her husband's old flame, passes by in her elegant Sunday best, Lampert stands alone and bemused by her dingy stove and unthinkingly touches her dress at the center of her chest before shrugging her shoulders. It's an unconsciously self-defining gesture of a type that lesser filmmakers would either lunge at and pounce on or never even attempt. While it is altogether more pointed than any given gesture within the fluid, long-take immersions of an Apichatpong or a Jia Zhang-ke, it is an early ancestor, part of the same aesthetic family.

In film after film, Kazan alternates between this kind of exquisite attunement to mood and place and an alternating (and more commonly noted) urge toward amplification, a trust in ongoing reality in conflict with a less personal imperative urge toward dramatic clarification. In *Splendor in the Grass* alone, Pat Hingle's overbearingly overbearing father alternates with the quieter work of Warren Beatty, Natalie Wood (prehysterics), and

Jack Palance (*left*) and Zero Mostel (*right*) as two criminals fleeing from police atop a New Orleans tobacco warehouse in a publicity still from *Panic in the Streets*. During the extended take, the camera remains stationary as the men enter the frame over the right-hand roof in the midground, charge to the rear, and then run back toward the camera. By maintaining the same framing for the entire duration, Kazan objectively situates the men's confused desperation within the specific location of the New Orleans docks and heightens the sense of realism. Photo courtesy of the Wesleyan Cinema Archives.

Lampert, as well as the pointed, needling, physical/vocal attack of the future Mrs. Kazan (and director of *Wanda*, 1971), Barbara Loden. But throughout the film, background mingles with foreground in a manner that is quite distinct from that of other films of the era. It's a matter of class, of course, the dark, pretentious expanses of Hingle's oil-financed mansion contrasted with the homey, gewgaw-stuffed coziness of Wood's family abode. But it's also a matter of air and light, the crazed, infectious excitement of a brilliantly colored New Year's Eve ball, the suspended summer stillness of that last scene. Similarly, anyone who has seen *Wild River* will remember the river crossings on the barge and the smoke drifting in the distance, the elated faces of the racist mob, the abandoned house at twilight through which Montgomery Clift and Lee Remick drift and delicately enter into their love affair, one gentle and hesitant turn at a time. The places look "right," but they also feel right — the atmosphere, the movement, and the behavior within any given space converge to allow every background to tell its own alternating story, sometimes in concert and sometimes in counterpoint with the action . . . as surrounding life always does.

Kazan is obviously not the only filmmaker of his era to pay close attention to the place-specific accoutrements of class. *A Letter to Three Wives* (1949), *All That Heaven Allows* (1955), *Bigger Than Life* (1956), and *The Best Years of Our Lives* (1946) are just a few random examples of class-conscious moviemaking. But in each case, the approach differs from Kazan's. The Joseph L. Mankiewicz and Douglas Sirk films both have a built-in, studio-dictated opulence that the Nicholas Ray and William Wyler films lack — in *A Letter to Three Wives*, the light falls evenly and advantageously on everyone and everything, a given of the studio era; in the Sirk, the impression of plushness underscores every scene, and Rock Hudson's bohemian lifestyle seems just as well-appointed and silky smooth as Jane Wyman's haute-bourgeois palace. In *All That Heaven Allows*, Sirk and Russell Metty, his cameraman, manage to harness the requisite opulence to their advantage, as a means of embodying and amplifying the peculiar dilemma in which Wyman finds herself . . . as has been noted in cinema studies departments around the world for over thirty years now. The control of light and color and varying distance in space, as every Ph.D. candidate knows, heightens the drama on the one hand and raises the levels of Bitter Irony on the other. In the Wyler, whose attention to class-specific housing elicited comparisons to *Greed* (1925) from both Manny Farber and James Agee at the time of its release, there is a strong imprint of the studio era undercut by a frankness of gesture and attitude, dictated by an urge to social truth in the immediate aftermath of the war. These cases differ from Kazan's filmmaking as it developed from his war-era debut through the end of his career in the late seventies. The settings and people on the periphery of *The Best Years of Our Lives* make a vivid impression, as does the contrast between the railroad kitchen and Paul Douglas's incongruously baronial lifestyle in *A Letter to Three Wives*. But in both instances, the backgrounds make their own vivid impressions, distinct from the impressions left by the human dramas within them.

The Ray film is a different case. As has often been noted, the house in *Bigger Than Life* is like a separate character, the staircase in particular. It is class-specific to be sure, as are the apartment complex in *In a Lonely Place* (1950), the honeymoon cottage in *They Live by Night* (1949), or the country house in *On Dangerous Ground* (1952) — not to mention the igloo in *The Savage Innocents* (1960). But in Ray, every space and every background is never less than tightly tied in a reciprocal, dynamic relationship with the characters as they strive to define themselves, to be understood by others and within their own minds. Environments are vividly imparted, but in quick glimpses that are remembered as sharp, even violent inflections, indicating a push-pull, convincingly unsettled relationship. If *Wind Across the Everglades* (1958) seems to move a little closer to Kazan territory, perhaps that's because it was written by Budd Schulberg and designed by Richard Sylbert, two of Kazan's principal collaborators. But just as Kazan is miles from the centrifugal Robert Mitchum–Susan Hayward–Arthur Kennedy rodeo-world relationships in *The Lusty Men* (1952), Ray is just as far from the rooftop scenes in *On the Waterfront* or the rich man's funereal calm that pervades most of *The Last Tycoon* (1976). The Vincente Minnelli of *Father of the Bride* (1950) and *Some Came Running* (1958) seems a little closer to Kazan, but while the environments in those films are unfailingly vivid, they are uniformly oppressive verging on nightmarish, looking back to Robert Wiene's *The Cabinet of Dr. Caligari* (1919) rather than forward to Apichatpong's *Blissfully Yours* (2002).

There are some interesting passages in Kazan's autobiography, *Elia Kazan: A Life*, in which he counters the exciting novelties of Lee Strasberg and the Group Theatre with the commonsense practices of certain old pros. From Osgood Perkins, father of Anthony Perkins (remembered as Johnny Lovo in Hawks's *Scarface*, 1932), Kazan learned how important props and their placement were to an actor. From John Ford, he learned the practice of allowing decisions about camera positions and blocking to be determined only after private early morning visits to the set, whether fabricated or genuine. On a more basic level, Kazan learned that the importance of the physical environment is basic to good theater — it is, for instance, central to Stanislavsky's thinking. Kazan is frequently cited as the first Method director and reflexively linked to Strasberg because of his participation in the Group Theatre and his role as cofounder (with Bobby Lewis and Cheryl Crawford) of the Actors Studio, whose operation was turned over to Strasberg in the midfifties. But apart from the fact that he was always pragmatically eclectic in his inspirations, Kazan had serious objections not only to the Method as developed by Strasberg but to Strasberg's tyrannical control and his inefficiency as a director (on the rare occasions when he actually directed a production, as opposed to a workshop scene). *Elia*

Kazan: A Life also contains a lengthy, withering description of Strasberg's celebrated midsixties production of *Three Sisters*. Kazan specifically objected to what he perceived as an excess of interiority among the three principal actresses: three inner-directed demonstrations of emotional intensity that relieved the play of its nuances and dramatic tension and dissolved all sense of place and time in the process. Apart from the fact that his favorite actor, Marlon Brando, was a devotee of Strasberg's archenemy Stella Adler, the interiority of the Method ran counter to Kazan's sensibility and what he considered good theater and cinema practice. Kazan, Sirk, Ray, Minnelli, and in a roundabout way Mankiewicz were all men of the theater, and they all understood the lessons of theater differently. In Kazan's case, it resulted in a refined sense of the all-but-erotic contact between people and their surroundings and the powerful, phantom role played by those surroundings in shaping people's makeup as social, spiritual, and sexual beings.

In Kazan's commentary on his own work, the viability of the environment always plays a central role. His disappointment with *A Tree Grows in Brooklyn* (1945) was with its excess of studio-bred "cleanliness." It is a Twentieth Century-Fox film made with the same kind of careful attention to detail and the same approach to working-class environment — pungent, eye-filling production design that always balances misery with expertly crafted homespun prettiness — as any other period piece of the era from Henry King, John Ford, or Henry Hathaway. By the same token, Kazan reckoned that Dorothy McGuire, although he admired her dedication, was too ethereal a creature to be playing a hardened, physically and spiritually depleted mother of three. People and how they are formed by places; places and how they inform and mingle with the lives of people — these mutual host/parasite relationships are always crucial for Kazan.

Like most filmmakers, Kazan saw his own career as a gradual climb away from the shadows of a dominant influence (in his case, the studios and all they brought to bear on his filmmaking) and an ever-expanding realization of his own ideas of character, story, and action. His first step up the ladder was with *Boomerang!* and then with *Panic in the Streets* (1950), two location films (shot in Stamford, Connecticut, and New Orleans, respectively) in the "docudrama" vein that began with Louis de Rochemont's productions and remained in vogue through the postwar period. These films were an antidote to *The Sea of Grass* (1947); one of the funniest passages in *Elia Kazan: A Life* recounts Kazan's gradual realization that his misbegotten MGM "western" was going to be filmed on Culver City soundstages, rather than

Kirk Douglas (*left*) and Elia Kazan (*right*) discuss a scene during production of *The Arrangement*. An adaptation of Kazan's second novel, the film contains many autobiographical elements and subjective sequences. Photograph by Frank D. Dandridge. Photo courtesy of the Wesleyan Cinema Archives.

out on the prairie, and filled out with second unit footage of the eponymous grass waving in the wind. Unlike Kazan's later films, *Boomerang!* and *Panic in the Streets* could have been realized in a studio, albeit in a slightly altered form, but they are more attentive to their environments and the way they are interwoven with the drama than, say, *The Naked City* (1948). Where the Jules Dassin film is remembered as a police procedural blended with a grab bag of vignettes from New York in the forties, *Panic in the Streets* leans more in the direction of a portrait of a city in which a police procedural takes place. At this early stage of his career as a filmmaker, one can clearly see the tensions that would become more pronounced later — the pull toward ruminative portrait of place, the life of a New Orleans café or a Connecticut street at night, adding up to much more than background flavor; and on the other hand, the dramatic instinct, tuned to the delineation and amplification of a courtroom battle or the power relationships between New Orleans gangsters. In *Boomerang!* Dana Andrews, Jane Wyatt, and the rest of the cast could hail from pretty much anywhere in the country — classic studio casting, "right" in the same sense that Hudson and Wyman are right as New Englanders in *All That Heaven Allows*. In *Panic in the Streets*, a different matter entirely, Zero Mostel, Jack Palance, and Paul Douglas are more New York than New Orleans, and all high-powered. Kazan struggles with these conflicting impulses throughout his career — actors who dominate and actors who blend into the environment, actors who overwhelm and actors who ruminate. Perhaps one of the many reasons Marlon Brando was the actor of Kazan's dreams was the fact that he reconciled these two tendencies.

Kazan has often stated that *On the Waterfront* was the film that marked the beginning of his real independence as a filmmaker, and he has been careful to note that he could only have made it after his HUAC testimony. In his personal narrative of his life, his testimony remains an unsettled matter, alternately a principled stand against the (very real) tyranny of the American Communist Party, an act of vengeance against the Party for rejecting him in 1936, a matter of survival, and, most interestingly for this discussion, an action so calculated to upset so many people that it forever dispelled the image of the agreeable facilitator, the "immigrant son," with which he had been saddled and which had led to his Group Theatre–era nickname "Gadg" (as in *gadget*: the guy who's always there to fix things when you need him). From then on, the misstep of *Man on a Tightrope* (1953) aside, there would be no more compromised portrayals of thorny issues like *Gentleman's Agreement* (1947) or studio-dictated adaptations of Broadway successes, no more falsifications à la *The Sea of Grass* or *Pinky* (1949). Environmental attunement becomes all-important — matters of mood, season, time of day. And while betrayal does play a part in these films, it seems to me that the more dominant conflict plays out around self-liberation, whose enactment often *results* in betrayal. In film after film, a sensitive and quietly introspective character undergoes a painful extrication from an overpowering mother or father, husband or wife (or stand-in for any of these). The split is realized with actors who are relatively quiet in their intensity, paired off against "bigger" and more blustering actors (Lee J. Cobb, Karl Malden, Pat Hingle, Andy Griffith, Richard Boone) who threaten to destabilize the other characters and the environment, and to up-end the movie itself. It doesn't take a genius to figure out the origins of this dynamic. It's fascinating to see Kazan's own conflict spill over into his art, again and again, as if he couldn't help but endlessly reenact his own drama of separation and individuation from his father, explicitly dramatized in the novel and the film adaptation of *The Arrangement* and elaborated one pain-filled detail at a time in *Elia Kazan: A Life*. As they struggle to become themselves, Kazan's heroes frequently edge his films toward a state of protective quietude, maneuvering the action into place- and time-specific moments delicately attuned to a sense of sheer being, alone and apart, safe from the emotional blackmail and dictatorial controls of others.

The hushed quiet of Robert De Niro's moments alone as Monroe Stahr in *The Last Tycoon* is emblematic in this sense. Pauline Kael once aptly likened the odd movie taking place around him to "a vampire movie after the vampires have left," and this may be a result of producer Sam Spiegel's very odd choice of Harold Pinter to adapt F. Scott Fitzgerald's unfinished novel.[1] Quiet menace is foreign to Kazan, who always flourished when there was more dramatic and psychological meat on the bone. But the uniformly brittle tone of the rest of this handsomely appointed movie actually creates an interesting background for the magical, aristocratic quiet of De Niro's scenes. There is real pain in his longing for Ingrid Boulting's excessively ethereal Kathleen Moore, but in a way the most satisfying stretch of the movie is its first half, as Stahr intervenes with a temperamental, Greta Garbo-ish star, gently sends a sell-out director on his way, or quietly inhabits his own solitude, accentuated by a luxurious, muffled quiet in perfect harmony with the airbrushed sleekness of Victor Kemper's cinematography (more redolent of the forties than the thirties) and Gene Callahan's production design, deco but not ostentatiously so — Stahr's office is realistically grounded in the idea of a young, powerful executive's sanctum sanctorum, while his home has just the right touch of slightly shopworn grandiosity left over from the twenties, a hint of Gatsby and *Sunset Blvd.* (1950). It's interesting that an artist like Kazan, who fought such a prolonged internal battle with the shadows of authority throughout his life, would end his career in cinema with a portrait of a man who is definitively alone. As envisioned by Kazan and De Niro, Stahr is a man at peace with himself and, for a time, even with his own discontent.

Solitude — *The Last Tycoon*. The internal balance between past and present, anguish and its acceptance — the end of *Splendor in the Grass*. And the sudden, unexpected harmony between two people — this is realized with an eloquence that seems almost unearthly in *Wild River*. Robin Wood once cited one of the film's key scenes, in which the characters played by Montgomery Clift and Lee Remick enter the abandoned house where she had lived with her late husband, in a long-forgotten collection of essays called *Favorite Movies*. His description is excellent. After noting the scene as

Chuck Glover (Montgomery Clift) intrudes on the quiet of the Garth family compound in a frame enlargement from *Wild River*. The film's lyrical pictorialism and ambivalent presentation of the protagonist make it a critical favorite.

"one of the finest things in the American — or any other — cinema,"[2] Wood zeroes in on one among a series of unfolding gestures between these two strangers who are trying to simultaneously acknowledge and instantly efface the undercurrent between them (a common balancing act when mutual attraction occurs) as they are also coping with the sudden confrontation between past and present: he works for the Tennessee Valley Authority (TVA) and has come south to purchase her grandmother's island in order to dam up the Tennessee River and prevent further catastrophic flooding; she has lived with her grandmother and isolated herself since her husband's death. Near the end of Wood's description of the film, he remarks on "the 'presence' of Carol's husband and their past together, marvelously created for us in the wealth of suggestions in the décor, and the girl's response."[3] This phantom presence, manifested in the leaves that have fallen on the bed, the broken furniture, and the fading wallpaper, is in constant silent dialogue with Remick's Carol and Clift's Chuck. Where Natalie Wood and Warren Beatty's walk through the arbor and the rundown farm house and out into the sun-baked afternoon is a matter of reconciliation with the disappointments of the past and a realigned vision of the possible, Clift and Remick's slow, tentative movements through the decrepit house hold multiple forms of tension in the most exquisitely refined manner — sexual, familial (should Remick convince her grandmother to leave in the name of progress or let her stay?), cultural (should Carol, a country girl, bed down with Chuck, an urban intellectual, in the house she once shared with her husband?). What's so interesting is that the tension is built into the reverie, so intimately tied to *this* place and *this* time of day, like a vivid memory in the process of forming.

One of the loveliest images in the film stands alongside D. W. Griffith and Ford at their pastoral best: a long shot of Clift and Remick drifting from her grandmother's house across the river on a barge to this house at the top of a slope, as smoke gently curls into the autumn air. The mood is deepened as they open the door and hear an African-American man singing "Hurry Sundown" as he ambles in the distance. They are caught in the harmony of the moment as they walk through the house, surveying the decay and damage, and as day gently turns to night.

According to Kazan, he shifted the power balance between Clift and Remick when he saw how nervous and tentative Clift was on the set. His youthful good looks had been marred after his accident during the production of *Raintree County* (1957), and Kazan did not allow him to drink during the shoot. This makes the coupling in *Wild River* distinctly different from those in *On the Waterfront* and *East of Eden*, in which the men find mother figures in the forms of Eva Marie Saint and Julie Harris, respectively. In *Wild River*, Lee Remick is the one crying out for solace, comfort, and protection, and Clift is the object on which she projects her longing. The fact that he is a somewhat unlikely candidate for the role of protector only deepens the scene, placing Remick at the dramatic fulcrum. The hint that Remick knows she is projecting impossible desires onto Clift and that he knows it as well adds another delicately webbed impulse, another layer of understanding just off the horizon. It's possible to infer a link between Remick's Carol and Barbara Loden, Kazan's lover at the time and his future wife (Loden appears in the film as a secretary). Where Kazan's first wife, Molly, was by all accounts a mother figure who provided a model for the Saint and Harris characters, Carol might have been modeled on the more forthright and aggressive Loden. However, explicit autobiographical links are easy to surmise and just as easy to discard. What's significant, I think, is the importance with which Kazan had always invested coupling in his films, which simultaneously reaches a summit, an endpoint, and an elegy in this singular scene, as the urge to solitude appears to have deepened within its creator.

Kazan's is one of the thorniest careers in American cinema. It needs to be approached scene by scene, moment by moment, as his turmoil, his conflicts, and his warring impulses play out through every interval of the creative process. These luminous pockets of serenity are precious because they are so hard won, instants of pure being sheltered from all the dramas of theater, cinema, and life.

NOTES

1. Pauline Kael, *5001 Nights at the Movies* (New York: Holt, 1991), 411.

2. Robin Wood, "The Seaweed Gatherers," in Philip Nobile, ed., *Favorite Movies: Critic's Choice* (New York: Macmillan, 1973), 166.

3. Ibid, 167.

Elia Kazan, Seen from 1973

PREFACE (2009)

Rereading this essay thirty-six years after I wrote it for Richard Roud's two-volume critical collection *Cinema: A Critical Dictionary: The Major Filmmakers*, I can't say that many of my positions or preferences regarding Kazan's work have changed. But in a few cases I've been able to amplify some of my original impressions. For my 2007 essay "Southern Movies, Actual and Fanciful: A Personal Survey" (to be reprinted in my 2010 University of Chicago Press collection *Goodbye Cinema, Hello Cinephilia*), for instance, I discovered that Kazan hired speech consultant Margaret Lamkin for his stage production of *Cat on a Hot Tin Roof* and then again for *Baby Doll* (1956), to ensure that all the southern accents heard were letter-perfect. And the significance of Kazan having given the names of former friends or colleagues to the House Un-American Activities Committee (HUAC) in 1952 — *not* in 1954, as my article stated — became a more prominent feature in his career profile when he was given a Lifetime Achievement Award in 1999, almost half a century later, from the Motion Picture Academy of Arts and Sciences. As controversial as this award was to some Academy members, it seemed to me then — and still seems now — rather hypocritical and myopic to assign more blame to Kazan than to any of the studio executives who actually implemented the Hollywood Blacklist and then kept it going for as long as it lasted, all of whom escaped public censure almost entirely. One of these executives, ironically and quite coincidentally, was Louis B. Mayer, the model for the villain played by Robert Mitchum in Kazan's last feature, *The Last Tycoon* (1976).

This film was even more of an anticlimax and letdown than its underexposed predecessor *The Visitors* (1972). There's an emblematic dialectic between these last two features, suggesting some of the span of Kazan's career — a personal, low-budget independent film and contemporary story, shot with unknowns in and around the Connecticut homes of Kazan and his son, followed by an impersonal, glossy studio package with a period setting, dripping with big names and shot on soundstages. To find rough counterparts in the first part of Kazan's career, one would probably have to reach for *Boomerang!* and *The Sea of Grass* (both made in 1947). But the faltering scripts in these last two films—overly didactic in the first case, shapeless in the second—give both of them the status of postscripts to Kazan's best work, so it still seems appropriate for me to have ended my 1973 discussion of his career with *Wild River* (1960).

As an unfinished novel, F. Scott Fitzgerald's *The Last Tycoon* steadily loses focus and coherence as it proceeds, and even if one accepts its curious idolatry of MGM producer Irving Thalberg as a role model, it's arguably inferior both as literature and as local portraiture to the two other major Hollywood novels written during the same period, *What Makes Sammy Run?* and *The Day of the Locust.* So it isn't surprising that the Kazan film, saddled with a sprawling Harold Pinter script that Kazan chose not to alter, never finds any secure footing, shedding its few virtues along the way. (Chiefly these are the finely tuned lead performance of Robert De Niro as Monroe Stahr, Kazan's own choice for the role, and an unusually intense one from Tony Curtis as one of the producer's leading players—along with a few incidental moments, such as a lingering close-up of Theresa Russell as a smitten college girl as she's leaving Stahr's office.) But the excellent Don Mankiewicz adaptation directed by John Frankenheimer for *Playhouse 90* in 1957 proves that it needn't necessarily have turned out that way, if Kazan had figured out some way of engaging with the material. The problem, as he admitted in his autobiography, was that his motivation for taking on this project had little to do with its own merits and a great deal to do with improving the health of his mortally ill mother by moving her to southern California—a ploy that, incidentally, didn't succeed.

Although I didn't mention it at the time, I was lucky to have seen three of Kazan's stage productions during the late fifties—*The Dark at the Top of the Stairs, J.B.,* and *Sweet Bird of Youth*—and still regard the third of these as one of his key achievements, far more important than any of the five features he directed after *Wild River.* (*Splendor in the Grass,* 1961, is still highly regarded in some quarters, but for me it's severely limited by the hectoring simplemindedness of its script and its stereotypical characters. Perhaps the only films scripted by or adapted from William Inge to have comfortably outlived their own periods are *Picnic,* 1955, and *Bus Stop,* 1956, in both cases mainly because of their casts and crews.)

Furthermore, I'm intrigued by the assertion of Robert Cornfield, the editor of the 2009 collection *Kazan on Directing,* that "Kazan's rise to directorial preeminence coincided with a crucial psychic shift in American culture [between] 1945 and 1955, [when] the per capita American income nearly tripled." (Cornfield hyperbolically calls the latter "the greatest increase in individual wealth in the history of Western civilization.")[1] I would also link the peaking of Kazan's talent during the fifties, like that of his friend Nicholas Ray, to his experiences during the thirties—the period when he first encountered filmmaking through his work on the leftist shorts *Pie in the Sky* (1935) and *People of the Cumberland* (1937). These experiences ultimately made *Wild River* the logical culmination of his film career. Ironically, *The Last Tycoon* is also set during the thirties, but the period as it's shown in the film is the converse of the kind of thirties that Kazan knew and understood firsthand.

J.R., 2009

*T*o view Kazan's development as either a progression or a regression is to assign a system to one of the most unsystematic careers in the American cinema. Even to regard his work as a totality is difficult, because the rules keep changing: how does one link *A Tree Grows in Brooklyn* (1945) with *The Visitors*—made over a quarter of a century apart—or *Wild River* with *Splendor in the Grass*, shot successively in 1960 and 1961?

Confronted with an extremely varied and uneven body of work, one is irresistibly drawn to the solace of formulas. In his conscientious, thoughtful study of Kazan (born 1909) in the Seghers series Roger Tailleur proposes a gradual movement from "third" to "second" to "first" person—a plausible enough theory, particularly when one comes to the later films, although Kazan seems to contradict it in an interview when he asserts that *The Arrangement* (1969) is "about Judith Crist's neighbor or Vincent Canby's cousin . . . [it's] about *you*, ya sonovabitch, in your button-down shirt!"[2] Andrew Sarris remarked in *The American Cinema*, more rhetorically than accurately, that "the Method of *A Streetcar Named Desire* (1951) has finally degenerated into the madness of *Splendor in the Grass*,"[3] when in fact, whatever position one takes towards either film, there is plenty of Method and madness in both of them.

Considering Kazan's status as an auteur, it is worth recalling that he was widely recognized as the equivalent of one for his work on the stage throughout the late forties and fifties—a man who persuaded Tennessee

James Dean goofs off and practices his target shooting in between takes during the filming of the carnival scene in *East of Eden*. In the background, cinematographer Ted McCord measures the strength of the available light falling on Rose Plumer. Earle Hodgins (*left*) plays the shooting gallery concessionaire. Photo courtesy of the Wesleyan Cinema Archives.

Williams to rewrite the ending of *Cat on a Hot Tin Roof*, and was believed to have played an important role in molding the conceptions of *A Streetcar Named Desire* and *Death of a Salesman*. It was observed more than once during the fifties that love had a magical way of stepping in and solving most of the characters' problems in the last acts of Kazan-directed plays, notably *Tea and Sympathy*, *Cat on a Hot Tin Roof*, *The Dark at the Top of the Stairs*, and *J.B.* — a recourse to a *deus ex vagina* was one wag's way of putting it. Ironically, there is a curious reticence in Kazan's handling of sex in films made during the same period: an unusual amount of tact is shown about the hero's extracurricular sex life in *East of Eden* (1955); in *Baby Doll* (1956) a central ellipsis makes it impossible to know whether the heroine and the

Sicilian ever sleep together; and in *Splendor in the Grass* the prostitute sent to the hero's hotel room abruptly disappears — in what looks like an editing error — before we can discover if they actually have had sex. By contrast, the transition from a broken mirror to a hose washing away trash in *A Streetcar Named Desire*, to stand for Stanley Kowalski's rape of Blanche DuBois, seems all too explicit.

As an indication of Kazan's reputation as a creative force, even a critic as unaccustomed to hyperbole as Eric Bentley wrote in 1953 that "the work of Elia Kazan means more to the American theatre than that of any current writer whatsoever."[4]

As the principal liaison between the students and techniques of the Actors Studio and the American cinema, Kazan's contribution and influence have been decisive; apart from "discovering" James Dean, Zohra Lampert, Jack Palance, Lee Remick, and Jo Van Fleet, among many others, he has directed some of the best performances ever recorded on film. His location shooting, which began with *Boomerang!* in 1947, and his sensitive use of local inhabitants, has given some of his films an authenticity of regional flavor which is rare in American films. In striking contrast to the sloppy approximations in such films as Richard Brooks's *Sweet Bird of Youth* (1962), Robert Mulligan's *To Kill a Mockingbird* (1962), John Frankenheimer's *I Walk the Line* (1970), and Sydney Pollack's *This Property Is Condemned* (1966), which can only make a native Southerner wince, the accents and background detail in Kazan's four excursions into the Deep South — New Orleans (*Panic in the Streets*, 1950), rural Mississippi (*Baby Doll*), rural Arkansas and Memphis (*A Face in the Crowd*, 1957) and the Tennessee Valley (*Wild River*) — are unparalleled in their accuracy; the only comparable example that comes to mind is Phil Karlson's *The Phenix City Story* (1955). (*Pinky*, 1949, and *A Streetcar Named Desire*, on the other hand, were both studio-shot, and look it.)

Despite these achievements, Kazan's work generally reflects and encourages equally scant amounts of critical detachment. Even in his most questionable enterprises Kazan can usually squeeze out the maximum amount of heat and tension implicit in any material. But if his talents are ultimately at the mercy of this material, how much of our response is dictated not by his abilities but by the material he is using?

Seen during adolescence, *East of Eden* (from John Steinbeck's novel) might be mistaken for naturalism; at a later age, it is likelier to look like expressionism; but how does one judge it "objectively"? A film which, like

its youthful hero, cries out for indulgence and sympathy, and offers a dazzling if spastic fireworks display in return, it is an experience designed to be
undergone, not an object to be contemplated; and one cannot look at that
experience without turning it into an object. Like most of Kazan's films, it
thinks with its guts, and it leaves one exhausted, but not wiser. When Cal
(James Dean) is violently dragged from his mother's presence down a dark,
narrow hallway in her whorehouse, screaming his protest and pleading
while he grasps a rail so tightly that the pimp pulling him tears off half his
sweater, the important thing is not that we are witnessing a symbolic birth
trauma, but that Kazan is doing everything he can to make us believe that
we are experiencing a real one. The tortured postures of Dean, as angular as
those in *The Cabinet of Dr. Caligari* (1919); the stark lighting and composition; the burst of highly charged anguish from Leonard Rosenman's score
and the exaggerated sounds of the violence; the pimp not just any pimp but
Timothy Carey, the quintessential B-film creep; the hyperbolical whoriness
of the bar at one end of the hall, the overwrought anger of the mother (Jo
Van Fleet) at the other — one either capitulates before it all or rejects it as
mad excess, but one can hardly sit there and watch it dispassionately.

East of Eden has been criticized for such "stylistic aberrations" as the tilted
angles in two scenes between Cal and Adam (Raymond Massey) and a
camera movement following Cal back and forth on a swing, but surely these
innovative uses of the CinemaScope format are motivated first of all by the
extravagance of Dean's performance; the camera's function is merely to set
off this spectacle as sympathetically and dynamically as possible. From the
opening pan that connects Jo Van Fleet crossing a road to Dean sitting on a
curb, the camera remains totally at the service of the actors. With the help
of Paul Osborn's script, Dean, Van Fleet, Massey, Julie Harris, and Burl Ives
all create characters who seem to extend beyond the confines of the story,
lending a certain verisimilitude to what is essentially an adolescent fantasy.
Certainly one's responses are largely determined by how much sympathy
one has with the emotional bias given to Cal; if the spectator feels "closer"
(by age or temperament) to Adam — and Massey's rich portrayal obviously
permits this — the film is bound to be more than a little irritating.

Similarly, one suspects that *On the Waterfront* (1954) falters in its final
section mainly because it is impossible for most spectators to feel, as Kazan
and Budd Schulberg (who wrote the screenplay) apparently did, that the
hero's status as an informer justifies the radical foreshortening of his character from a complex human being — perhaps Marlon Brando's densest and

A frame enlargement from *America America* illustrates Kazan's
use of aperture framing and compressed depth staging to focus the
viewer's attention. In the scene, the protagonist, Stavros (Stathis
Giallelis, *middle*), watches his Anatolian Greek father demean
himself by kissing the hand of the Turkish governor.

most fully realized role — to an icon of a suffering Christ. Admittedly, this
notion is a logical culmination of the "individual versus the mob" theme
that informs the film from the outset, observable even in the contrasts in
Leonard Bernstein's score — a solo French horn (heroic) behind the credits,
stormy percussion (threatening) behind the opening scene. But confronted
with the brilliance of Brando's performance — largely a matter of details
having little to do with this theme, like his gesture of trying on Eva Marie
Saint's glove in their first long scene together — it is difficult not to feel that
this notion is finally bent out of shape; and unless one is as obsessed with
the idea of informing as the film implies one ought to be, the final emphasis
is bound to seem somewhat false and misleading — a drastic oversimplifica-
tion of most of the issues involved. (*East of Eden*, it should be noted, ends
with some less than convincing piety of its own, when Adam's bedroom is
lit in a way that suggests a cathedral.)

On the basis of interviews and other external evidence, it is evident that
East of Eden and *On the Waterfront* both contain elements that relate quite
personally to Kazan — the father-son relationship in the former, the issue
of becoming an informer in the latter. (In 1954 Kazan supplied names of

former Communist associates to HUAC; other "friendly" witnesses included Schulberg and Lee J. Cobb, who acted in *On the Waterfront.* In *The Visitors,* scripted by Kazan's son Chris, informing again becomes a central issue.) Indeed, a particular stylistic emphasis is given to these elements which makes them the pivotal points in each film: Adam's refusal of Cal's gift shown in the most extreme of *East of Eden's* tilted angles, Terry Malloy's "confession" — made successively to priest and girlfriend — highlighted by the fact that it is unheard (the first time, the actors walk away from the camera; the second time, a boat whistle covers it up).

In reviews of *East of Eden* and *Baby Doll,* Truffaut suggested that Kazan's unity was to be found neither in shots nor in films but in scenes, and the longer the scene the better. It is a persuasive idea, and one that helps to explain why *Baby Doll* survives as one of Kazan's most controlled and successful works. Built almost exclusively around very long scenes, first between Carroll Baker and Karl Malden, then Baker and Eli Wallach, and then all three together, it sustains its peculiar brand of black comedy until the last scene, when the tone abruptly shifts to bittersweet pathos. None of the three leads has ever given a better performance: Malden's top-heavy puggishness is for once turned into a marvelous comic instrument as he assumes the mulish pride of Archie Lee, Tennessee Williams's engaging variation on Faulkner's Jason Compson — a villain we love to hate, whose angry tirades ring like lyrical cadenzas; Wallach, as the sly Sicilian, conveys an icy intensity of "grace under pressure" that suggests enormous reserves of energy; while Baker's girlish eroticism prefigures, and very likely influenced, the sorts of parts that Tuesday Weld would later expand upon. Possibly because *Baby Doll* is the least ambitious of Kazan's mature works (excepting only *Panic in the Streets,* an expert thriller) and is not burdened, except incidentally, with conveying any profound social or emotional truths, even the most questionable devices — such as the use of local blacks as Greek chorus — are handled with a measured ease which makes them work. Most impressive of all is the lengthy seduction scene staged in and around the crumbling mansion, a virtuoso acting exercise that runs (with brief interruptions and diversions) for nearly an hour.

But if Kazan works best in his longest scenes — usually those, one should add, with only two characters — what are we to make of his more recent films, where the scenes have become progressively shorter and more fragmented, and the overall unity sought is a thematic consistency binding together a mosaic? This trend can already be seen in the scattershot hysteria of *A Face in the Crowd*, where the montage sequences serve to convey both Schulberg's simplistic sociological notions (a housewife watching television and declaring, "Ain't that the truth!") and the exciting if overaccelerated rise to power of the hillbilly hero. But even more than this film and other earlier works — well-intentioned, offensive nonsense like *Gentleman's Agreement* (1947) (Be nice to Gregory Peck because he's a Gentile playing a Jew) and *Pinky* (Be nice to Jeanne Crain because she's playing a black girl playing a white); Cold War agitprop like *Viva Zapata!* (1952) and *Man on a Tightrope* (1953); and Manichean psychodramas like *On the Waterfront*, *East of Eden*, and *Splendor in the Grass* — *America America* (1963), *The Arrangement*, and *The Visitors* are ostentatiously thesis films, and the details seized in individual shots and short scenes are stacked together to support the overriding arguments.

In *America America* and *The Arrangement* — parts I and III of a still unfinished quasi-autobiographical trilogy — the grandness of the conceptions theoretically justifies this procedure; a geographical-cultural density is attempted in the first, a psychological-chronological depth in the second, although even here the best scenes are invariably the longest ones: Stavros's confession of duplicity to his fiancée in the apartment that has been furnished for their marriage; Eddie and Florence Anderson thrashing out their own marriage in a hotel suite. (Women tend to figure for Kazan, here and elsewhere, as the Great Imponderables, but it is interesting that the best acting in both films generally comes from women, perhaps because they're allowed a greater range and more leeway.) But if these works take up serious and commanding themes which make them intermittently compelling, they are limited in each case by Kazan's lack of objective distance from his heroes: Stavros's monomaniacal wish to get to America is matched only by Kazan's monomaniacal insistence on the moral duplicity which this requires, repeated in nearly every scene, and scarcely helped by the monotonous performance of Stathis Giallelis, who chiefly dramatizes his dilemma by covering his mouth and glaring intensely. Kazan's novel *The Arrangement*, whatever its faults, betrayed an R. D. Laing–influenced concern about the definition of sanity that permitted a searching examination of its hero's situation; the film reduces this question to such narrow dimensions that the issue of "selling out" begins to center less around Eddie Anderson and more around the question of why Kazan chose to cheapen the most interesting aspects of his own novel.

Fragmentation in *The Visitors* — principally a matter of crosscutting between simultaneous scenes — serves mainly to create crude juxtaposi-

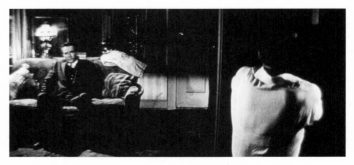

A frame enlargement from *Wild River* demonstrates Kazan exploiting the width and depth of the CinemaScope composition to emphasize the simultaneous separation and union of Chuck Glover (Montgomery Clift) and Carol Garth (Lee Remick).

tions, inhibiting the narrative flow and making the exposition rather laborious. A daring experiment in low-budget, super-16mm shooting that deals with the horror of the Vietnam War and the domestic violence that ensued from it, it features a remarkably strong, believable performance by a nonprofessional (Steve Railsback as Nickerson) and raises a lot of questions; but too many of these revolve around the film's own methods and assumptions. Why does the protagonist, who reports the rape and murder of a Vietnamese girl by his fellow soldiers, wait until two of these men turn up for revenge, months later, before telling his girlfriend about the incident? Is the girl's flirtation with Nickerson credible by any criteria but the most didactic? After establishing the *machismo* of the visitors and the girl's father a dozen different ways, to the point of caricature, why push the point even further by underlining that they like their steaks rare, while the informer likes his "nearly burnt?" If the latter truly abhors violence, why does he strike the first blow in his climactic fight with Nickerson? (The same problem turns up elsewhere in Kazan — in *East of Eden*, when the peace-loving Aaron viciously turns on Cal; more centrally in *The Assassins*, Kazan's second novel, when the nonviolent hippie hero Michael ends up murdering a sympathetic ally to express his cynicism about social injustice. Are all of Kazan's "pacifists" imposters?)

In striking contrast to this garish overkill is the quiet, understated control of *Wild River*, Kazan's best film — an elegiac meditation on the relationship between social progress (the construction of a Tennessee Valley Authority dam in the late thirties) and individual intransigence (the refusal of an old woman, Ella Garth, to vacate her premises before her island is flooded), including the most complex and finely detailed love story in all Kazan's work. Here one finds an editing style that succeeds beautifully in expressing and amplifying the theme: by continually cutting from medium shots to long shots, Kazan moves from considering the characters on their own terms to situating them in the natural settings which help to identify them — the land, fields, buildings, and river which are never only backdrops to the story, but form an integral part of it. As many have noted, the theme and style are quite Fordian; at the end of the first meeting between Chuck (Montgomery Clift), the TVA agent, and Ella (Jo Van Fleet) on the latter's porch, after her granddaughter Carol (Lee Remick) says to Chuck, "If I was you, I'd go now," and the family withdraws into the house, Kazan cuts to a long shot of Chuck framed though the closing door that unmistakably echoes the final shot of *The Searchers* (1956).

In an extended scene between Chuck and Carol the same principle is used differently, to even greater effect. As Carol tries to learn whether Chuck will take her away with him when his job is over, their dialogue is shown in angle/reverse-angle, emphasizing the emotional distance between them by isolating each in separate shots. When Chuck finally indicates that he *does* intend to leave without her, she starts to cry, at which point there is a cut to both of them in a single shot — Carol standing against a wall in the right foreground of the CinemaScope frame, Chuck sitting on the sofa in center background — a transition which, coinciding with Carol's tears, defines the moment when their separate lives become irrevocably linked.

Paul Osborn, who scripted *Wild River* as well as *East of Eden*, and Jo Van Fleet, who makes extraordinary contributions to each, are undoubtedly responsible for much of the distinction of both films, but obviously much credit is due Kazan as well. It is paradoxical that all three collaborated on two works which are so radically different, and which reveal Kazan at his most rhetorically effective and his most classically restrained. From the sensitive directing of Peggy Ann Garner in *A Tree Grows in Brooklyn* to the spectacular helicopter shots in *The Arrangement* — two examples out of dozens — the films of Kazan are full of isolated achievements. But *Wild River* represents an isolated achievement of its own: a masterful integration of the social with the personal, the romantic with the practical, the historical with the contemporary, the subjective with the objective, the local with the universal — a fusion of long scenes with a broad vision that creates Kazan's one achieved masterpiece.

NOTES

1. Robert Cornfield, "Introduction," in Elia Kazan, *Kazan on Directing* (New York: Knopf, 2009), x.

2. Roger Tailleur, *Elia Kazan* (Paris: Éditions Seghers, 1971), 48, 61, 79.

3. Andrew Sarris, *The American Cinema: Directors and Directions, 1929–1968* (New York: Da Capo Press, 1996), 158.

4. Eric Bentley, "*What Is Theatre?*" in *The Dramatic Event* (New York: Atheneum, 1968), 110.

LEO BRAUDY

"The Director, That Miserable Son of a Bitch"

Kazan, Viva Zapata! *and the Problem of Authority*

My advice and warning to people starting out in
this field is not to surrender authority to anyone.

ELIA KAZAN

A strong man makes a weak people.

VIVA ZAPATA!

Whenever the discussion turns to a particular film director, the whole question of the auteur theory reemerges, with its as-sumptions — or at least its conjectures — about personal style, aesthetic control, and, most basic of all, the equivalence between authority and value: What makes a Kazan film and what makes it good? What is his signature as a director? After the great pioneering directors who began their careers in the 1910s and 1920s — D. W. Griffith, John Ford, Fritz Lang, Jean Renoir, Alfred Hitchcock, and others — Kazan represents a new genera-tion, fully aware of those who have gone before but intent on making his own way. As Kazan himself said in a 1973 talk at Wesleyan, although the auteur theory was "partly a critic's plaything," nevertheless "the director is the true author of the film."[1] And he spent the rest of his time arguing in great detail the need for the director to have a wealth of knowledge, of dramatic forms, of literature, of the physical forms of theater, of acting, of history, of all physical environments, including city and country, of topography, of war — the list, if not endless, abounds.

When Andrew Sarris first brought the auteur theory of François Truf-faut and *Cahiers du Cinéma* to America, there were responses heralding the writer, the actor, the set designer, et al. as equally if not more responsible for the ultimate value of the film. But Kazan by 1973, about ten years after auteurism had hit American shores, was hardly being exclusive. Writers in particular he considered essential, although he also insisted that the direc-tor have a hand in the final script, and his annotations of scripts in the

Wesleyan collection show how constantly he made his opinion known. Any comparison between the final shooting script and what appears on screen in a Kazan film demonstrates his involvement. And his most common comment is "how can I show this without telling it?" The text is what the writer gives him, but, as he says, the subtext is what the director directs, and the more the text can be conveyed by subtext, the happier Kazan seems to be.

With that attitude, it's easy to assume that writers had a tough time with Kazan. Budd Schulberg's script for On the Waterfront, for example, first published in 1980, twenty-six years after the film appeared, often bears little resemblance to what appears on the screen. Is this competitive? Is it Schulberg getting his own back? But Schulberg always spoke highly of his relation with Kazan, and of course they made A Face in the Crowd (1957) after On the Waterfront (1954) and had yet another project in mind, although it ultimately went nowhere. As Schulberg has said, his experiences in Hollywood soured him on working within the studio system: "I thought I had left filmmaking forever after the war. I hated the way [writers] were treated." But when they sat down to work on On the Waterfront, "Kazan and I really meshed, so much that we could almost read each other's mind. . . . [He] was marvelously open to suggestions."[2] Brenda Murphy's book on the collaborations between Kazan and Tennessee Williams makes with even more detail the same point of Kazan's active collaboration with the writers whose work he was staging. And all of them seemed to come out of the experience with positive feelings. Arthur Miller as well considered Kazan to be the only director he knew who understood the relation between any particular moment in a play and the overall shape of a play.[3]

We could ask a similar question about Kazan's other great strength, his work with actors. Anyone he has directed has stories about Kazan's whispered words before scenes: sometimes fairly straightforward, as when he whispered "Jeffrey" in Eva Marie Saint's ear before a love scene with Marlon Brando in On the Waterfront, to indicate that she should feel toward him as she felt toward her husband, Jeffrey Hayden; sometimes more manipulative, as when he would increase the tension between Anthony Quinn and Brando in Viva Zapata! (1952) by playing on their insecurities as well as their desire to be friends to get the differing degrees of camaraderie and competitiveness he needed for the film.[4] But by the same token actors as well have primarily positive memories of their experience with Kazan as director. Whatever their irritation at the time, they seemed to have felt, like Schulberg, Miller, and others, that they were all in it together, and Kazan's

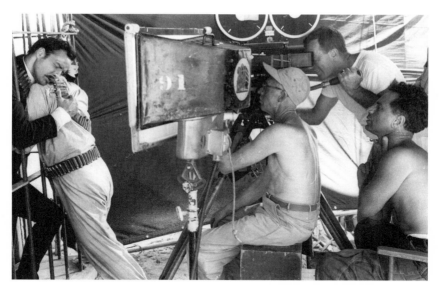

Elia Kazan (*far right*) watches Marlon Brando (*far left*) during the filming of a scene in *Viva Zapata!* Photo courtesy of the Wesleyan Cinema Archives.

authority as director was entirely in the service of showing them and their work to best advantage, what Kazan called "the mutual effort to excel at any cost."[5]

Viva Zapata! offers some interesting ways to get at this special quality of Kazan's directorial imagination and practice because more than any of his films, it directly faces the question of authority, what it means to be in charge, and the toll it takes. At the heart of *Viva Zapata!* there is a profound ambivalence about the idea of the leader, especially the self-promoting leader who, like Porfirio Diaz (Fay Roope) at the beginning of the film, adorns his public rooms with larger-than-life portraits of himself. The cult of personality is never mentioned, but it plays like an undercurrent in the film, which Kazan, in the often reductive way he treated the politics of his films, described in interviews as akin to a direct punch in the nose to Stalin and fascist dictators.[6] In their remarks on the film, both Kazan and John Steinbeck, who wrote the script, emphasize their effort to explore how revolutions so often institutionalize themselves as dictatorships. Kazan especially pushed this point in the exchange over *Viva Zapata!* in the *Saturday Review of Literature* the year the film was released. The contretemps started with Hollis Alpert's review, calling much of the dialogue (like the line in

In a frame enlargement from *Viva Zapata!* Emiliano Zapata (Marlon Brando) steps out of a group of Mexican peasants to implore President Diaz (Fay Roope, *foreground left*) to protect their land.

my epigraph) "stock phrases . . . a homely philosophy that falls sourly on the ear," and accusing Steinbeck and Kazan of having made Fernando, the character played so archly by Joseph Wiseman, into a doctrinaire ideologue in order to deflect "the criticism of those quick and eager to smell scarlet rats."[7] A few weeks later Laura Z. Hobson—the author of *Gentlemen's Agreement*, for whose movie version Kazan had won an Academy Award— wrote in a column that she was puzzled by Alpert's account of a film she admired and then weighed in with an account of Steinbeck's research and his interpretation of the events dramatized in the film. Finally, a week later, Kazan himself contributed a long letter, defending the film and emphasizing that it was exactly Zapata's renunciation of power that drew him to the subject. He also argued that the hostility with which the possibility of filming in Mexico had been received had been due to this theme: "No Communist, no totalitarian, ever refused power. . . . The man who refused power was not only no Communist; he was that opposite phenomenon: a man of individual conscience."[8]

Richard Schickel justly calls *Viva Zapata!* "Kazan's most overtly ideological movie, the one in which he most openly stated the political ideas, and ideals, he would go on worrying for the rest of his life."[9] But politics here seems to me less important as an animating force than the whole question of heroism: Can the leader work for the good of the people, or will he be ultimately absorbed by the very system he seeks to bring down? It's a political question that slides easily into analogy with an aesthetic question: Can the director work with his collaborators as an ensemble, or is his own position of authority too far above them for creative interchange? To a great extent it was a question that came up in interminable Group Theatre arguments during the 1930s, as it would in the Left politics of the 1960s — one reason why the activists of the Students for a Democratic Society considered the film seminal for their movement and its own "power to the people" ethic of participatory democracy, even though it had been condemned by other leftist critics. But the antiauthoritarian vision of *Viva Zapata!* also alludes to the forces that come into play outside the bounds of an individual film: the producers and bean counters of the studio system. According to John Womack, Jr., Zapata in fact never really had the power (presidential, as the movie implies) to abdicate, although he did renounce the military coalition with Villa and went home. Yet the key for both Kazan and Steinbeck is the refusal of power.[10]

The problem with power is not only that one might get a swelled head and become a portrait-painted "hero." The way the enigmatic Fernando moves opportunistically from one side to another Kazan in his letter identifies as a "Communist mentality. . . . He typifies the men who use the just grievances of the people for their own ends, who shift and twist their course, betray any friend of principle or promise to get power and keep it."[11] But a more sinister presence is the nameless character who in turn is Diaz's secretary, then Madero's, then Zapata's, then Fernando's. Perhaps the real problem is not opportunism or an urge to political power but bureaucracy.

I don't want to reduce Kazan's aesthetics to his politics, or his politics to his aesthetics, but to point out how interwoven they are. Strikingly, Kazan has said that he first became interested in the Zapata story in the mid-1930s, after the success of Wallace Beery in *Viva Villa* (1934), but also when Kazan was beginning to chafe against his subordinate jack-of-all-trades role in the Group Theatre that won him the nickname "Gadg," and the psychic shadow of always being on the outside looking in, yielding what John Lahr has called "the outcast's desire for revenge."[12] Zapata similarly is torn between the desire to join an official society — his premeditated willingness to trade proverbs in the courtship scene with Josefa (Jean Peters) — and his emotional directness when he sees injustice. Intriguingly similar to Kazan's picture of his younger self in his autobiography, Zapata's own longings for respectability get him into trouble. They represent a desire to be accepted by an older generation, an older tradition, that mirrors Kazan's frequently mentioned conflicts with his own father, and invokes as well the array of father-son conflicts that form the spine of so many of his films. Such Oedipal clashes know no boundaries of political right and wrong. There

A frame enlargement from *Viva Zapata!* depicts Zapata (Marlon Brando) uncomfortable with his new power. Kazan frames Zapata behind the president's desk receiving the supplications of peasants from his village much as former President Diaz did, visually encouraging the viewer to compare and contrast the two leaders.

may be anger against repressive and dictatorial father figures like Diaz, but there is also no great love for the ineffectual liberal paternalist Madero (Harold Gordon), who even has a good word for General Huerta (Frank Silvera), who will order his murder: "He's got good qualities too."

Fernando from this angle is less the political opportunist than the word-person, "the man with the typewriter" who is always more worried about structure than meaning. "This is all very disorganized," he says despairingly when he first meets Zapata and his small band of insurgents. In the more autobiographical allegory I am suggesting, Fernando's emphasis on words and logic is the foil to the often inarticulate side of Zapata, who conveys more with his face and his gestures than with his words, and on his wedding night insists that his middle-class bride teach him how to read from the Bible.

What choice then does *Viva Zapata!* give its audience between the necessary corruptions of government and the lonely but finally impotent individual, whose only influence seems to be the posthumous power of his martyrdom? Part of its strength as a film, I would argue, lies exactly in its ambiguous relation to any explicit political solution. It certainly traffics in ideology, but its answer is not a treatise but a movie, whose ideals are more coherently understood in relation to the community of the Actors Studio, which Kazan cofounded with Cheryl Crawford and Robert Lewis so that actors might have a home where they could work on and discuss their craft. The contribution each person in an ensemble makes to theater is usually more obvious than it often tends to be in the more star-oriented world of film. Here is the crux of the seeming Kazanian paradox of the two quotations I have used as epigraphs. The director must have authority, but his authority is based on the knitting together of the preexisting strengths of his performers and crew. This is the auteur as collaborator, resembling the way Jean Renoir and John Ford often worked with what Renoir called his *équipe*, the dynamic group with whom his own role as director could most easily mesh.

Tied to this vision of community in *Viva Zapata!* is the sense of place that Kazan had been exploring since *Panic in the Streets* (1950), which he considered to be his first effort to break away from the confines of the stage, where he knew "only how to talk actors into doing what I wanted them to do."[13] In *Panic in the Streets*, however, it's the ambience of New Orleans as a city that plays an important role, whereas more often it is the country that most compellingly inspires Kazan's emotions. Griffith and Ford among the Americans, Jean Renoir and Marcel Pagnol among the Europeans, stand behind Kazan in this acute sense of the relation of environment to action and character. But a special charge also comes from Kazan's politics, as if he set out explicitly to contradict the urban bias expressed by Marx's phrase "the idiocy of rural life." In *Viva Zapata!* particularly, but also in *East of Eden* (1955), *Baby Doll* (1956), *Wild River* (1960), and *America America* (1963), the land is primary. As Zapata says in the film, "Our cause was land and not a thought . . . liberty, not a word." Perhaps Kazan's own communism might therefore be considered less Marxist and more like the critique of Marx by Peter Kropotkin—an anarchist, land-oriented view of politics that tends to believe that law is always an excuse for tyranny. As Diaz says in the first scenes of *Viva Zapata!*: "Verify your boundaries, my children. Facts, facts. You must have patience." To which Zapata's answer is, "These men make their tortillas with corn, not patience."[14]

In *Elia Kazan: A Life*, Kazan mentions Marcel Pagnol as a particular favorite of his, a connection that is rarely explored. In Pagnol's films, set for the most part in his native Provence, the characters grow out of their soil as immediately as the peasants who come to rescue Zapata after he is captured by the *rurales* emerge from the craggy land and hillsides. It's a kind of solidarity that is imitated in Stanley Kubrick's *Spartacus* (1960) when in Dalton Trumbo's script the defeated army refuses to incriminate Spartacus individually and each man insists instead that he is Spartacus—the leader diffused into each one of his followers. In the Wesleyan archives there are letters in which Kazan expresses some discomfort with changes in the script that introduced lines like "A strong man makes a weak people." But in the argument over the historical accuracy of the depiction of Zapata and his abdication, as well as its connection to the anticommunist politics of Steinbeck and Kazan, little note has been taken of similar attitudes voiced in Bertolt Brecht's *Galileo*, which premiered in Los Angeles in 1947: "Pity the country without heroes. Pity the country that needs heroes." Is *Viva Zapata!* then the crossroads at which Brecht, Trumbo, and Kazan come together? It's another seeming paradox of those postwar times, perhaps more mediated by the flexible bonds of aesthetic coherence than the iron law of political ideology.

In the less reflective applications of the auteur theory to films, the director has power over all the elements, especially the actor and the writer. But when Kazan disengaged himself from what he was so accomplished at as a theater director in order to discover what he needed to learn about film, he not only became sensitive to the shaping power of environment but also discovered an ambivalence about his own authority, a fruitful bad conscience about being a director. Ultimately, I think Kazan is most interesting as a director when he is most ambivalent, ambivalent not in the sense of uncertain but in the sense of staging and exploring conflicting values, which when reduced to abstractions are contradictory but when embedded in character are complex. Ambivalence in art lasts, while certainty stays fixed in its period. Like the uncertain line in *Viva Zapata!* between self-display and vulnerability — Diaz's portrait on the wall and Diaz's portrait pulled down, Brando stripped to the waist on his wedding night and Brando's bullet-riddled body at the end of the film — politics and aesthetics, ideology and feeling, blend together in *Viva Zapata!* to create a film whose meaning continues to entice, confuse, and enlighten.

NOTES

1. Elia Kazan, "On What Makes a Director," in *Kazan on Directing* (New York: Knopf, 2009), 237.

2. Quotations from Budd Schulberg are from interviews conducted in Los Angeles with the author in the spring and summer of 2004 in preparation for writing *On the Waterfront* (London: British Film Institute, 2005).

3. "Arthur Miller Ad-Libs on Elia Kazan," in Matthew C. Roudané, ed. *Conversations with Arthur Miller* (Jackson: University Press of Mississippi, 1987), 70–71.

4. Elia Kazan, *Elia Kazan: A Life* (New York: Knopf, 1988), 429–30; Richard Schickel, *Elia Kazan* (New York: HarperCollins, 2005), 243–44.

5. Elia Kazan, "The Pleasures of Directing," in *Kazan on Directing* (New York: Knopf, 2009), 252.

6. Jeff Young, *Kazan: The Master Director Discusses His Films* (New York: Newmarket Press, 1999), 93.

7. Hollis Alpert, "Kazan and Brando Outdoors," *Saturday Review of Literature*, February 9, 1952, 25–26.

8. Laura Z. Hobson, "Trade Winds," *Saturday Review of Literature*, March 1, 1952, 6–7; Elia Kazan, "Elia Kazan on *Zapata*" (letter to the editor), *Saturday Review of Literature*, March 5, 1952, 22–23.

9. Schickel, *Elia Kazan: A Biography*, 247.

10. John Womack, Jr., *Zapata and the Mexican Revolution* (New York: Knopf, 1968), 127–28.

11. Kazan, "Elia Kazan on *Zapata*," 22.

12. Foreword to *Kazan on Directing*, xi.

13. Kazan, *Elia Kazan: A Life*, 375.

14. Similarly, one of Zapata's final charges against Fernando when Zapata leaves office is that he has no attachments to people or to land: "No wife, no woman, no home, no field." Womack quotes an interview Zapata gave on leaving Mexico City in 1914: "I am going to work at discharging the men who helped me so I can retire to private life and go back to farming my fields" (Womack, *Zapata and the Mexican Revolution*, 128).

Kazan's a man of natural responses;
he's always true to himself — for good
and bad. He just can't be bothered living
by any of the made-up rules.

CLIFFORD ODETS

VICTOR S. NAVASKY

Mr. Kazan Goes to Washington

A Case Study in Misguided Ambivalence

W hen I first interviewed Elia Kazan way back in 1973 for the book that became *Naming Names*, I asked him how he felt about his April 1952 testimony before the House Un-American Activities Committee (HUAC), in which, at the committee's insistence, he named former Party comrades in the Group Theatre, and thereby avoided being placed on the ubiquitous blacklist that then haunted Hollywood. He told me he didn't want to talk with me about that, and he gave three reasons:

First, he had read an essay I had written where I had referred to his "peddling" paperback rights to his novel, *The Arrangement*, and "until you take back that slur" he didn't want to talk with me.

Second, he was going to write about it in his own way at his own pace, and maybe after that we could talk about what he had said.

And third, to convey the dilemma he faced in all of its nuanced complexities would require a novelist's ability to recreate the context of the times, and he was a novelist, and I wasn't, ergo . . . (The wise guy in me refrained from asking whether that meant that he would be writing another work of fiction.)

Subsequently, he did agree to talk with me, but (for the reasons listed above) not about his testimony. Nevertheless, in a number of interviews connected with my book, he would bring up the subject of informing, but once-removed, as it were. For example, once, as we talked, he invited me to join him in watching John Dean, who was appearing before the Senate Watergate Committee in its televised hearings. Neither of us was unaware that Dean was an informer who might be said to be engaged in socially constructive betrayal. On another occasion, Kazan mentioned a jury on which he had served that had been about to acquit a guilty man because the only evidence against him was provided by a police informant, until Kazan and the critic Alfred Kazin, who was also on the jury, had intervened and carried the day. He lent me the transcript of a trial involving a Jewish Defense League police informer who was being persecuted by the police. And when we ran into each other on a Broadway bus a few days after Solzhenitsyn's *Gulag Archipelago* was published, Kazan observed, "Isn't it interesting that all of that was going on while all of what you're looking at was going on?" The implication: if he was right about Stalinist brutality, perhaps he was not altogether wrong to name the names of those who denied Stalinist brutality.[1]

The one person he had talked with at considerable length about his testimony was the French critic Michel Ciment. His message: that the choice confronting him (to cooperate or not to cooperate) was one that would cause pain either way, but all things considered, he did what he thought was the right thing to do; and that since in certain contexts to inform could be an act of honor, it was simplistic to condemn all informers. Here is some of what he told Ciment:

> I don't think there's anything in my life toward which I have more ambivalence, because, obviously, there's something disgusting about giving other people's names. On the other hand . . . at that time I was convinced that the Soviet empire was monolithic. . . . I also felt that their behavior over Korea was aggressive and essentially imperialistic. . . . Since then I've had two feelings. One feeling is that what I did was repulsive, and the opposite feeling, when I see what the Soviet Union has done to its writers, and their death camps, and the Nazi pact, and the Polish and Czech repression . . . it revived in me the feeling I had at that time, that it was essentially a symbolic act, not a personal act. I also have to admit . . . that there was a personal element in it, which is that I was angry, humiliated, and disturbed — furious, I guess — at the way they booted me out of the Party. . . . I had a choice between two evils, but one thing I could not see was [by not saying anything] to continue to be part of the secret maneuvering and behind-the-scenes planning that was the Communist Party as we knew it. I've often since then felt on a personal level that it's a shame that I named people, although they were all known, it's not as if I were turning them over to the police, everybody knew who they were, it was obvious and clear. It was a token act to me, and expressed what I thought at the time.[2]

Then, in 1988, in his 848-page memoir *Elia Kazan: A Life*, he did write about it in his own way and at almost interminable length, sharing in concrete detail his initial thoughts and second and third thoughts. When he first appeared before the Committee he talked freely about himself and his own brief (eighteen-month) membership in the Party when he had been in the Group Theatre in the early thirties. But he declined to name others. Then, before his second appearance in which he did name other Party members in the Group, he tells of advance conversations he had with a number of those whose opinions he valued, among them the playwright Arthur Miller. "What the hell am I giving all this up for?" he rhetorically asked his former (and future) collaborator. "To defend a secrecy I didn't think right and to defend people who'd already been named or soon would be by someone else?" As he explains, "I said I'd hated Communists for many years and didn't feel right about giving up my career to defend them. That I would give up my film career if it was in the interests of defending something I believed in but not this."[3] Miller, according to Kazan, told him to do what he thought he had to do.

But when he met with the playwright Lillian Hellman to tell her what he meant to do, she listened and then left, he later learned, in silent protest. In *Elia Kazan: A Life* he writes, "I believe now that she wanted me to become the 'villain' I became. Life was easier for Lillian to understand when she had someone to hate, just as her plays were easier for her to construct when she had a 'heavy' to nail. It simplified the issues. Later I heard her reaction to me, the old familiar one: He sold out! He did it for the money! It was not the reason. In the end, when I did what I did, it was for my own good reasons and after much thought about my own experiences. I did what I did because it was the more tolerable of two alternatives that were, either way, painful, even disastrous, and either way wrong for me. That's what a difficult decision means. Either way you go, you lose."[4]

In his book, he even added a thoughtful note of self-doubt when he wrote, as if asking himself: "What good deeds were stimulated by what I'd done? What villains exposed? How is the world better for what I did? It had just been a game of power and influence."[5] But for me, he also writes apropos *On The Waterfront* (1954) in which dockworker Terry Malloy (Marlon Brando) takes the unpopular but morally mandatory action of testifying against the corrupt labor boss Johnny Friendly (Lee J. Cobb, who in real life also named names before HUAC): "When Brando, at the end, yells . . . 'I'm glad what I done — you hear me? — glad what I done!' that was me saying, with identical heat, that I was glad I'd testified as I had."[6]

Eleven years later, in 1999, Kazan's name-naming was recycled yet again when the Academy of Motion Picture Arts and Sciences honored him with its Lifetime Achievement Award. Outside, protesters picketed, while inside a fair number of objecting luminaries sat stone-faced, symbolically declining to join the applause when Kazan received his Oscar. As one objector put it, "since part of his lifetime achievement was to cost others in the profession their jobs, he shouldn't be honored." At the time, my joke noir was that he deserved the award for his filmmaking, but they should print the names he named on the back of it, to remind him and everybody else of how he behaved when it counted. But the historian Arthur Schlesinger, Jr., who had no use for HUAC, nevertheless made the retrospective case for Kazan, arguing that informing isn't always a bad thing (think Nazis, think Mafia) and that "Mr. Kazan's critics are those — or latter-day admirers of those — who continue to defend Stalin after the Moscow trials, after the pact with Hitler, through the age of the gulag. One wonders at their presumption in condemning the horrors of Stalinism — horrors that the entire world, including Russia, acknowledges today."[7]

But then after the meltdown of the former Soviet Union, after the partial opening of various Soviet intelligence archives, the release by our own National Security Agency of the so-called Venona intercepts (thousands of pages of translated interceptions of communications between the Soviets and their agents in this country), the publication of various memoirs and such, it became evident that the Soviets had more spies in this country than was previously understood (certainly by the Left); and that the Communist Party of the United States of America (CPUSA) had not only been financed by Moscow, but was used as a base for Soviet espionage. Books like *Joseph McCarthy: Reexamining the Life and Legacy of America's Most Hated Senator*, by Arthur Herman, argued that the senator was essentially right after all. Even a freethinker like Nicholas von Hoffman wrote an article in the *Washington Post* (April 14, 1996) that asked, "Was McCarthy Right about the Left?" and answered in the subhead: "The Reds Were Under the Bed While the Liberals Looked Away." His point: "An adequate history of the McCarthy/Truman period, one that gives proper attention to the class, ethnic, religious, and cultural antagonisms of those times, has not yet been written. But enough new information has come to light about the Communists in the U.S. government that we may now say that point by point Joe McCarthy got it all wrong and yet was still closer to the truth than those who ridiculed him."[8]

If, indeed, the new consensus historians are right, and the newly released materials document the existence of a real Red Menace, then don't all of those who denounced Kazan and other cooperative witnesses as informers and stool pigeons owe them an apology? And don't those who want to learn what lessons history has to offer owe liberal anticommunists like Kazan, who chose to cooperate with HUAC, a reassessment, and ultimately, perhaps even their gratitude?

Richard Schickel, Kazan's posthumous biographer, would say, yes they do. Essentially what he says in *Elia Kazan: A Biography*, published in 2005, is that much as we might deplore HUAC and its crude methodology, "in the late forties and early fifties, it incontrovertibly appeared to be a harsh and permanent fact of American life. If you were unlucky enough to be caught in its sights, you had to deal with it as a reality, which, generally speaking, forced this choice on a witness: betrayal of long-lost colleagues who had, at one time, betrayed you; or abandonment of your present life and career for people you no longer respect, like, or share the values of."[9] Since the Communists had betrayed all Kazan stood for, why should he protect them?

Schickel quoted a portion of an essay he wrote for *Time* containing a point I had not seen elsewhere: How, he asked, could anyone expect people like Kazan "to assert blind, retrospective loyalty to a cause they had abandoned for good principled reasons? By that time (1952) Kazan, like many others, had acquired new, better and more pressing obligations — to the hard-learned truth about a secretive party controlled on virtually a day-to-day basis by Moscow, to the art that defined him more accurately than any politics, and above all, to new relationships."[10] That, Schickel says he was trying to say, "is the way people who are not ideologues live their lives."[11]

My problem with the Schickel analysis (as well as with the way Kazan would describe one horn of his dilemma) is that it misidentifies the values at stake. The question of naming names aside, the issue wasn't to-protect-or-not-to-protect Communists; it was whether to cooperate with and thereby help legitimize an essentially corrupt wrecking expedition of an enterprise — HUAC, and its co-Red-hunters. The HUAC hearings were not the fact-gathering occasions they purported to be, since as is well documented, the Committee already had the names they were ostensibly seeking. The Hollywood hearings were a form of American show trial that functioned as what I have called elsewhere degradation ceremonies. Their targets were not spies but for-the-most-part well-meaning former comrades who had joined the Party however many years ago because they believed, misguided though they may have been, that it was an effective way to fight the Great Depression, racism, fascism (or, as the character actor Lionel Stander put it, "to meet broads"). If Kazan wanted to expose the activities of the former comrades he felt had betrayed him, not to mention the international Communist conspiracy, without simultaneously strengthening the forces of domestic repression, he always had the option of rewriting that famous ad he took in the *New York Times*, arguing that the way to fight against totalitarian secrecy was with democratic openness (including the naming of names). He might, for example, have used half of the ad to denounce totalitarian secrecy, and the perfidious CPUSA, and then, scrupulously avoiding any hint of moral equivalence, used the other half to denounce the depredations of McCarthyism and the ways the HUAC hearings undermined our open society through its systemic antidemocratic assumptions, rituals, and procedures.

A debate still rages (although in a small room) among historians on whether the newly released archival material "proves" that this or that Left personage was a spy. Alger Hiss, I. F. Stone, Ernest Hemingway (yes, Ernest Hemingway!), among others, are all mentioned in the archives in ways that lead some post–Cold War culture warriors to call them agents. But of course none of this had anything to do with the Hollywood hearings that began as a search for Communist propaganda and ended by stigmatizing former political activists.

Kazan did not "sell out" in the sense that he did it for the money. Kazan did not face an agonizing dilemma — he truly believed the Communists (the "totalitarians") represented a social evil, and would have preferred not having had to name names. Kazan did resent the way his old comrades in the Group Theatre did business ("The secret caucuses before, the clever tactics during, the calculating positioning of our 'comrades' in the meeting hall to create the effect of a majority when the fact was that we were a small minority"),[12] but it was sadly ironic that he chose to protest Moscow's clumsy attempt at manipulating the Group through our own homegrown antidemocratic arts-bully, that is, HUAC. And most important, Kazan for all of his brilliance as a socially engaged actor, writer, director intent on using his art to make this a better society, ended up acting in a way that lent legitimacy to an antidemocratic institution whose project would undermine the artistic values he fought for, for so much of his life (and purported in his *New York Times* ad to uphold).

The bottom line:

Kazan the reluctant informer, under intense political pressure, ended up inconveniencing, and in some cases wounding, his former comrades in the Group Theatre. Kazan the whistle-blower told the truth as he knew it about the brutality of the USSR under Stalin and its toadies in the CPUSA. But Kazan the congressional witness, although he had his reasons, by cooperating with HUAC ended up helping to perpetuate an institution and project that contradicted the democratic values he so passionately purported to embrace.

NOTES

1. Victor S. Navasky, *Naming Names* (New York: Viking Press, 1980; reprint, New York: Penguin Books, 1991), 211. Citation is to the Penguin edition.

2. Michel Ciment, *Kazan on Kazan* (New York: Viking Press, 1974), 83–84.

3. Elia Kazan, *Elia Kazan: A Life* (New York: Knopf, 1988; reprint, Cambridge, Mass.: Da Capo Press, 1997), 460. Citations are to the Da Capo Press edition.

4. Ibid., 462.

5. Ibid., 685.

6. Ibid., 500.

7. Arthur Schlesinger Jr., "Hollywood Hypocrisy," *New York Times*, February 20, 1999, New York ed., sec. 4.

8. Nicholas von Hoffman, "Was McCarthy Right about the Left?" *Washington Post*, April 14, 1996, late ed., sec. C.

9. Richard Schickel, *Elia Kazan: A Biography* (New York: HarperCollins, 2005), 264.

10. Richard Schickel, "Cinema: An Oscar for Elia Kazan," *Time*, March 8, 1999.

11. Schickel, *Kazan*, xxvii.

12. Kazan, *Kazan*, 459.

BRENDA MURPHY

Man on a Tightrope
Kazan as Liberal Anticommunist

*P*erhaps abetted by Elia Kazan in his autobiography and comments in interviews, *Man on a Tightrope* (1953) has been treated by most critics as a straightforward attack on Communism that he was more or less forced to undertake. It may be more productive to see the 1953 film as part of a cluster — including *Boomerang!* (1947), *Panic in the Streets* (1950), *Viva Zapata!* (1952), and *On the Waterfront* (1954)—that express the evolving liberal anticommunist position Kazan was working out for himself in the late forties and early fifties. As Thomas Pauly has suggested, all of these films focus on the individual, typically what Kazan called "the man of individual conscience," in conflict with a corrupt authority.[1] As Kazan's views on Communism changed in the context of contemporary events, however, so did his positioning of the liberal individual. Thus the honest lawyer in the 1947 *Boomerang!* is in conflict with a corrupted justice system, a typical liberal concern. But in 1950, the uniformed public health official in *Panic in the Streets* actually *represents* the system, protecting the people, who would behave hysterically if they knew their danger, against the threat of contamination by ignoring the law and the Constitution, a position that reflects one of the justifications that was used for the actions of the House Un-American Activities Committee (HUAC) and McCarthyism in general. With *Viva Zapata!* Kazan and John Steinbeck, two disaffected former leftists, created a film about a revolutionary in which the most significant moment, according to Kazan, is when he "turn[s] his back on power," when he renounces the revolution he has led.[2]

When he began working on *Man on a Tightrope*, Kazan had effectively been outed by HUAC. He had been forced to expose his disaffection with Communism, something he later insisted needed to be done, but the means of doing so mirrored the tactics that had been used by the Communist Party against him nearly twenty years before. And now he was being told by the studio — Spyros Skouras via Darryl Zanuck — what political message to convey in his film, a perennial complaint against the Communists. Although it is overtly about a circus that escapes from Communist control to Western freedom, *Man on a Tightrope* is also deeply informed by Kazan's own response to his treatment by the American government. The threat of Communism that he dramatized is the threat to the artist's right to creative freedom and self-definition, exactly the threat that he was facing.

It is well known that after his brief flirtation with the Communist Party in the early 1930s, Kazan came to hate Communism, or more specifically the American Communist Party (cpusa). But his hatred was more a personal than an ideological matter. He said in his autobiography that he left the Party because it sought to shame him, to make him confess his sins, to apologize and grovel to the Party's representative. There he tells the story of "The Man from Detroit," which he wrote down after his resignation from the Communist Party in 1936. According to Kazan, because he was reluctant to follow the Party's directive for the actors to take control of the Group Theatre away from its directors, a "Leading Comrade" from the uaw in Detroit had been sent to correct his thinking. After listening to the man's analysis of him, with its implication that the Group should censure but forgive him, Kazan wrote that he recognized "the door was being held wide open for me to walk back into favor, except that to judge by the cow eyes of my pitying friends, I was expected to make that walk back on my knees." He stopped listening. A vote for censure was taken, and he was the only one who voted "for me."[3] Before he went to bed, he wrote a letter resigning from the Party. In his autobiography, written fifty years later, he said that the meeting taught him all he needed to know about the workings of the cpusa. He understood the police state from The Man from Detroit: "I know what I'm reading about when I see the words 'authoritarian rule.' The man was not only stopping people from thinking; he was setting up a ritual of submission for me to act out. . . . He'd come to make us all frightened, submissive, and unquestioning. The assumption of human cowardice on which he operated was so profoundly insulting that it didn't penetrate totally until years later. By then I was another man."[4]

During the 1940s, Kazan managed to remain admired by the Left, working on such socially conscious projects as *All My Sons*, *Death of a Salesman*, *Gentleman's Agreement* (1947), and *Pinky* (1949), while becoming what he later referred to as the "blue-eyed boy," Broadway's most sought-after director and a respected and very well-compensated Hollywood director as well. This status collapsed with his public testimony before HUAC on April 10, 1952, another ritual of humiliation, but this time one to which he submitted. Kazan testified twice before HUAC, once in executive session in January and then publicly in April. Describing the room in which the first interrogation took place, he said that "a film director could not have devised a more humiliating setting for a suppliant" and that "what these fellows were conducting was a degradation ceremony, in which the acts of informing were more important than the information conveyed. I didn't doubt they knew all the names they were asking for."[5] Kazan refused to give the names of his colleagues in the Group Theatre in his first testimony "as a matter of personal conscience," though he did refer to others in the Party.[6] After a good deal of soul-searching anguish and consultation of his friends, he asked to be heard again, naming the members of the Group Theatre unit and several others.[7] Kazan's behavior was no different from that of a number of other disaffected former Communists, but he became the public face of the informer because of the aggressive action he took the day after his testimony, placing an ad in the *New York Times*, which he later said was written by his wife, Molly, justifying his exposure of people who had been in the Party and calling on others to do the same. "Secrecy serves the Communists," he stated, "at the other pole, it serves those who are interested in silencing liberal voices. The employment of a lot of good liberals is threatened because they have allowed themselves to become associated with or silenced by the Communists. Liberals must speak out."[8] Kazan said in his testimony that "the last straw" in his break with the Party came when he "was invited to go through a typical Communist scene of crawling and apologizing and admitting the error of my ways. I had had a taste of police state living and I did not like it."[9] The irony of this statement was lost on HUAC, but it was certainly something Kazan was aware of.

The effect of Kazan's course of action was that he was rejected by both sides, shunned by the Left and still considered suspect by the Right. "I was on a great social griddle," he wrote, "and frying."[10] Although it was generally assumed that he had caved in to the demand to submit to HUAC in order to preserve his Hollywood salary, he always insisted that since he was now considered damaged goods, the salary he could command in Hollywood was considerably reduced. The offer from Zanuck to direct *Man on a Tightrope* came on April 17, just five days after his testimony was reported in the *New York Times*. In his autobiography, he admits that the assignment was partly intended as a proof of his anticommunist bona fides, a pressure to which he bowed in accepting the assignment. There he dramatizes an exchange with Zanuck that was actually conducted through letters and telegrams. He portrays Zanuck as saying that Kazan's sincerity was doubted and he would be attacked again unless he made the film. Kazan wrote that he had read the script by Robert Sherwood and balked at taking the assignment because it was "badly written, all-black or all-white characters, typical propaganda stuff, and I'd only be doing it to satisfy a pack of red-baiters who want my ass," whereupon Zanuck said of the screenplay: "It's true. It happened exactly that way." Kazan quotes Zanuck as saying that a lot of people, including him, still had questions about where he stood, and himself as replying "I don't care . . . I've done all the crawling I'm going to do."[11] Upon reflection, he wrote, he had decided that his knee-jerk reaction against the story about the circus that had jumped the border to freedom was a trace of his old loyalty to the Communist Party. He decided to go to Bavaria to see the Cirkus Brumbach, on which the story was based, and "If I found out that what I'd read in Sherwood's script was true and not pumped-up propaganda, I'd make the film; if not, not."[12] Zanuck sent Sherwood to go along with him. In the autobiography, Kazan says that it was meeting the people in Cirkus Brumbach that convinced him: "I was not dealing with a faulty scenario; I was dealing with an event in history. There was only one conclusion I could come to: I had to make this film to convince myself—not others—that I was not afraid to say true things about the Communists or anyone else, that I was still capable of free inquiry, that I was no longer a Party regular in my head."[13]

The account in the autobiography makes a good story, as well as a useful narrative for conveying what Kazan wanted to convey about the making of the film: that firsthand experience with people who had suffered directly from the oppression of a Communist regime validated his own actions and made him stronger and more self-reliant when dealing with his critics. At the end of the experience, he was determined, he said, "not to look for support or friendship where I'd once had it. I determined to look everyone in the eye when I got back and tough it out."[14] But the documentary evidence shows that things did not come about exactly as Kazan suggested they did. The offer to make the film actually came by letter from Zanuck, not in person, and the only allusion to Kazan's HUAC troubles was an opening paragraph in which Zanuck said that he agreed with Spyros Skouras, the right-wing head of Twentieth Century-Fox, "about the present situation" and that he was just as eager as Skouras "to have you make a picture now."[15]

Elia Kazan appears with an unknown circus performer, one of the extras in *Man on a Tightrope*. Kazan shot on location in West Germany using the same troupe, Cirkus Brumbach, whose story was the subject of the movie. Photograph by Karl Ewald. Photo courtesy of the Wesleyan Cinema Archives.

He then went on to explain the situation with "Man on the Tightrope [*sic*]": Robert Jacks, his son-in-law and a young producer at Fox, had found the story in an obscure English magazine and shared it with the director Henry Hathaway, who had become "a sort of co-sponsor of the operation."[16] Zanuck was proposing "*confidentially*" to take the project away from Hathaway and give it to Kazan, putting Hathaway instead on a big Technicolor extravaganza he was planning, *Queen of Sheba*.[17] Zanuck's main concern was to get Kazan's agreement to do the picture before Hathaway got wind of his plans. He asked Kazan, "a good friend of Sherwood's," to talk with him about the draft he was working on, and "if it appeals to you, then please get in touch with me."[18] After reading Sherwood's treatment, Kazan sent a letter and a telegram conveying his dissatisfaction with it, and told Zanuck that he intended to meet with Sherwood and talk out his objections with the writer.

In a long letter to Zanuck on May 10, Kazan outlined his problems with the Sherwood script as it was beginning to take shape. Overtly anticommunist details were minor in his list of concerns. He made an offhand suggestion that the "heavies," the secret police, were too heavy, particularly Fesker, and reminded Zanuck that the real secret police don't wear leather coats and walk in unison. Molotov's business suit, he reminded him, concealed his "authoritarian heart."[19] He thought the second of what were originally two interrogation scenes should be cut because it was redundant. He also observed that one of the weaknesses of the love story between the circus owner Cernik (then called Barova) and his young wife Zama, besides its simply not being a good story inherently, was the "'iron curtain between us' material." This was "so much malarky!" he wrote, adding that their situation would be the same in the United States "or wherever! The Russians and the Commies are always blaming the 'system' for everything. Why should we go in for the same foolishness?"[20] Kazan also objected strongly to several conventional elements in the script, including the opening of the film, which Sherwood had set during a circus performance. He complained that this was the most banal way of starting a circus movie. Kazan wanted Sherwood to cut an extended chase sequence in which Cernik goes in search of Tereza and Joe, and he did not like the ending, which originally had Zama, not Cernik, dying heroically. He also wanted to restore the situation in Neil Paterson's original story, in which Zama was not a performer and Cernik's daughter was not a headliner.

Kazan's main complaint about the script, a complaint he voiced consistently throughout his lifetime whenever he was asked about the film, was that the two love stories, those between Cernik and Zama, and Cernik's daughter Tereza and Joe, the AWOL American GI, were "out of proportion" in the film, at the expense of the escape scene, which he thought should always be kept central.[21] In place of the conventional plot elements, Kazan thought the film should focus on the escape as the central element of the story rather than the lovers, and end with "the arrival of the circus into the *Free World*—and what this means!" If anything, he was asking for the script to be more propagandistic rather than less so.[22] He also thought they should emphasize the "backstage" aspect of the circus, showing the circus performers as unique people—"individualists," as he called them—rather than anonymous performers. To do something new, he said, the film should take an insider's perspective, letting the audience into life "behind" both the circus and the Iron Curtain. Finally, Kazan argued that the film should be shot in Europe and that he and Sherwood should go there together to research it, making a pitch for the necessity of avoiding movie convention and penetrating to the truth in the story, because it was "something red hot, something that will be seen and judged by the rest of the civilized world, and judged by very serious standards because it deals, in miniature, with the central issue of our day."[23] This claim was somewhat overblown, but from where Kazan was standing, it certainly seemed true.

Kazan eventually got his way in almost everything he brought up in the letter. He and Sherwood went to Bavaria and spent time with the people from the Cirkus Brumbach, who eventually were used in the film to portray the Cirkus Cernik. The beginning and ending were altered. The film opens with the traveling circus being brutally forced off the road to make way for a military convoy, and the mirror ending dramatizes the daring escape, as the circus parade makes its break across the border from Czechoslovakia into Bavaria, and the heroic death of Cernik (Fredric March), as he insists that the escape go on after he is shot by the Communist spy Krofta (Richard Boone). The police are bureaucrats rather than thugs, alternately bullying and bullied, sometimes lost amid their stacks of paper. As Fesker, Adolphe Menjou is not so much the heavy as the jaded, ironic policeman, outthinking the government bureaucrats, a figure reminiscent of Claude Rains in *Casablanca* (1942) but resolutely playing against his dapper image. *Newsweek* referred to him as "a sinister man with dandruff."[24] The second interrogation scene was indeed cut, and there was little of an ideological nature in the dialogue. The conservative *Saturday Review* noted with approval that despite the film's "strong political overtones," it contained no "anticommunist speeches, the characters are never allowed to become grotesque political symbols." In fact, the reviewer commented that the credibility of the Communist officials was one of the strengths of the film: "They are defeated by the rules they live by, not by the cleverness of the anti-Communist hero."[25]

Sherwood's long chase scene was also cut. Cernik simply leaves the circus to find Tereza (Terry Moore) and Joe (Cameron Mitchell), arrives on the scene, hears from Tereza that Joe is an American rather than the Communist spy Cernik had suspected him of being, and they all head back to be led by Joe across the border. To Kazan's chagrin, the "love stories" play a prominent role in the final cut of the film, which was made by Zanuck in Kazan's absence. Kazan had made the most of the romantic scenes during the filming, however. The scene in which Tereza and Joe swim in the swiftly moving river was described in one review as "one of the great erotic idyls of movie history."[26] Kazan also succeeded at showing the "backstage" of the circus, the circus people going about their daily lives, and he did a very effective job of building suspense throughout the escape sequence and making the escape seem at once quixotic and courageous, naive and daring, "individualistic," as he would say. To sum it up in *Variety's* concise language, "*Man on a Tightrope* is taut 'chase' for O.K. b.o. In all situations. . . . The political overtones are underplayed."[27]

In his notebook for the film, Kazan wrote that the theme was "simple and rudimentary." . . . "It is Liberty + Freedom. It needs no verbalizing."[28] He noted that the "unideologic" hunger for freedom should shine from the characters' faces. He also described the film as "AN ODE TO INDIVIDUALISM" with a dominant mood of pride. The emphasis on the individual is to be expected, but the type of individual Kazan was elevating in the film was quite different from Dr. Clinton Reed in *Panic in the Streets* or D. A. Henry Harvey in *Boomerang!* Circus people, he wrote, "essentialize the odd, the eccentric, the individualistic, the anarchistic, the perforce lonely." Although romantic and drawn to each other, they are also distrustful of each other, because they are also "the unregimentable, the outcasts by choice, the fiercely alone." That this is much the way Kazan was seeing himself at this point in his life probably had a good deal to do with his identification with the circus people during the making of the film. Along with the longing for freedom, he told himself he must emphasize the theme that "they retain their own selves under all pressures" — something he was trying very hard to do himself. In an odd political characterization, he wrote: "they are the epitome of the democratic citizen. In a phrase, they are romantic anarchists."[29] This may have been Kazan's view of democracy, but it certainly was not the view of democracy he had recently encountered in Washington.

In contrast to the circus people, Kazan characterized the "Servants of Totalitarianism" as rigid, humorless, suspicious, and fearful, always on the lookout because any private soldier might be either a spy or the head man. These qualities were certainly shared by the die-hard anticommunists in Washington, who flourished by creating an atmosphere in which everyone was encouraged to have fear and suspicion toward his or her neighbor, who could be a Communist or an informer. Interestingly, Kazan wrote that what these people were seeking was "the safety of being in a state of constant approval," noting that the circus people were revolted both by the need for approval and by the "THREAT behind the good-boy approval. Just as much as by the VERY REAL THREAT of withdrawing the good-boy approval."[30] This is the major psychological consequence of his testimony that he talks about in his autobiography and elsewhere. After his testimony, he said there were days "when I'd long to be forgiven, when I yearned to return to my old innocence; those harmonious times of long ago. Other days I became rambunctious, and what I longed for was a fight. I felt myself toughening. I enjoyed the apartness, had to. If I was a wolf, I'd be a lone wolf, not a herd animal." He came to believe that an artist "can't have much that's truthful to say" when "everyone likes him."[31] It was this conjunction of feelings that he sensed in, or projected onto, the circus artists, and he decided that it was their passion for their own artistic integrity as well as their essential maverick quality that led to their break across the border, to find a place where they would be free to practice their art as they wished, without seeking anyone's approval. "In the circus, as in any democracy," he wrote, "politics is secondary. . . . They just want to be a circus. But under certain conditions, they can't be a circus — i.e. they can't live their normal lives — so they're prodded to a political step."[32]

Kazan most often likened the character of Cernik to the screenwriter Robert Sherwood, proud, aloof, reserved, unyielding. But he also imputed qualities to Cernik that he claimed for himself. Like Kazan's famous "Anatolian smile," which pragmatically hid his feelings of injury and rage, Cernik's "meekness & humbleness always has something two-edged about it . . . it smells not kosher to the Communists. They resent him without knowing why. But it makes the circus people adore him without knowing quite why. His PRIDE, gives them pride. And pride is necessary to go on under humiliating circumstances."[33] This is most evident in the interrogation scene, where Cernik plays the cooperative and naive circus owner in order to keep his circus going. The casting of Adolphe Menjou, one of the prime cooperative HUAC witnesses, as an agent of the Ministry of Propaganda and of the formerly blacklisted Fredric March as Cernik has been seen as an ironic circumstance in the making of the film. Kazan was fully aware of this, and he makes full use of the resonance of these roles in his filming of the interrogation scene and in Menjou's own subsequent arrest by the police, which he plays with the polished sangfroid of Claude Rains at the end of *Casablanca*.[34]

The interrogation scene was filmed in the underground chambers of the Royal Residence in Munich, a low-ceilinged, winding, cavernous cellar that produced the oppressive effect Kazan was looking for. The wine bins in the cellar were used as file organizers for the police, with each compartment labeled with the name of a suspect, including the name of the real Czech archbishop Josef Beran, who was imprisoned for resisting the Communist regime. On the wall are large portraits of Stalin and Lenin and a smaller

In a publicity still, Commissioner of Police Fesker (Adolphe Menjou, *left*) questions Karel Cernik (Fredric March, *right*) during his interrogation in *Man on a Tightrope*, Kazan's first film after his testimony before HUAC. Photo courtesy of the Wesleyan Cinema Archives.

one of Czech president Klement Gottwald. In keeping with Kazan's view, the police are represented as bureaucratic functionaries rather than thugs. The Sergeant (Philip Kenneally) and the Police Chief (John Dehner) are jammed into a cramped space behind a desk, with the young Sergeant, who conveys the orders of the Party to the subservient Police Chief, literally looking over the Chief's shoulder and breathing down his neck as he conducts his work. After the Chief interrogates Cernik, the Sergeant critiques the interrogation, chiding the Chief for saying that the State, rather than the people, owns the circus, and the Chief apologizes abjectly and thanks him for setting him straight. Contrasting these two born bureaucrats is Adolphe Menjou's Fesker, who as a member of the Ministry of Propaganda is physically and psychologically aloof from them. He lies on a couch reading the newspaper during the interrogation and only becomes interested toward the end when he senses that Cernik is not the humble clown he is playing in the interrogation.

During the interrogation, March plays Cernik as cooperative, deferential, and ready to be instructed by the police but still trying to present his side of things. The major accusation against him is that he has not followed the directive he has received about his own clown act. At issue is a skit in which the other clown kicks him twenty-seven times in the backside, trying to get him to kick him back, while Cernik flinches but does not otherwise react. On the next kick, he turns on the clown and plants a big kiss on him, which, he says, always brings a laugh from the audience. Besides the obvious Christian overtones of this bit — turning the other cheek, responding to injury with love rather than revenge — it also carries a subtext that Kazan was looking for. There is a bit of the Anatolian smile in this clown, the trickster, the irrepressible artist who secures his revenge by startling his adversary and getting a laugh, thus winning the contest through superior wiles rather than brute strength. The Communist regime had objected to this routine and had insisted that Cernik change the bit so that he represented an American Negro worker and the other clown a Wall Street imperialist, a change that would obviously render the bit heavily propagandistic and irrelevant to the Czech audience, robbing the original of its joy, surprise, and art.

The research material Kazan received from the studio shows that this sort of government pressure was not a far-fetched scenario. There was a concerted effort in the Communist countries of Eastern Europe to get rid of traditional clowning and replace it with something more ideological. The Communist *Literary Gazette* said that "the jokes and scripts for clowns must be revised with serious social satire as their base and a school should be established where young clowns can make a deep study of social political subjects."[35] A Hungarian newspaper reported that the plan for the eleven circuses in that country was that "the clowns, wearing red wigs, giant shoes and loose dresses, who stultified the people with their hackneyed and stupid anecdotes, will disappear." In their place "new luminous artists" will take the center ring and "recite instructive Chastushkas (Russian 4-line rhymes), which speak of daily problems and are of a constructive character; the fight against the kulaks, the economic plan, etc."[36] The Czech and East German circuses were under similar orders to change.

During the interrogation, Cernik explains quietly and reasonably that the new material simply isn't funny. Audiences didn't laugh at it. He says that they worked on the bit for a long time but simply couldn't get a laugh, so they went back to the old routine. For his disobedience, he is ordered to do the skit the way he was instructed, to pay a fine, and to fire one of his performers who has a French flag, all of which he takes humbly, but when his movement permit is taken from him, he gets upset and objects that inability to travel will cripple "my circus." This sparks the Chief's rebuke that it is the State's circus, not his. Circuses have been nationalized, and he is simply the manager. Fesker has been detached from the interview to this point, but his interest is piqued when he recognizes Cernik's pride, his internal refusal to bow to authority while he outwardly plays the humble role, a quality that Kazan had noted was central to his character. Fesker advises him that he should also smash his radio so there will be no suspicion that he is listening to broadcasts from Radio Free Europe, which sends the bureaucrats frantically searching through their papers to find a reference to Cernik owning a radio. When they later tell him there is no reference, Fesker says, archly, "Isn't there?" When the Sergeant refers to Cernik as a "dull, uncomplicated clown," Fesker says he is wrong, that Cernik is a complicated man, a "profoundly shrewd, subtle, dedicated man." This earns Fesker the enmity of the Sergeant, who says he is out to make fools of the police, and makes a phone call to have him watched. This foreshadows Fesker's arrest later in the film, when he looks up at the flag flying from the building and says, "Sooner or later, it happens to all of us."

The threat to artistic freedom and creativity by government control and oppression is intensely felt throughout the film, and the embattled individual here is not an agent of the government, as in *Boomerang!* and *Panic in the Streets*, but an outsider who is persecuted by it, a position Kazan could now feel with empathy. The enemy of freedom is meant to be the Communist government, with its secret police, its stupid bureaucrats, its ubiquitous soldiers. The compelling visual metaphor of the ragtag but valiant circus parade as it makes its break for the border and creative freedom offers a powerful statement of the ability of art to resist the oppression of authoritarian government. It seems likely that this carnivalesque assertion of creative freedom was Dionysian rather than Apollonian on Kazan's part, an artistic expression of his own irrepressible resistance to his feelings of oppression, his own "ode to individualism."

The ending of the film, with its long escape sequence, has been generally recognized as its most powerful and most original element, and it is one that was invented for the film. The escape of the Cirkus Brumbach, on which the screenplay is loosely based, was not nearly as dramatic as the escape in the film. While they were wintering in East Berlin, Gustav Brumbach gradually had all his circus wagons painted brown and installed false bottoms in them so his drivers could smuggle the circus across the border into West

In a publicity still, the performer Kalka (Hansi) shoots the government mole Krofta (Richard Boone) as his colleagues at the Cirkus begin their escape across the Iron Curtain in *Man on a Tightrope*. Photo courtesy of the Wesleyan Cinema Archives.

Berlin a few wagons at a time, under cover of being a small carnival or a convoy buying feed for the animals. Each time they returned, they brought back one wagon fewer. Although this made for a number of close shaves at the border, it was not the dramatic break that occurs in the film. The inspiration for this scene was a Czech train engineer who executed a daring border crossing by not stopping his train at the border town of Asch (Aš), his last stop, but roaring through the station and taking the train a half mile into Germany. He and thirty-two other passengers sought political asylum in the United States; the seventy-seven other passengers opted to return home. This escape was dubbed the "Freedom Train" in the Western press, and received a good deal of attention.[37]

In the film, the Cirkus Cernik combines both strategies, as Cernik and his trusted colleagues carefully plan their escape across the border but make the break in the most simple and daring way possible: under the cover of being a circus parade en route to entertain the border guards, they advance all the way to the river that is the borderline with Bavaria and then break for freedom across the bridge. Because it was Zanuck who made the final cut, it is not clear how responsible Kazan was for the powerfully building suspense throughout the ten-minute sequence, which cuts between the carnivalesque circus performers in their costumes doing their parade routines and the border guards, at first suspicious and grumpy, then slowly drawn in, and then laughing and thoroughly enjoying the show, many of them leaving their posts to watch the performers more closely. Caught off guard by the performers, they don't respond quickly enough to stop the flight across the border, which is directed, of course, by Joe, the American soldier who is, as Cernik says, "trained in this sort of thing." Having established the individual characters of a number of the circus performers earlier in the film, Kazan uses close-ups and medium shots of the individuals, as each performer practices his or her art with great professionalism under tremendous pressure, juxtaposed with shots of the whole procession, the image of the irrepressible freedom of art as it moves along the road, and shots of the soldiers, the threat that pursues them. As they cross the bridge, we see shots of individual crossings and acts of bravery, shots of the soldiers desperately shooting at the performers, and shots of the controlled chaos as the whole caravan makes its way across. Besides providing a satisfying ending, Kazan also managed to convey his sense of who these people were and why they escaped. It is finally their art, their professionalism, their courage, and their stubbornness that wins them their freedom, qualities he tried to emulate when he returned home to the United States.

Kazan tended to downplay the significance of *Man on a Tightrope* throughout his life. When he was asked about it in interviews, he returned to the same topics — Zanuck's insistence that he make the film and his interference with the editing, his own friendship with the crew, and what he learned from working with East German artists, the victims of an oppressive regime. The film is perhaps more personally significant than he cared to admit, however, coming at a crucial point in the development of his art and his politics, which were deeply connected at this time. In 1952, he had a need to produce his own "ode to individualism," a celebration of the artist's pride and dedication to creative freedom. Like Cernik, he had shown the humble face of cooperation with an oppressive agency of the government, but he believed that his free artistic soul remained untouched. In making *Man on a Tightrope*, he could attack the repression of artistic freedom by a Communist regime, thus answering his critics on the Left, at the same time that he was celebrating the power of art to resist authoritarian repression, thus divorcing himself from the extremists on the Right. In celebrating creative freedom and individualism, he was marking out his position as a liberal anticommunist artist, one that he would assert more confidently in his direction of Tennessee Williams's *Camino Real*, another treatment of the free spirit's resistance to oppression, and his defense of the informer in *On the Waterfront*.

NOTES

1. See Thomas H. Pauly, *American Odyssey: Elia Kazan and American Culture* (Philadelphia: Temple University Press, 1983), 139–214.

2. Elia Kazan, "Elia Kazan on *Zapata*" (letter to the editor), *Saturday Review* 35 (April 5, 1952), 22.

3. Elia Kazan, *Elia Kazan: A Life* (New York: Knopf, 1988), 130–131.

4. Ibid., 131.

5. Ibid., 446–47.

6. Brian Neve, "Elia Kazan's First Testimony to the House Committee on Un-American Activities, Executive Session, 14 January 1952," *Historical Journal of Film, Radio and Television* 25, no. 2 (June 2005), 266.

7. For Kazan's testimony, see Neve, "Elia Kazan's First Testimony," 251–72, and House Committee on Un-American Activities, *Hearings Regarding Communist Infiltration of Hollywood Motion-picture Industry*, 82nd Cong., 2nd sess., pt. 7, April 10, 1952.

8. Kazan, "A Statement" (advertisement), *New York Times*, April 12, 1952.

9. C. P. Trussell, "Elia Kazan Admits He Was Red in '30's," *New York Times*, April 12, 1952, 8.

10. Kazan, *Kazan*, 472.

11. Ibid., 476.

12. Ibid., 476.

13. Ibid., 477.

14. Ibid., 482.

15. Darryl Zanuck to Elia Kazan, April 17, 1952, Elia Kazan Collection, Wesleyan Cinema Archives, Wesleyan University.

16. Neil Paterson's novella, originally entitled "International Incident," first appeared in the British magazine *Lilliput*. As a tie-in with the film, it was published by Random House as *Man on the Tightrope* in 1953.

17. *Queen of Sheba* never happened, but Henry Hathaway did direct *Niagara* for Fox in 1953.

18. Darryl Zanuck to Elia Kazan, April 17, 1952.

19. Elia Kazan to Darryl F. Zanuck, May 10, 1952, Kazan Collection.

20. Ibid.

21. Ibid.

22. Ibid.

23. Ibid.

24. "New Films: *Man on a Tightrope*," *Newsweek*, 41 May 11, 1953, 102.

25. "*Man on a Tightrope*," *Saturday Review*, 36 May 30, 1953, 30.

26. "New Films."

27. "*Man on a Tightrope*," *Variety*, April 1, 1953, 6.

28. Elia Kazan, notebook for *Man on a Tightrope*, Kazan Collection, n.p.

29. Ibid.

30. Ibid.

31. Kazan, *Kazan*, 472.

32. Kazan, notebook for *Man on a Tightrope*, n.p.

33. Ibid.

34. Kazan told Jeff Young that March was blacklisted and that he had "got him the lead in the picture by pulling a lot of strings and throwing my weight around." As for Menjou, he felt: "there's no reason why if I got one side work, I shouldn't get the other side work. A man is an artist first" (Jeff Young, *Kazan: The Master Director Discusses His Films: Interviews with Elia Kazan* [New York: Newmarket Press, 1999], 113).

35. "Circus Clowns Ordered to Turn to Stalin for Inspiration," *Literary Gazette*, n.d., clipping, Kazan Collection.

36. Ibid.

37. See "Czech Engineer Flees with Train and 111 Passengers to Germany," *New York Times*, September 12, 1951, 1, and the summary of press coverage in *Rescue*, 5, no. 2 (Winter 1951), 1.

For being such a gentle man Kazan can sure raise more hell than anyone I have ever known. It is awfully difficult for some to accept men possessing as many talents as Kazan. But he shall never be defeated by any outside influence or criticism. There's too much energy and creative urges to hold him back from doing what he thinks is right.

ROBERT SURTEES

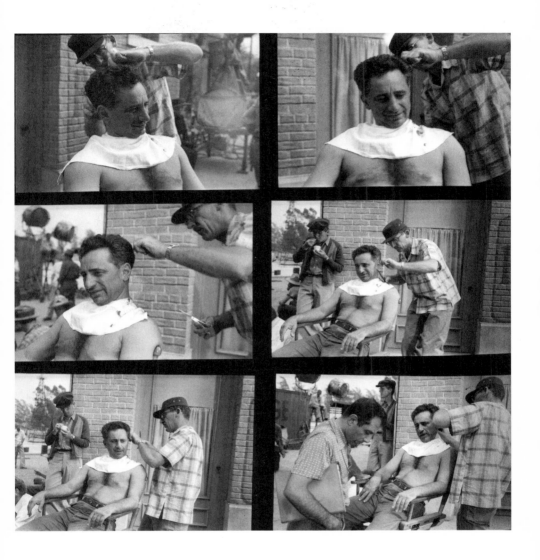

"Independence" and the "Art Film"
Baby Doll *and After*

In the thirties it was a common view in the Group Theatre in New York that "going Hollywood" and going to Hollywood was to some degree a process of "selling out." Elia Kazan's writings are littered with references to the remoteness and artificiality of Los Angeles life compared to that of New York, and to the tendency of Hollywood actors to have a "wax fruit" look. In his most personal film, *America America* (1963), the director was engaged not only by the immigrant struggle, but by an analogy to his own life and the quest for artistic autonomy. His notebooks of the time make an explicit comparison between the film's Anatolian Greek protagonist, his eyes on New York, and his own younger self as a studio director in the forties. The temptations of family life in Constantinople — a central sequence — are related to his own deliverance from the fate, as he saw it, of remaining in Hollywood (with a "house in Bel Air") as a career contract director. A note in the script suggests: "Stavros (you) goes to America, as you went into the world of ART."[1]

Kazan's frustration with aspects of studio production became evident in 1951 when Warner Bros. was complicit in the additional cuts imposed by the Legion of Decency on the version of *A Streetcar Named Desire* (1951) that was approved by the Production Code Administration (PCA). The *Hollywood Reporter* felt that the film would need "specialized selling and exploitation," including long runs in the "classic and art houses," although Kazan always felt that the combination of sex and sensibility would have a broad appeal, and was proved right on this film, if less so with his second film project with Tennessee Williams.[2] At the time the director wrote to the film's composer, Alex North, explaining that he was fed up with the "manufacturing process in relation to pictures" and that his experiences had fed his "determination again for the nth time to go out and make some pictures independently." By 1954, working for Warner Bros. as (for the first time) a producer-director, Kazan told Paul Osborn, his screenwriter on *East of*

Eden (1955): "Do I sound like Hollywood has gotten to me a little?" Yet his desire for more creative autonomy was always balanced by a preference for the finance, prestige, and distribution clout of a major studio.[3]

This impatience was further enhanced by the studios' blanket rejection of his and Budd Schulberg's 1953 pitch for what would be *On the Waterfront* (1954), prior to the intervention of independent producer Sam Spiegel. It was the commercial and critical success of Spiegel's Horizon production of the film, for Columbia Pictures release, that facilitated the director's move to activate his own production company and allowed him to assemble, in part from television, a regular East Coast crew. Kazan was also to acknowledge that his working relationships during *On the Waterfront* had encouraged in him a new outlook on his filmmaking. In particular he cited his work with Polish-born cinematographer Boris Kaufman, the brother of Dziga Vertov and Jean Vigo's key collaborator in the early thirties. Kazan remembered that he and Kaufman, who was also to work on *Baby Doll* (1956) and *Splendor in the Grass* (1961), worked "as artists, not as men paid to manufacture entertainment, and not as technicians with mechanical problems." Other Kazan "regulars" in this period included costume designer Anna Hill Johnstone and a young New York production designer, Richard Sylbert, who played a key role in helping his director find the crumbling Mississippi mansion that became the central location and symbol for *Baby Doll*.[4]

Newtown Productions, named after the estate Kazan had purchased in Newtown, Connecticut, in the late thirties, was chartered in April 1950 as a vehicle to produce and present plays and motion pictures. It had a small office on Broadway, and its three directors were Kazan, his wife and longtime advisor, Molly Day Thatcher Kazan, and his lawyer, William (Bill) Fitelson. By the midfifties, studio financing and distribution of independently produced films was becoming a common arrangement. In 1956, when half the films distributed by the studios were independent in this sense, Warner Bros. advanced over $25 million to independent producers, compared to $1.5 million in 1946. A January 1955 agreement between Newtown and Warner Bros. provided for the making of *Baby Doll* and *A Face in the Crowd* (1957), neither of them "presold" in terms of established stars or literary properties. The latter film, as Denise Mann has shown, referred directly to the independence issue by exploring the ambivalent relationship between the creative individual and an emerging East Coast culture industry of agents, advertisers, and political elites. The key motive for Kazan seemed to be to increase his creative autonomy, and that of his writers. In a letter of

November 1955 to Budd Schulberg, the director argued that "I didn't start this fucking company to hurry or be hurried."[5]

Baby Doll represented an emerging art cinema practice, with no established Hollywood stars and ambivalent characters and narrative. Whereas *A Streetcar Named Desire* had been a long-running Broadway success, the screenplay for *Baby Doll* was an original, very loosely adapted from two of Williams's early plays. Kazan encouraged Williams to work on the project in early 1952, and the next year a contract was signed with Warner Bros.; but it was only in 1955, after the success of *On the Waterfront*, that the final screenplay slowly took shape under the impetus of the Newtown contract. This agreement gave first cut to the director unless two previews indicated to the financing studio that changes were required, while it also imposed responsibility on the production company, Newtown, to obtain a PCA seal. Kazan was never tempted by the option of releasing a film without a seal — as Otto Preminger did with *The Moon Is Blue* (1953) — having already rejected an offer to film Robert Anderson's risky play *Tea and Sympathy*, some time before Vincente Minnelli's censored version was made at MGM in 1956.[6] There were certainly tensions in the Newtown–Warner Bros. relationship: Kazan grudgingly agreed to use the studio's processing facilities but successfully resisted pressure to title Williams's adaptation *Tiger Tail Road*. His calculation was that his strong personal relationship with Jack Warner, demonstrated in their correspondence (and in part reflecting their common immigrant background), would provide his company with maximum autonomy, and that the studio would help him resist the inevitable Production Code pressure and then sell *Baby Doll* effectively to a broad audience. (Kazan later wrote to Warner thanking him for help with the PCA). The final cost of the film was approximately $1.2 million, and allowed Kazan the relatively generous rehearsal time and shooting ratio he wanted; after filming was completed he thanked Warner for "wa[i]ving the penalties you could have exacted because I went over budget."[7]

There was a trend toward the art film in fifties America, although the notion was not clearly defined in marketing terms. The decade saw a growth in first-run art film houses (there were 80 in 1950 but 450 in 1963) and an increase in film festivals and magazines concerned with the art of the cinema, prompted initially by the greater exhibition of European films. A central element of Kazan's move to independent production was his desire to better and more freely represent in film the work of the playwrights and novelists whom he knew or had worked with in the East. The playwright

A publicity still from *Baby Doll* suggests the seductive power of Silva Vacarro (Eli Wallach) over the young, unhappily married Baby Doll (Carroll Baker). Photo courtesy of the Wesleyan Cinema Archives.

and screenwriter Robert Ardrey saw his friend as wanting to "make available to the screen the writing of first class people," although Ardrey also pointed out that it was not an easy matter to combine "the creative freedom that a director must have with the creative freedom that an author must have."[8] With *Baby Doll* Kazan did much to organize and order his writer's work, but he also wanted to break away from the tendency in his earlier films to build sympathy and audience engagement around a particular character: he told Frederic Morton as he finished filming in Brooklyn: "I'm beginning to break out of my formula — as in *Baby Doll*." He used his new authority to bring a distinctive and adult cinematic form to a wider public, combining realism with the bizarre, sex with comedy, and contemporary social observation with a universal story. As one study suggests, two prejudices limited the early recognition of *Baby Doll*: against "considering movies an art form and the less acknowledged prejudice against considering comedy as a serious form of art." Combining sex and comedy was perhaps even more difficult territory at that time.[9]

The *Baby Doll* screenplay that slowly emerged in the first half of the fifties was set in rural and small-town Mississippi over two days. The story concerns a nineteen-year-old child bride, Baby Doll Meighan, who lives in a dilapidated mansion with her husband, Archie Lee, who is twice her age. In a definitive assessment, Baby Doll describes her husband as "a mess." We learn that there is an agreement that their marriage not be consummated until Baby Doll's twentieth birthday, two days hence. The only other inhabitant of the once grand building is the sister of Baby Doll's dead father, an ancient and rather addled visitor and sometime cook, Aunt Rose Comfort. Archie Lee's livelihood, such as it is, is based on the operation of a run-down cotton gin that employs, in the segregated society and economy of the South at this time, a number of local black workers. A Sicilian immigrant outsider, Silva Vacarro, buys a rival gin, and when it is burnt down he rightly suspects that Archie Lee is responsible. Vacarro engages in an extended "seduction" of Baby Doll, with the objective both of revenge and of obtaining proof of the crime. Suspecting himself to be a cuckolded husband and fearful of losing his wife completely, the drunken Archie Lee finally goes wild with a rifle and is taken away by the local marshal. Tennessee Williams warned Kazan against a "heavy" ending, which he felt would be inappropriate to the nature of the piece, mentioning that he felt his friend's film work was sometimes marred by final bursts of excess.[10] The extent of sexual relations between Vacarro and Baby Doll is left unclear, but their encounter awakens something, if only a sense of adultness, in the young woman. In the film Vacarro leaves, promising to return; Baby Doll tells Aunt Rose in the final line, supplied by Williams with location filming half completed, "We've got nothing to do but wait for tomorrow, and see if we're remembered, or forgotten."

A key obligation on Newtown was to obtain a Production Code Admin- istration seal, yet filming began without agreement with the censors, and with the producer-director flatly resisting pressures to reduce Archie Lee's "sex frustration," something Kazan saw as crucial to the Williams story. The tension of this studio-independent "partnership" is caught in the director's letter to Warner from the location hotel in Greenville, Mississippi. At this time, November 1955, with no agreement on a seal on the horizon, Kazan was keen to stiffen Warner's resolve to resist both the censors and those within the studio who were skeptical about the commercial prospects of the new venture:

> In general, Jack, it seems to me that with fewer and fewer people leaving their TV sets and their homes after supper, we must, we MUST strike out for exceptional subject matters and really unusual treatments of these subject matters. In one sentence we are now obligated, AS A MATTER OF SELF PRESERVATION, to put on the screen of Motion Picture Theaters ONLY what they cannot and will never see on their TV screens at home. Our industry now is in a desperate situation, and we must be bold and fight for our lives. TV is improving fast, and getting bolder every day. The wide screen gimmick cannot keep our head above water much longer. We've got to break our own taboos and strike out for increasingly un- usual and daring material. Either that or just quit and sign up with the TV guys.[11]

The completed film was eventually granted a seal, despite several ob- vious violations of the Code, but, as with *A Streetcar Named Desire*, the PCA's judgment cut no ice with the Legion of Decency. A month before the film's New York opening in late 1956 the Legion gave the film a C (Con- demned) classification, finding it to be "morally repellent both in theme and treatment." In an act that set something of the critical and popular agenda, making it harder to appreciate the film's comedic virtues, Cardinal Francis Spellman of New York, from the pulpit of St. Patrick's Cathedral, denounced *Baby Doll*, sight unseen, as unpatriotic and immoral. A massive Broadway sign, using the image of Baby Doll stretched out in a crib, sucking her thumb, may have reinforced this reading of a work that the reviewer for *Time* called "possibly the dirtiest American-made motion picture."[12] Arthur Knight's comment in his review that it "makes no effort to reward the good and punish the wicked" can be taken as a broader reflection on the weakened enforcement of the Production Code, as well as a comment on

The Broadway billboard for *Baby Doll*. The Catholic Legion of Decency condemned the film for its salaciousness. Photo courtesy of the Wesleyan Cinema Archives.

the way the film differed from mainstream Hollywood practice. The *Motion Picture Herald* characterized the film less as entertainment than as part of a "school of picture-making" associated with foreign producers. Long-term *New York Times* critic Bosley Crowther compared the film unfavorably with Fellini's *La Strada* (1954), but the fact that he made the comparison at all is significant. Writing at the time in his production notebook for the film, Kazan felt that the "nearest thing to it is Pagnol, who also mixes comedy and tragedy!"[13] In directing *César* (1936), from a screenplay based on his own play, the French playwright and filmmaker Marcel Pagnol had used local locations and sound that captured the texture of life in Marseilles.

Baby Doll's lack of a clear resolution and its moral ambivalence, together with its strange landscape and game playing, its "hide and seek," suggest something closer to avant-garde theater. A parallel might be made with Joseph Losey, who moved to Britain in the early fifties as a consequence of the Hollywood blacklist. Losey's own use of space to denote struggles for dominance, and the role of an outsider as a catalyst, is seen most clearly in *The Servant*, his 1963 collaboration with Harold Pinter. (Meetings on the stairs feature in both films.) The social aspects of Kazan's film, capturing something of the benighted American South of its time, have been neglected, yet its enduring strength is as a small-scale study of human and semicomic struggles for respect and survival.

Another element of Kazan's new venture consistent with his earlier work was a concern with contemporary social issues. (Williams was indeed at one point fearful that Kazan would overload his story with "social significance.") The director seemed particularly determined to show that his cooperative testimony before the House Un-American Activities Committee in 1952 had not diluted the realist, semidocumentary strain in his work. Before the filming of the interiors at a refurbished Warner Bros. studio in Brooklyn, location work was based in the small town of Benoit, Mississippi, where the nearby mansion perfectly represented the crumbling edifice of the old white South. Built in 1848, it had once been at the center of a plantation, so the black characters are in some sense the ghosts and spirits referred to in the screenplay. The director's most noticeable addition relates to the twenty or more roles for local black people, compared to only three references to black characters in the published Williams script.[14] Five local residents were also flown to New York for the scenes in the café, including the real sheriff of Benoit and his deputy, and a black waitress whose performance of "I shall not be moved" seems to signal the wider world and the political resistance to come.

The film works as a universal tale of cuckolding and revenge, but it also captures life in the Deep South before the economic boom and the civil rights movement that would eventually transform it. It was at or near to the time of filming that Emmett Till was murdered in the Delta, and Rosa Parks refused to move from her seat on the bus in Montgomery, in the neighboring state of Alabama, acting as a catalyst for the rise to national prominence of the southern civil rights movement. In *Baby Doll* the African-American characters — passive as they may be — do tell a story, constituting a collective chorus that challenges the authority of the white characters, and in particular Archie Lee. PCA vice president Jack Vizzard was to see in the film a contemporary political subtext about the effort of "trashy whites" to sustain the status quo, and was also struck by what he called the "spirit of self-assertion of the new independents," meaning the new independent production companies.[15]

Small-scale as it might be, *Baby Doll* illustrated Kazan's efforts, as his own producer as well as director, in harmonizing and coordinating the work of cast and crew. Boris Kaufman's black-and-white cinematography and Richard Sylbert's art direction integrated location and studio material and served both the realist elements of the project and the sense of a world cut off from the more celebrated "success stories" of American life of the time. Visually the film is a study in whites and off-whites, bleached by the sun, while Kazan as director emphasizes again his preference for exploiting the moment and the location to serve the emotional dynamics of the work, rather than using preplanned, storyboarded effects. The grounds of the mansion are consistent with its location on Tiger Tail Road, out beyond the regular visits of the garbage trucks, but they also suggest a bleak, almost elemental site for the playing out of the story. Set in late fall (election time), the film was shot in December and January, and the actors sucked ice cubes before shooting to ensure that their breath did not show in the close shots. Kazan takes full advantage of the location's well and old plantation bell, while Richard Sylbert, assisted by his brother Paul, assembled the props that were given expressive use in the film, from the antique car, a Pierce-Arrow, to the elaborate swing that is the centerpiece of the long "seduction" scene.[16] Kazan also introduced the composer Kenyon Hopkins to poststudio American filmmaking, and his score, directed by the Warners head of music, Ray Heindorf, combines pop, jazz, blues, and rock-and-roll influences, and lightly suggests the story's mix of innocent and erotic possibilities.

The professional actors in *Baby Doll* had little Hollywood experience, and all worked at the Actors Studio, which Kazan had jointly formed in New York in 1947. Kazan decided on Carroll Baker for the role of Baby Doll after checking with George Stevens on the yet-unreleased *Giant* (1956), and after Tennessee Williams had seen her play the role at an Actors Studio tryout. Eli Wallach's first film role, as Silva Vacarro, was in *Baby Doll*; Karl Malden (Archie Lee) was making his fourth film appearance for the director; and Mildred Dunnock (Aunt Rose) had been in the Broadway cast of *Death of a Salesman*. All these principals, together with Lonny Chapman (as Vacarro's manager) and the unaccredited Rip Torn and Madeleine Sherwood, were Actors Studio alumni, while the other speaking parts, including the town marshal, were played by locals.

Laughter is important to the tone of the film. In an early scene in which Lee enters Baby Doll's bathroom, provoking first cries of laughter and then screams, the frustrated and "wet" suitor is left alone with the camera, rather like Oliver Hardy contemplating "another fine mess" with his audience. Vacarro's own charm may be just a tactic, but his at times frightening single-mindedness is finally disturbed by the "mutual attraction" that he and Baby Doll establish. Archie Lee adopts a comic persona as part of his desperation, "performing" as the man of status and authority in the community and blowing his horn, as in the early scene, with increasing impotence. Baby Doll Meighan's cries turn to laughter, as she walks with Vacarro by the pigsty (as the seduction begins), and Baker's subtle performance suggests a degree of self-knowledge as she copes with the predicament engineered by her late father. The use of framed photographs of her "Daddy," owner of the Kotton King Hotel, is a device Kazan often uses in his films, from *On the Waterfront* to *The Last Tycoon* (1976), to suggest the spell cast on characters by the past.

A particularly effective example of the film's ensemble playing comes with Archie Lee's early trip downtown to consult his doctor. While Baby Doll spars with a young dentist (played by Rip Torn in his first screen role), Archie Lee suffers the double embarrassment of making a public spectacle of the distance between his desire — for a woman twenty years his junior — and his capacity. It is suggested that Lee is impotent and also possibly a cuckold; the black "workers" have already suggested, before Vacarro's arrival, that there have been other gentleman callers. In the doctor's office, a nurse (Madeleine Sherwood) watches Archie Lee's humiliation. When the doctor (played by Kazan's friend, the Actors Studio lawyer John S. Dudley) prescribes a minor sedative the nurse tells Lee "it's not going to help what's wrong with you one bit." All the while a small skull on the doctor's desk casts a beady eye on the proceedings. Seen at the time through the related perspectives of sex and sordidness, *Baby Doll* in fact works as a black comedy about small town sex and life, and about a benighted and bizarre social realm (half *Waiting for Godot*) still waiting to catch up with modernity and the ideals of the New Deal.

In immediate commercial terms the Newtown venture was unsuccessful. Perhaps because of the intervention of Cardinal Spellman and the Legion, *Baby Doll* was slow to cover its costs, while Kazan saw *A Face in the Crowd* (1957) as a financial disaster. He later reclaimed both films from Warner Bros. and hired Julian Schlossberg, subsequently the founder of Castle Hill Productions, to promote them. Kazan's next film as producer-director was *Wild River* (1960), made in Tennessee under his original contract with Twentieth Century-Fox. Fox's complete lack of interest preserved Kazan's autonomy but contributed to its box office failure and lack of contemporary critical appreciation. Only *Splendor in the Grass* (1961), again made for

Warners under a contract similar to that for *Baby Doll*, was commercially successful, in part at least because of its controversy (the agreed-on release print was again challenged by the Legion) and a more sophisticated marketing campaign that was tailored for the film and addressed to an emerging youth audience. Kazan felt under even greater pressure to use the Warner Bros. facilities, and with Newtown failing to produce a clear hit, the studio was reluctant to fight his battles with the Legion. Kazan threatened to sue the studio at one point, when he felt that Warners was going to concede further cuts; he argued that he could have earned $1 million in salary in that time, but "I preferred $125,000 in order to make a fine work independently and without interference."[17]

At the beginning of Kazan's "independent" career *Baby Doll* demonstrates the mastery of his work with actors and his inventiveness in realizing a script in terms of location and mise-en-scène. The Newtown work came before a notion of "independence" or "art cinema" was clearly established in industry or marketing terms, but has come to be widely appreciated. The vulnerabilities of the central characters in *Baby Doll* seem to generate greater sympathy now than then, and in the off-white mansion Kazan and Sylbert found a unifying and resonant emblem. Following *Splendor in the Grass*, the director again turned to Warner Bros. to finance his semiautobiographical immigrant epic *America America*, after another independent deal collapsed while the crew was gathering in Istanbul. Studio marketing executives, echoing earlier comments, referred to the new film as having "staying power" only in "art houses or theatres that run special attractions." Kazan commented at the time: "Maybe it just isn't a picture for general release. Maybe, like some other of my pictures, it should get art-house treatment. *Baby Doll* should have."[18]

NOTES

1. Elia Kazan, notebook for *America America*, Elia Kazan Collection, Wesleyan Cinema Archives, Wesleyan University. For further discussion see Brian Neve, *Elia Kazan: The Cinema of an American Outsider* (London: I. B. Tauris, 2009).

2. "'Desire' Powerful Drama," *Hollywood Reporter*, June 14, 1951, 4.

3. Kazan to Alex North, n.d., Alex North Collection, Margaret Herrick Library, Academy of Motion Picture Arts and Sciences, Los Angeles; Kazan to Paul Osborn, April 19, 1954, Paul Osborn Papers, Wisconsin Center for Film and Theater Research, State Historical Society of Wisconsin, Madison; Kazan, *Elia Kazan: A Life* (London: Andre Deutsch, 1988), 533.

4. Kazan to Museum of Modern Art, Film Department, September 5, 1980, Kazan folders, Museum of Modern Art, New York.

5. Douglas Gomery, *The Hollywood Studio System* (London: BFI and Macmillan, 1986), 122; Janet Wasko, *Movies and Money: Financing the American Film Industry* (Norwood, N.J.: Ablex, 1982), 118; Kazan to Budd Schulberg, November 7, 1955, Budd Schulberg Correspondence, Kazan Collection; on "independence" and *A Face in the Crowd* see Denise Mann, *Hollywood Independents: The Postwar Talent Takeover* (Minneapolis: University of Minnesota Press, 2008), 169–91.

6. Kazan to Jack Warner on *Tea and Sympathy*, October 9, 1953, legal file, *East of Eden*; reference to January 1955 contract, legal file, *America America*, both in Warner Bros. Legal File Collection, Doheny Library, University of Southern California, Los Angeles.

7. On discussion of the *Tiger Tail Road* title, Kazan to Jack Warner, November 7 and November 9, 1955; Kazan to Steve Trilling (postmarked November 16, 1955); statement of finances for *Baby Doll*, January 1, 1957, all in Warner Bros. Archives, University of Southern California, Los Angeles; Kazan to Jack Warner, March 1, 1956, Kazan Collection.

8. Barbara Wilinsky, *Sure Seaters: The Emergence of Art House Cinema* (Minneapolis: University of Minnesota Press, 2001), 2; Robert Ardrey to Kazan, November 27, 1955, Ardrey Correspondence, Kazan Collection.

9. Frederic Morton, "Gadg!" (*Esquire*, February 1957), in William Baer, ed., *Elia Kazan Interviews* (Jackson: University Press of Mississippi, 2000), 24; Anthony C. Hilfer and R. Vance Ramsey, "*Baby Doll*: A Study in Comedy and Critical Awareness," *Ohio University Review* 11 (1969), 85–88.

10. Albert J. Devlin, ed., *The Selected Letters of Tennessee Williams*, vol. 2, *1945–1957* (London: Oberon Books, 2006), 597.

11. Kazan to Jack Warner, November 15, 1955, Warner Bros. Archives.

12. Review of *Baby Doll*, *Time*, December 24, 1956, 61.

13. Arthur Knight, "The Williams-Kazan Axis," *Saturday Review*, December 29, 1956, 22–24; Charles S. Aaronson, review of *Baby Doll*, *Motion Picture Herald*, December 8, 1956; Bosley Crowther, "The Proper Drama Of Mankind," *New York Times*, January 6, 1957; Kazan, notebook on *Baby Doll*, Kazan Collection.

14. Tennessee Williams, *Baby Doll: The Script for the Film* (London: Penguin Books, 1957).

15. Jack Vizzard, *See No Evil: Life Inside a Hollywood Censor* (New York: Simon and Schuster, 1970), 206–8.

16. See Richard Sylbert and Sylvia Townsend, *Designing Movies: Portrait of a Hollywood Artist* (Westport, Conn.: Praeger, 2006), 45–58.

17. Kazan to Jack Warner and Ben Kalmenson, May 25, 1961, Kazan Collection.

18. Elia Kazan, interview by Bob Thomas, *Oregonian*, March 14, 1964, clipping, legal files, *Baby Doll*, Warner Bros. Legal File Collection.

SAM WASSON

The Search for Humor and Humanity in *Baby Doll* and *A Face in the Crowd*

I no longer hide it; it's out in the open, my perennial scowl.
Which is why my smile, when it does appear, is so dazzling.
The sheer surprise of it! That's supposed to be a joke.

ELIA KAZAN

Kazan is so angry!

When we think of his great films, his iconic films, what comes to mind, above all else, is ferocity. Everything, no matter how tame, is in Kazan's hands imbued with operatic, even dangerous vehemence. Extremity spares no person or theme, and it permeates the director's oeuvre so completely it has become synonymous with our sense of his style. Indeed, Kazanesque, if such a word were to exist, would undoubtedly signify a film or staged narrative deeply involved with ideas of injustice, dramatized with histrionic savagery.

This sometimes grating combination of passion and polemics, which critic Robin Wood called "The Kazan Problem" in an essay of the same name, is largely responsible for the polarizing effect the director's pictures had, and continue to have, on filmgoers. "If it is impossible to watch without embarrassment," Wood writes of *Splendor in the Grass* (1961), "it is also impossible to watch without admiration. Often one admires and writhes at the same time. It is partly a matter of distinguishing between effects one would call 'strong, forceful, direct' and effects one would call 'crude, vulgar, obvious.'" ("One considers sending him to Stanley Kramer for lessons in tact and reticence," he adds.)[1] Andrew Sarris, writing in 1963, agreed. With a certain degree of ambivalence, he labeled Kazan's vociferousness "more excessive than expressive."[2] Pauline Kael, in a rare instance of Sarris-assent, was right behind him. "One also knows," she wrote in her review of *The Arrangement* (1969), "that Kazan is building up the pain as proof of the significance of his message, that he has always been a pain peddler, that he developed the school of theater in which one screams when no more than a grimace is appropriate—until honest emotions are devalued, because who would notice them?"[3]

Keeping with *Splendor in the Grass*, think for instance of Pat Hingle's performance as the raging, spitting, sweating father of Bud Stamper (Warren Beatty). Whether one thinks his choices appropriately intense or just plain overarticulated will vary with taste, but there's no question that from the very moment we meet him, Hingle, as directed by Kazan, has given flesh to a kind of evil Falstaff, hell-bent and robust, and very likely the most flavorful father in American movies. Always on the hunt, Ace Stamper makes a jungle of his home, screaming at everything and everyone, shoving his interlocutors against walls and furniture, and gesturing with all limbs in all directions at once, like a whirling firecracker or the Hindu god Shiva—if he were shot through with a barrel of testosterone. It is amazing work; amazing the way any feat of great size amazes us, but one can't help but wonder, as Hingle sweats through his next shirt, if his ferocity hurts the movie or helps it.

The answer is both. The problem, as always, is the character's place atop Kazan's soapbox. Were Kazan, John Cassavetes, or Ace Stamper one of the guys from *Husbands* (1970), this kind of delirium would go unchallenged; in fact, it might even be admired (the more Cassavetes pushes his subjects, the more thrilling his experiments become). But here, within the context of Kazan's dialectical world of good and bad and dos and don'ts, Hingle's performance, no matter how viscerally compelling, rigs Kazan's defense of kids versus parents unfairly in the former's favor. Empathically, it's a fixed fight. Morally, that makes it propaganda.

But hold on. How could Kazan—a filmmaker deeply interested in human intricacy—succumb to such a reductive absolute? Why does he stack the deck when he has a winning hand?

Perhaps because there are two Elia Kazans. One, the heated lobbyist, is a man in honorable pursuit of encouraging change. He has taken an unhappy look at the world—its strictures, its tyrannies, and its hypocrisies—and comes to the camera angling to strike out against it. The other Kazan, his doppelgänger, is a Method-minded artist deeply engaged with the kind of acting he once described as "intense and truly emotional, rooted in the subconscious, therefore often surprising and shocking in its revelations . . . Acting is more than a parade of emotionalism. . . . It is—or should be—a human life on stage, that is to say, behavior: total, complex, complete."[4] Of course, the dual interests of the lobbyist and the psychologist add value to

Kazan's films—the lobbyist shines a light into the darkness and the psychologist adds darkness to the light—but regrettably, as Kazan's influence over Hingle demonstrates, they cannot coexist. What is forfeited, ironically, is what Kazan identified as the primary goal of his cinema. "If I can portray a sense of 'humanness,' that's all I want," he said to Jeff Young. "That's why I admire Renoir so much. Everybody in his pictures, representing all points of view, is sympathetic. It comes from the soul of the man. And I've got it in me. I don't think I've ever quite done it."[5]

Renoir? *Kazan?*

It would be difficult to think of two more antithetical filmmakers. True, both are invested in theatricality; true, both are deeply committed to the work of their actors; but the crucial difference is that Renoir, whose cinema is characterized by a forgiving generosity of spirit, is, by virtue of his benevolence, unable to see the world through a binary lens. ("The easy paths of cynicism and sentimentality have never appealed to him,"[6] wrote Sarris.) In this light, the notion of humanness, which demands a nonpartisan view of character, becomes problematic. It raises the question, was Kazan truly interested in the complex psychological portraits he is credited for, or was he too angry to see people as clearly as he saw their predicaments? If so, what kind of humanness does that bestow on his pictures?

Key to Renoir's success as a humanist, to, as Kazan says, "representing all points of view," is his willingness to laugh where another would shout. As David Thomson notes, this doesn't make his films soft; it makes them treacherous. He writes, "The extraordinary weaving of laughter and tears is not so much warming as a warning to tread warily in life. Recollect the title [*The Rules of the Game* (1939)], and it becomes clearer that Renoir is reproducing the fraught indecisiveness of the game."[7] Without indecision, without uncertainty, Elia Kazan was also without humor. Until he found it—*if* he found it—his dream of humanness would stay a dream.

Part of the problem is that Kazan's innate dialecticalism craves not uncertainty but justice. On the very first page of his autobiography, he writes, "The fact is I *am* mad, most every morning. I wake up mad. Still."[8] That hostility, translated through cinema, becomes one of the hallmarks of his visual style. In a controversial piece written for *Sight and Sound*, Lindsay Anderson, future director of the insurrectionary *If . . .* (1968), described the results—and it wasn't pleasant. "This is hysterical filmmaking," he wrote. "Every incident, whipped up by tricks to a quite spurious dramatic intensity: music to shock and scare, effects that boom, dialogue incomprehensibly shouted or mumbled in a theatrical affectation of realism, looming close-ups that seek to impose their mood on us by sheer size, jazzed-up cutting and compositions meaninglessly bold. A style, in short, of horrid vulgarity; to which the notion of *decorum* is unknown; using every possible device to batter and bemuse."[9] This was written in 1955. The film was *On the Waterfront* (1954).

This view is overstated. "Hysterical filmmaking" needn't be pejorative (isn't that Eisenstein? Dziga Vertov?), but the fact is, Anderson's got Kazan by his Achilles heel. In rising up against the status quo with every weapon in his arsenal, the director inculcates his characters with frenzies of feeling that are antithetical to complex emotion. Rather than humanizing them, this tendency can objectify Kazan's people, taking them from characters to illustrations of a particular point. We can see strains of it even in the young Kazan — Kazan the actor — studying at the Group Theatre. "After a few weeks of work," he wrote in *Elia Kazan: A Life*, "I began to have an idea of what the artistic leaders there, the directors and the veteran actors, thought of me. The verdict was unfavorable: 'Kazan has a great deal of energy but no actor's emotion.' No emotion! A strange judgment to pass on a man who was a closet hysteric."[10] They had a good point. After all, the Method is predicated not on volume (as it would sometimes seem) but on equanimity. "That's the essence of the Stanislavsky system," Kazan said. "You justify everyone's point of view. Drama is best when you're dealing with opposing feelings within the audience and they don't know who's right."[11] Is that *On the Waterfront*?

How, then, would Kazan ever achieve complex humanism? Could he, like Renoir, learn to laugh instead of shout? If so, what would it look like? Would it be funny?

Was it even possible in light of "hysterical filmmaking?"

To find out, we might consider a brief phase in Kazan's career — two films made back-to-back between 1955 and 1956 — in which he endeavored, for the first time, to take a newer, lighter approach.

The first was *Baby Doll* (1956). "I don't think it's a big film," Kazan said, "it's not a heavy, pompous film pregnant with meaning."[12] He called it a black comedy. But why now, after all the years of earnestness? "As I got older," he explained to Jeff Young, "I began to feel the charm and the attraction of foolishness under tension, which is by the way what you usually find. The picture expresses the affection I have for the foolish of the world. I mean, you can't take *Baby Doll* seriously. It's like a fairy tale. It's ridiculous, improbable, unrealistic."[13]

This doesn't sound like Elia Kazan; it sounds like Kazan trying to be the *opposite* of Kazan, and it suggests that in order to achieve a state of antiseriousness, the director believed he had to be frivolous. (Kazan said, "I used to tell Wallach, 'Come on Eli, it's not realistic.'"[14] But what about the Method?) What results is the impression that comedy — in Kazan's mind a flight from gravitas — is antithetical to human conduct, and ultimately, human dignity. Place this against the director's claim of feeling affection for his characters, and *Baby Doll* becomes a film of deeply muddled points of view, contradictory, not complex. One need only look at the picture's opening images to see how that muddle thwarts its comic opportunities and keeps the viewer from joining Kazan in laughter.

The film opens with a tortured establishing shot of the setting: a dilapidated antebellum mansion surrounded by twisted, leafless trees. We cut then to an off-putting, low-angle shot of Archie Lee (Karl Malden) standing before the house, shouting up to a hard-to-see black man on top of the roof. From this distorted angle, realistic proportions are all off; Malden towers over the mansion, which itself seems to be only steps ahead of him, but the fact of the tiny figure on the roof means that in truth, the house is farther away than we might have thought. Spatially speaking, it's a trompe l'oeil, an improbable image.

Laughter is often predicated on improbability, but these contrasts are too disorienting to be funny. We need to feel secure if we are going to laugh, and with these opening images (and the images to come), which evoke Anderson's "hysterical filmmaking," Kazan has confused improbable exaggeration with his intended result, absurdity. The successive image — a reverse shot of the one before it — follows suit. With the camera high above Malden, presumably from the man on the roof's point of view, the shot instantly diminishes him, shrinking him, in effect, from the size of a giant to a midget in the space of a cut. Sitting off to the side of the shot (an irregular composition once again) is an older black man, who watches Archie impassively. His blank silence makes Malden's already overblown performance seem even more — to borrow Kazan's word — ridiculous.

Of course, ridiculousness, like improbability, is a reliable source of humor, but this shot reroutes Kazan's supposed amusement right into contempt. His hostility is reiterated in the chorus of black farmhands, chuckling at Archie from the sidelines.[15] "Ain't you gonna help him?" one says; "I'm retired" is the answer. But we can't laugh with them because Malden's performance, typical of Kazan in its force, contains too much conviction to be anything but compelling, and leaves no room for the kind of latent

In a publicity still from *Baby Doll*, Silva Vacarro (Eli Wallach) brandishes the "affidavit" he coerced Baby Doll (Carroll Baker) into signing to prove that her husband, Archie Lee (Karl Malden), burned down Vacarro's cotton gin. Vacarro takes his revenge on Archie Lee by seducing Baby Doll. Photo courtesy of the Wesleyan Cinema Archives.

foolishness that invites genuine laugher. So why do the farmhands laugh? As southern black men, they stand at the utter apex of helplessness, and yet they hoot at Archie Lee all throughout *Baby Doll*. One even laughs when the mill owned by Silva Vacarro (Eli Wallach) burns down. But why, when what they observe is just as menacing?

"It's my father's sly face," Kazan wrote in *Elia Kazan: A Life*. "I call it the Anatolian Smile, the smile that covers resentment. And fear. I see the cunning in that smile. . . . Where did it come from — on me, I mean — that mask to hide a truer feeling?"[16] The black onlookers in *Baby Doll* are Kazan's stand-ins, and as an on-screen audience, act as our intended surrogates as well. Their amusement sheds light on what it is Kazan himself finds funny (read: contemptible) about Archie Lee and Vacarro, and represents an effort to undermine, through humiliation, whatever authority they have left. Take the following exchange (Archie has just delivered Baby Doll an ice cream cone. She's been waiting in the car):

ARCHIE LEE: Yesterday on Front Street, a man called out to me and said, "Hey, Archie Lee, has your wife outgrown the crib yet?" Three or four others ha-ha'ed at me. Public humiliation.

BABY DOLL: Private humiliation is just as painful.

ARCHIE LEE: There's no torture on earth to equal the cold torture a woman inflicts on a man. There's no torture to compare with it.

It's that torture, that humiliation that, in Kazan's mind, Archie Lee deserves (Kael called it pain peddling). As the mercenary oppressor, a man who takes — from the land, from women, and from others' pockets — Archie Lee is a vintage Kazan-adversary. Thus does *Baby Doll* lose out on being, as Kazan said, "a film pregnant with meaning" and becomes instead invested in the director's long-standing polemic. Evidence of his partisanship persists throughout the picture, often in the sort of exaggerated visual strategies detailed above, but also in the performances themselves. Malden's choices, for instance, his brusque movements, his yelling, and his wild eyes are as reliant on notions of power technically, from an acting standpoint, as they are thematically, from a narrative standpoint. His mammoth style, in other words, reflects both the Malden/Kazan sensibility as well as Archie Lee's ugly vehemence, and asks us to regard him as Kazan does — Malden's clownish nose does — as a tyrant humiliated. We are meant to laugh through the Anatolian smile.

There are other instances of humiliation, buttons Kazan affixes onto the ends of scenes like punch lines, as if to remind the viewer that these people, no matter how powerfully they present themselves, are actually ridiculous. In one, Archie Lee, following his bathtub skirmish with Baby Doll (played, coyly, off-screen), defeatedly spits out a mouthful of water; in another, Vacarro, watching Baby Doll run off the porch in search of Archie Lee, curses her in flummoxed Italian. These codas, which follow tyrannical demonstrations on the part of Archie Lee and Vacarro, attempt to upend brutality with humor, and in so doing, perpetuate Kazan's contempt for the powerful.

It is a contempt he asks us to share. Throughout, Vacarro's predatory pursuit of Baby Doll is underscored by tight close-ups, often crunching their faces uncomfortably close in the frame, or against pieces of scenery, like the stairway railing, a column on Archie Lee's porch, or, most memorably, a wooden plank of a double-sided swing (and even in a kiss). These types of compositions are so aggrandizing of Vacarro, and recur so regularly, that

Kazan's comic efforts to disgrace him are seriously impaired. In these pictures, his forcefulness is just too convincing. The dot of white light Kazan shines in Wallach's eye lends him a sinister glint, further urging the director's attitude on us: Vacarro is more frightening than foolish. The Anatolian smile has widened to the point of resentment.

And so, in trying not to be serious, in trying to play levity, it becomes clear that the director is only hiding his rage. Because of it, *Baby Doll* is actually as serious, and as damning, as ever.

A significant roadblock between Kazan and his interest in complex humanism is that his indigenous visual, thematic, and emotional sensibility is predicated on power; and power engenders antagonists; and antagonists undermine his efforts at pervasive sympathy, or ambivalence. This is why, with the tenets of "hysterical filmmaking" applied, he left the population of *Baby Doll* without recourse. Humor and humanism are the casualties.

Again, we might ask, would the director ever approach his destination? Could he find a way to regulate the two Kazans, thereby actualizing an equanimity that allows him to see his characters' human follies without contempt? Could he smile the Anatolian smile without sneering? In other words, could he forgive?

Enter *A Face in the Crowd* (1957).

Kazan said the film "makes me laugh more than any other film I made."[17] This may sound incredible, but the fact is *A Face in the Crowd* is a Kazan comedy; cheerless, yes, but with a sense of humor that is never at odds with the director's sensibility, one that, contrary to Kazan's ideological agenda, offers even the most hateful character a touch of humanity. With this framework — one of satire — the two Kazans can work in rich counterpoint, laughing and critiquing simultaneously. Unlike the otherwise dialectical worlds of *On the Waterfront* and *Splendor in the Grass*, *A Face in the Crowd* contains a conceptual and humanistic complexity unique in the director's estimable body of work.

It seems the material forced him into it. Kazan knew that if the character of Lonesome Rhodes was going to have a credible rise to popularity, he'd have to be appealing. How else would he be able to seduce an entire county? Casting Andy Griffith, a basically funny personality with considerable comedy experience, was Kazan's way of answering the question. In Griffith's hands, power — ordinarily a dogmatic stumbling block for Kazan, and as we've seen, profoundly serious — would become synonymous with humor. "One thing that a lot people overlooked," the director said, "is that Fascism

Lonesome Rhodes (Andy Griffith) reveals his tender side to Marcia Jeffries (Patricia Neal) in a publicity still from *A Face in the Crowd*. Marcia's attraction to Rhodes is central to the film's presentation of him as charismatic yet dangerous. Photo courtesy of the Wesleyan Cinema Archives.

always had attractive elements of populism in it."[18] That's Rhodes. It's another way of framing the Anatolian smile, and in *A Face in the Crowd*, Kazan makes it the very subject of his film, not his attitude toward his characters.

"I wanted to have an amusing picture," he said "and still have a lot of 'warning' in it."[19] "Hysterical filmmaking" is, quite readily, the ideal means of synthesizing these disparate elements. Within the context of a personality both fearful and entertaining, its bold, exaggerated techniques do not, as Lindsay Anderson warned, "impose their mood on us by sheer size"; rather, because they exaggerate an already ambiguous personality, Kazan's aesthetic choices celebrate and criticize Rhodes justly, in equal proportion. They do visually what the hot and cold love of Marcia Jeffries (Patricia Neal) for Rhodes does emotionally: that is, ask us to consider Rhodes as both a source of incredible charisma and, simultaneously, danger. That's ambivalence.

To underscore this dualism, to draw us, through Marcia, both into and away from Rhodes, Kazan privileges his audience with multifaceted reaction shots of Patricia Neal. Whether she is beaming in adulation or frozen in horror, her responses to Rhodes — namely his own Anatolian smile — do a great deal to complicate Kazan's attitude toward his subject. Sounding off at the expense of Mr. Luffler, his program's major sponsor, Rhodes offers the following piece of perspective to all those at home: "I don't reckon a Luffler mattress will break your back," he says ruefully, "but it sure ain't no world shaking message." This gets him an off-screen laugh from the live studio audience and a smile from Marcia, watching proudly from the wings. Griffith's Anatolian smile is full of charm and stinking with contempt (Luffler is tagged "The Mattress Aristocrat"), but Kazan, in allowing us access to Marcia's delight, is emphasizing the former; later, when Marcia begins to resist Rhodes, his grinning charm will be undermined by a reaction shot of her — who now sees through him — that emphasizes the latter. Not only do these reactions add complexity to our feelings about Rhodes, they imbue the character of Marcia, and ultimately *A Face in the Crowd*, with a complexity in line with Kazan's definition of humanism ("representing all points of view"). It is interesting to note that *Baby Doll* is almost without reaction shots.

Within the context of "hysterical filmmaking," Kazan's use of close-ups generates a substantial portion of *A Face in the Crowd*'s strongest comic passages. The Vitajex commercial is a case in point. Employing many of the tactics Anderson criticized, including shouted dialogue, theatrical affectations, looming close-ups, and jazzed-up cutting, Kazan indeed fashions a montage "of horrid vulgarity," but this time, his rhetoric, refined by satire, makes "hysterical filmmaking" hysterically funny. "I also like the scene in the ad agency in New York," he said. "I thought it was hilarious. In the end what it came down to is that what you sell in America is not what's in the product, but what's in the ad."[20] Of course, Kazan's contempt for power is still here, but it's directed at institutions, not people. The media is the villain, and Kazan uses "hysterical filmmaking" to satirize it. "I also wanted a lot of cuts," he said, "which meant shooting more set-ups. I wanted a slam-bang style."[21] That style, with its self-reflexive emphasis on camera technology, laughs harder at the TV than it does at the faces on it.

Kazan's application of extreme close-ups, namely those of Andy Griffith, asks us to scrutinize, challenge, and ultimately reconsider the authenticity of what we're seeing. *He smiles*, we observe, *but is he really happy?* Is that hard, loud laugh Griffith gives Rhodes hysteria or hysterical? By contrast, close-ups of Pat Hingle in *Splendor in the Grass* are mostly redundant. No matter where he is in the shot, even if it's deep in the frame, his intensity always puts him downstage center. And another thing: where Hingle's sweaty underarms reiterate, yet again, what we already know about him, Griffith's perpetually wet face and forehead work in revealing counterpoint to his wholesome, corn-fed laugh. (Kazan must have had a spritzer on the payroll at all times.) Perspiration tells us Rhodes is straining, that he's performing, which means Kazan is asking us to consider Griffith's "slam-bang" hysteria, unlike Hingle's, within the context of the very idea of representation. It registers as real because Kazan is suggesting it isn't.

But remember, we need to *like* Lonesome Rhodes. If his characterization is going to be truly complicated, we need to find ourselves empathizing with him. From Kazan's directorial standpoint, it means that he has to ration his own stylistic hysteria, and encase it in moments of sober, levelheaded filmmaking. That way, we will see off-camera Rhodes as Marcia Jeffries sometimes sees him — as a true and wholesome man. To this end, Kazan shoots their domestic scenes with mostly eye-level two shots and a close-up or two peppered in to elicit doubt. This straight-ahead, almost classical strategy is utterly antihysterical; it intends to show us Rhodes, as Kazan would say it, without "that mask to hide a truer feeling." Here at last is power reduced to human size.

Unfortunately, it doesn't quite come off, for the very simple reason that Rhodes doesn't seem to have a truer feeling. He's only Anatolian smile, and all the fear, cunning, and resentment that go along with it. Kazan's attempts to humanize him, therefore, fall flat in comparison to the moments of satirical hysteria he constructs so deftly. "I don't think I blended the styles quite right," he admitted, "I mean the satiric and the tragic. That's a very hard blend to achieve. I think I came close, but I don't think I achieved it."[22] Neither did he ever bring Griffith's performance down to a level befitting those eye-level shots, which in the final analysis suggests that Rhodes was a character Kazan hated more than he loved, remaining slightly more polemical than human. However, in *A Face in the Crowd*, Kazan walks that line better than he ever did or ever would. The result may be idea-heavy, but it's admirably close to "representing all points of view." "Without that ambivalence," Kazan said, "the whole film wouldn't be worthwhile."[23]

That's what makes *A Face in the Crowd* the most challenging Kazan picture: his polemics, his tendency to shout above his material, is filtered through humor, making the problematic matter of volume the butt — as well as the conduit — of the joke.

After considering *Baby Doll* and *A Face in the Crowd*, one may wonder if Kazan's private comic repertoire, the kind of laughter he laughed off the set, extended beyond his Anatolian smile. Or was he as derisive as his films? Personally, he was known to laugh at the impolitic sentiment spoken aloud, in crude terms, when someone, including himself, was busted for bullshit. For Richard Schickel, a personal friend and one-time interviewer of Kazan, the director's laughter was more elusive. "I never once heard him crack a joke or for that matter respond to one," he wrote in response to the question. "He was basically an ironist and a rather gloomy observer of the passing human scene. That does not mean he was not great company. He was full of anecdotes about behavior on the set, but usually they were not funny ones. And he often told stories in which he was the butt of some directorial misjudgment of his own, and he had the most wonderful way of insinuating his way into your confidence, again, often enough, by showing how he had misjudged some professional situation. . . . What he had instead [of humor] was a charm that never quite masked his intensity."[24] An intensity that served his passion for passion, but one that often overcame his love.

NOTES

1. Robin Wood, "The Kazan Problem," *Movie* 19 (winter 1971–72), 29.

2. Andrew Sarris, *The American Cinema* (Chicago: University of Chicago Press, 1968), 158.

3. Pauline Kael, "Kazan's Latest Arrangements," *New Yorker*, 22 November 1969, 211.

4. Elia Kazan, *Elia Kazan: A Life* (New York: Knopf, 1988), 90.

5. Jeff Young, *Kazan: The Master Director Discusses His Films: Interviews with Elia Kazan* (New York: Newmarket Press, 1999), 230.

6. Sarris, *American Cinema*, 74.

7. David Thomson, *The New Biographical Dictionary of Film* (New York: Knopf, 2004), 745.

8. Kazan, *Kazan*, 3.

9. Lindsay Anderson, "The Last Sequence of *On the Waterfront*," *Sight and Sound* 24, no. 3 (January–March 1955), 130.

10. Kazan, *Kazan*, 64.

11. Young, *Kazan*, 250.

12. Elia Kazan, interview with Stuart Byron and Martin L. Rubin, *Movie* 19 (winter 1971–72), 9.

13. Young, *Kazan*, 226.

14. Ibid., 228.

15. Blacks will laugh again at whites in *East of Eden*, *A Face in the Crowd*, *Wild River*, *Splendor in the Grass*, and look on through *The Arrangement*. "I did it *here* consciously," Kazan said of *Baby Doll*. "I thought, 'The blacks are sitting down there, and they're laughing at these fucking whites.'" Kazan, *Movie* 19.

16. Kazan, *Kazan*, 4.

17. Michel Ciment, ed., *Elia Kazan: An American Odyssey* (London: Bloomsbury, 1988), 86.

18. Young, *Kazan*, 235.

19. Ibid.

20. Ibid., 244.

21. Ibid., 237.

22. Ibid., 235.

23. Ibid., 253.

24. Richard Schickel, email exchange with the author, August 16, 2009.

Elia Kazan with his marvelous wiles, tripping

the latches of the secret little doors that lead into

the always different personalities of each actor.

That is his secret; not merely to know what must

be done, but to know the way to implement

the doing for actors trained in diametrically

opposite schools, or not trained at all. He does

not "direct," he creates a center point, and

then goes to each actor and creates the desire

to move toward it. And they all meet, but for

different reasons, and seem to have arrived

there by themselves.

ARTHUR MILLER

A Straight Director's Queer Eye

1951–1961

*L*et's start with a contradiction. On one hand, an admission: Including the phrase "queer cinema" and "Elia Kazan" in the same sentence is a stretch. And on the other, an assertion: Any director who, in the space of a decade, put Marlon Brando, James Dean, Montgomery Clift, and Warren Beatty before his camera, two of them in roles that were among the most sexually iconic of their careers, may have contributed more to the (homo)eroticization of the American male movie star than even he realized.

It's tempting to label this underexplored thread within Kazan's work the Cinema of Inadvertency. The director was, after all, heterosexual and by most accounts a man of robust carnal appetites — the index of Richard Schickel's excellent 2005 biography includes separate entries for "philandering" and "womanizing."[1] He was also (with some notable exceptions) more interested in using film to explore the lives and characters of men than of women. In any number of his movies, from *A Streetcar Named Desire* (1951) and *Viva Zapata!* (1952) to career-twilight works like *The Arrangement* (1969) and *The Last Tycoon* (1976), the protagonists are complex, charismatic men — some brutish, some closed off, some self-loathing, but always assumed to be worthy of deciphering, and treated in a way that quickens your appetite for a more intimate glimpse of them.

To make you look at his men the way he wanted you to look at them, Kazan, on occasion, turned his camera into a woman. He sometimes used it as a kind of perspectival stand-in for a female protagonist, attuning it to her viewpoint, her appetite, even her passion. To gaze on Marlon Brando in full rut in *A Streetcar Named Desire*, or on Warren Beatty, the beau ideal of a full-lipped, sensitive high-school jock in *Splendor in the Grass* (1961), is to experience them not only through the eyes of Vivien Leigh and Natalie Wood, but through their frank lust. And in those Production Code days when homosexuality was an untouchable subject and gay moviegoers had

Stanley Kowalski (Marlon Brando) tells his sister-in-law Blanche DuBois (Vivien Leigh) about the significance of the Napoleonic Code in a publicity still from *A Streetcar Named Desire*. Brando's aggressive physicality both attracts and frightens the frail and fluttery Blanche. Photo courtesy of the Wesleyan Cinema Archives.

to seek solace in subtext, any movie that presented a man's sexuality through the lens of desire *for* him (rather than desire *from* him) could invite gay moviegoers into a parallel ghost narrative in which they could identify with the desire, and even with the desirer.

But suggesting that all this was nothing more than an accidental by-product of Kazan's taste for powerful and magnetic male characters under-credits the director, who, after all, worked closely on *A Streetcar Named Desire* and *Splendor in the Grass* with two gay writers, and who chose, time and again, to return to a portrayal of male sexual attractiveness as something so powerful — a perfume and a poison — that it could drive you mad, as, in a way, it does Blanche DuBois in *Streetcar* and Deanie Loomis in *Splendor*. Desire for men in these movies is a kind of sickness, a weakness or fever that, whatever else it may be, is certainly not what the prevailing psychoanalytic orthodoxy would then have called normative. Like homosexuality as defined sixty years ago, it's a deviation that needs to be cured. Even a much saner, more centered woman than Blanche or Deanie can succumb. In *A Face in the Crowd* (1957), the seen-it-all Marcia Jeffries (Patricia Neal, never anybody's fool) falls so hard for the sweaty, sexy bastard Lonesome Rhodes (Andy Griffith), despite his belief that "a guitar beats a girl every time," that her own temperature rises; she starts to glisten the day they meet. (In a concurrent plotline, Lonesome also seduces, professionally speaking, a man, an uncharismatic beta male played by Walter Matthau.) Only when it's almost too late does Marcia manage to pull herself out of a death-spiral of attraction. Just as it does at the end of *Splendor in the Grass*, the fever of desire finally breaks; Marcia, all but shattered by her craving for Lonesome, comes to her senses. In the film's final shot, Neal and Matthau's characters, both recovered from their follies, gaze up one last time at the man for whom they had both swooned. And if anyone truly doubts that something about male erotic allure was deeply rooted in Kazan's psyche and made manifest in his work, consider this: In his hands, even Andy Griffith became a reasonably credible sex object.

Before examining Kazan's men, some background on his attitudes about homosexuality—and himself—is in order. Schickel writes that Kazan, a "swarthy, runty, big-nosed outsider" who was acutely conscious of his status as the son of immigrants, "always identified with gays as people, like himself, who were 'different,' outside the American mainstream."[2] It's a point Kazan himself made in his admiring description of Tennessee Williams as "the complete outsider. . . . The centers of civilization that he found agreeable were . . . those populated by his own kind: artists, romantics, freaks of one kind or another, castoffs, those rejected by respectable society. . . . We both felt vulnerable to the depredations of an unsympathetic world."[3] In his autobiography, Kazan wrote bluntly that he "never warmed to the so-called masculine virtues. . . . I've lived apart from the male world and its concerns. . . . Men have to be constantly proving something that is not worth proving—their muscles, their fearlessness, their affluence, the strength of their erections." In the same passage, he noted that "many of the men I've liked best have had strong 'feminine' characteristics." As well as Williams and *Splendor in the Grass* screenwriter William Inge, he included Marlon Brando on that list.[4]

But Kazan's identification with homosexuals wasn't merely analogous, a professed kinship of outsiders; it may have been more personal, since Kazan himself knew what it was like to be excluded from the sexual mainstream. Looking in the mirror, he was tormented by that unbeautiful mug of his; in fact, he begins his autobiography by talking about how much he has always disliked his face. And perhaps his body as well — throughout his childhood, Kazan was fascinated and frustrated by a massively endowed first cousin in his father's employ (his dad would actually show this nephew's huge appendage off to select customers). Kazan, who himself felt that he was "an embarrassment" to his father, thought that this immense member — which he never saw himself — made his cousin a rival for his father's affection and admiration.[5] Small wonder that he emerged from that bizarre point of reference as a pimply and awkward teenager who felt almost congenitally inadequate. Kazan recalled his lonely, sexually frustrated high school and college life as "eight years of unspeakable torture." He felt rejected by both men and women — and both spurnings truly hurt. During those years of sexual draught, he wouldn't fantasize about having sex with women himself, but about what the men he wanted to be were doing with the women he wanted to be with. At Williams College, when he was shunned by a group of Waspy fraternity brothers, "it hurt for four dark, cold years, and in the blackest part of my heart," he wrote sixty years later. "I still haven't forgiven the men who rejected me."[6]

One does not need to argue that Kazan was homosexual (even latently) to acknowledge, then, that his own coming of age did not describe a prototypical heterosexual arc. Those words reflect the lasting sense of injury of someone who, from a tender age, educated himself to observe male sexuality from a distance — a wounded boy who looked with envy at men who seemed comfortable in their own bodies. Kazan was a kid who learned from early adolescence to read and decode the elements of male sexual appeal, a pattern of behavior that any gay man who spent a portion of his youth in the closet will recognize instantly.

Kazan, of course, survived those tough years and proceeded into adulthood as a straight man. But his sexually agonized adolescence appears to have given him great sympathy for gay men, even if, to achieve that sympathy, he needed to define homosexuality as a state of extreme vulnerability and, perhaps, of emotional arrestedness. (It should be pointed out that at midcentury, Kazan was hardly alone in misunderstanding homosexuality in those terms, and was more benevolent about it than many of his contemporaries.) With the exception of the renegade Tennessee Williams, the homosexuals to whom Kazan was sympathetic were, in his view, not men, but lost boys, a definition to which he held fast in both drama and life. It's telling how many of the characters in plays Kazan helped usher into existence fulfill that prototype—not just the nervous teenager in Robert Anderson's 1953 *Tea and Sympathy*, whose tragedy, Kazan wrote, "would be the imposition of a sexual choice upon him by the hearty, uncomprehending, male world, before he is ready," but also the morbidly sensitive, almost certainly gay Tom Wingfield in *The Glass Menagerie*, and the very young, vulnerable, suicidal husband of Blanche DuBois, never seen but referred to in *A Streetcar Named Desire*.

Kazan carried the same definition into his personal relationships. He understood his *Wild River* (1960) star Montgomery Clift not as the gay man he was but, curiously, as "a sexual borderline case . . . an insecure boy. . . . Monty's sexuality was that of a child waiting for his mother to put her arms around him."[7] William Inge, well into his forties when Kazan worked with him, is given the same peculiar characterization as "childlike," a "psychically damaged . . . boy."[8] And of his *East of Eden* (1955) star James Dean, whose homo- or bisexuality now seems beyond dispute, Kazan wrote, "His imagination was limited; it was like a child's . . . he had to be coddled and hugged or threatened with abandonment."[9]

The director's complicated professional relationship to this subject began early in his career. Although his film version of *A Streetcar Named Desire* arrived in 1951, Kazan had been intimately involved with the play since early 1947, when Tennessee Williams had written him an admiring note and asked him to read an early draft.[10] By the time the movie opened, Kazan had put his imprint on hundreds of lines, and it remains evident even in the severely compromised screenplay that, under Production Code strictures, whitewashed Stanley's rape of Blanche and omitted any references to the homosexuality of Blanche's late husband.

Talking about *A Streetcar Named Desire* purely as a film text of Kazan is inappropriate, since the drama and character psychodynamics are primarily Williams's work. But Stanley Kowalski was, by the time of filming, a kind of joint creation of Williams, Kazan, and Marlon Brando, and the different ways writer and director described the character are revealing. In the stage directions for his play, Williams introduces Stanley as an exuberant and even generous life force: "Since earliest manhood the center of his life has been pleasure with women, the giving and taking of it, not with weak indulgence, dependently, but with the power and pride of a richly feathered male bird among hens."[11] But Kazan's description of Stanley, taken from his 1947 notebooks, is considerably darker: "He's completely self-absorbed ... supremely indifferent to everything except his own pleasure and comfort ... he's desperately trying to drug his senses, overwhelming them with a constant round of sensation so that he will feel nothing else." (Remarkably, given the casting, Kazan added, "He's going to get very fat later.")[12]

It's Kazan's vision, not Williams's, that seems to prevail in Brando's filmed performance. Sexy but impatient and animalistic, his Stanley, furious when his poker night with the boys is interrupted and warning the smitten Mitch away from Blanche, could well fit the description Kazan later wrote of Ace Stamper, the domineering brute of a father in *Splendor in the Grass*, a character he felt was "a base and unawares homosexual. He is only happy in the company of men. . . . He doesn't like it when he sees a man in love" with a woman.[13]

There's no reason to think that Kazan, Williams, or Brando thought Stanley was a repressed homosexual (especially since Brando's later, completely dissimilar performance in *Reflections in a Golden Eye* (1967) offers ample and florid evidence of what he thought a repressed homosexual looked like). But Kazan's camera, throughout *A Streetcar Named Desire*, sees Stanley through Blanche's eyes, and Blanche — Williams's surrogate — is, in some ways, the playwright's disguised and self-loathing version of a gay man. She's given to ornate self-dramatization, she has already married a gay man once, she observes with wry revulsion her own appetite for unformed boys ("I've got to be good — and keep my hands off children," she says in one of the play's only camp lines) as well as her attraction to near-anonymous sexual encounters; finally, in the last stage of her journey toward oblivion, she is thirsty for dangerous rough trade, even if that rough trade happens to be her sister's husband. Kazan doesn't queer Stanley; with considerable help from Williams, he queers Blanche — and makes us look at Stanley through her "abnormal" attraction to him.

Kazan made most of his movies at a time when overt homosexual content and perspective was not an option, so it may be said that his use of a woman with a sick passion for a man, and his camera's endorsement of that febrile need, were akin to what he must have imagined self-punishing homosexuals feel like. A decade after *A Streetcar Named Desire*, he returned to some of the same themes in *Splendor in the Grass*, a film over which, with Inge writing under his supervision, he exerted even more authorial control. Made at Warner Bros. soon after the studio's high-gloss teen-lust melodrama *A*

Deanie Loomis (Natalie Wood) swoons for Bud Stamper (Warren Beatty) in a publicity still from *Splendor in the Grass*. Deanie's overwhelming sexual desire for Bud takes an unusually masochistic turn. Photo courtesy of the Wesleyan Cinema Archives.

Summer Place (1959), *Splendor in the Grass* was (very successfully) pitched to the same young audience as a story of two beautiful young people madly in love with each other, reminiscent of *Peyton Place* (1957). But what unfolds on screen is something else entirely — a story of the deranging power of unladylike hunger for a beautiful man. The first time we see Deanie (Natalie Wood), she's in a car, kissing Bud Stamper (Warren Beatty), and looks almost faint from the need to take him in. Kazan then follows her home, where she wonders, "Is it so terrible to have those feelings about a boy?"

The answer — yes — animates the entire dramatic action of the film, as we are pulled into an obsession that eventually lands Deanie in a mental institution by a camera that endorses her viewpoint, lingering worshipfully on Bud, even following him into the school shower to capture him, self-entranced, in a private moment. Bud's sexuality is not transactional; a beautiful boy-man, a star athlete, and something of a cipher, he is objectified perhaps more than any male character had ever been in a Hollywood romance. It's quite possible that Kazan's aching memories of watching (and wanting to be like) the handsome boys with whom he went to school were in play here. Beatty's lithe, graceful Bud could have been a lad out of the director's youth; the film is set in 1928, when Kazan himself was about Bud's age.

Beatty later said that during the making of the movie, he thought Kazan "didn't like good-looking guys," and Kazan's feelings about the character seem powerfully conflicted; Bud is a decent boy, but also the insensitive, even cruel cause of Deanie's disintegration.[14] With her passion as its motor, *Splendor in the Grass* plays as an almost hysterical case study of self-destructive sexual need for an only transiently obtainable straight boy. And a queer reading of the film, especially in the context of its middle-aged gay screenwriter's hopeless crush on Beatty, is hardly a challenge, since Kazan commits fully to Inge's clear belief that Bud must be completely desired by the viewer for the film to make sense. In the movie's most shocking scene, Bud, for one moment, realizes the power he has over Deanie (whose ambiguously gendered name cannot be an accident), and he starts to become aroused by his own cruelty. "You're nuts about me, aren't you?" he says to her as he leans against a wall, closing his eyes in a semimasturbatory fugue as the voracious Deanie slides down to crotch level. "At my feet, slave. Tell me you love me, tell me you can't live without me."

"I would go down on my knees to worship you . . . I would. I would," she says in reply. "Where's your pride?" he asks her later, appalled as she keeps pursuing him. "I haven't any pride," she says. These torrid, masochistic-orgasmic exchanges — in a studio movie from 1961! — are many things, but nobody would call them heteronormative. In fact, they hew remarkably close to a voguish sixties dramatic notion of homosexual relationships as twisted power struggles.

Kazan presents Bud Stamper as a more sensitive Stanley Kowalski in training, a young man learning to use and abuse his sexual charisma (tellingly, Inge leaves him settled down in working-class squalor with a Stella of his own). But both characters are pretty clearly heterosexual; a queer reading of either film depends entirely on how much one is willing to accept the "inappropriate" sexual hunger of a woman as a stand-in for the "inappropriate" sexual hunger of a gay man. However, in two other Kazan movies from the period, the homosexual subtext is integrated into the hero himself. Both *Wild River* and *East of Eden* deploy, as protagonists, the "feminine" men — Montgomery Clift and James Dean — Kazan professed to prefer in life, and in both films, the neurotic sexual uncertainty with which they infuse their characters materially changes the plot and dramatic impact.

In *Wild River*, the effeteness of the hero is, in part, built into the text. Chuck Glover, sent by the Tennessee Valley Authority into the sticks to convince an old woman to abandon her home on a river island that's about to be flooded, is a city boy among country men; he represents progress and enlightenment but also the kind of unmasculine, urbanized refinement of someone who's gotten too far away from the land, from physical work, and from his own body. As played by Clift (who made the movie a couple of years after the accident that paralyzed part of his face, and spent much of the production fighting his impulse to drink), this tremulous, timorous quality is so extreme that Chuck's blossoming relationship with a beautiful young widow named Carol (Lee Remick) becomes, in some ways, the story of a woman trying to attract a man who seems to have almost no sexual appetite; Chuck's hold on masculinity is so tenuous that he can't even bring himself to make a move.

Kazan himself seems to have been of two minds about Clift's near-queer interpretation of *Wild River*'s hero. In his autobiography, he recalls extraordinary frustration that Clift was utterly unable to make himself believable in a seduction scene with the luminous Remick. "She seemed dominant," he wrote, "and Monty seemed sexually uncertain. In one scene, Monty, at the instant of arousal, slumped to the floor. I cursed him under my breath as a limp lover." Kazan was then forced to reconceive the scene with Remick as the aggressor; she "was taking him, not vice versa."[15]

But although the director refers to this alteration as an "accident of [Clift]'s personality," there's some evidence that he conceived Chuck as sexually problematic from the beginning. "I wanted their scenes to show ambivalence," he told Clift's biographer, Patricia Bosworth; "attraction, repulsion, fear, love."[16] And in an interview with Michel Ciment, Kazan said that in *Wild River*, "I tried to make everything as close as I could . . . to myself. . . . This role was no problem, because I said, well, this is the way I was then. I was shy, uncertain with girls . . . I took him from myself, because I knew what my own weaknesses were, which are not the same weaknesses I have now."[17]

The conception of Chuck as an uncertain boy who's very shaky about taking his first steps toward a sexual relationship with a woman might have worked less complicatedly on screen if Kazan had cast a twenty-five-year-old (the age he originally intended Chuck to be). But Clift was pushing forty by the time the film was shot; his creased, injured face had taken on the blank, stricken stare that characterized his later work, and in some of his scenes with Remick, he comes off as a closeted gay man trying to convince himself that he can make it work with her. As in *Splendor in the Grass*, the most intensely romantic scenes are shot through with masochism. "You can't get enough of me right now, can you? Tell me! Tell me!" begs Carol, aching for any sign that it might be true. Chuck doesn't offer much of a reply. Later, in their climactic encounter, she says to him, "I love you! I love you! I love you! Don't say anything. Don't say a thing. I'm afraid of what you might say."

"I don't know what to say," he replies, defeated.

"Oh, God," she says, equally defeated. "That says it all. I heard you. I asked you and you said no. I heard you."

Chuck and Carol eventually end up together, but only after a group of "real" men beat the daylights out of him and literally throw her into the mud for loving him. He demonstrates his complete inability to defend himself or her, revealing his "feminine" quality in an especially shaming way, and when he sees that she is willing to accept him anyway, he flies her off to the city — his world — as the movie ends. It looks unlikely to become a typical marriage, but since Carol already has two children, Chuck may be more useful for companionship than for sex, and she may offer him the outward contours, if not the reality, of a "normal" life.

Any queer reading of *Wild River* rests, at least in part, on the idiosyncratic asexuality of Clift's performance, and on the peculiarity of casting him in a role for which Kazan really wanted Brando. But in truth, the film — and its approach to its hero — is in many ways a close echo of a movie Kazan directed five years earlier, *East of Eden*. In that film, in the casting and performance of James Dean, in the substantial reshaping of John Steinbeck's source material, in the staging, and even in the camera angles, Kazan created one the most sexually diffident male protagonists of the decade, and put him at the center of a near-gay near-epic.

In adapting *East of Eden*, Kazan and screenwriter Paul Osborn jettisoned the first two-thirds of the novel. What remains is a quasi-biblical parable reset in California farm country (Dean is Cal, the Cain character; Richard Davalos is his brother Aron). The presence of Julie Harris as Aron's girlfriend Abra is meant to set up an archetypal midfifties Hollywood love triangle: the good (but bland) brother, the bad (but hot) brother, and the girl they both want. But that's not how *East of Eden* plays out. In his first film, Dean is not particularly dangerous or dark — nor is he nearly as interested in Abra as Abra is in him. Instead, he's the emblem of a Kazanian feminine boy-man. In every possible way, the director cues us to perceive Dean as diminutive, vulnerable, and frail. He's first shown sitting on a curb, looking up with a half-surly, half-anxious squint as if bracing for an injury. Throughout

Abra (Julie Harris) tries to encourage Cal Trask (James Dean) in a production still from *East of Eden*. Her eyes are on him, but is he interested? Photo courtesy of the Wesleyan Cinema Archives.

the film, Kazan shoots him to appear as small as possible — in almost every grouping, he's placed low in the frame, and made to look shorter than the people with whom he's standing, even the women. When he kneels before his mother (Jo Van Fleet), he's tiny; when he's with Julie Harris, he hunches over in a protective crouch. He can barely even stand on his own two feet — Kazan has him lean on objects for support whenever one is handy.

Dean is feminized from *East of Eden*'s first moments, when a whore addresses him derisively as "pretty boy." He starts the movie by saying about a woman "You tell her I hate her," and then quickly scolds himself for his ineptitude, serving as a perfect avatar for the teenaged Kazan: "I should have gone right on in there! I should have gone right on in there and talked to her." When we next see Cal, he's hiding alone in the bushes, watching his brother with Abra, following them, trying to understand what a "normal" relationship between a boy and a girl looks like. Later, Abra and Aron cuddle in an icehouse, while Cal hides in a corner, spying on them. While they make out, he rhythmically bangs the long, hard shaft of a grappling hook, an unhappy solo act.

Moviegoers of the time would naturally have believed that Cal is pining for Abra, but Kazan thwarts that notion more than once — it's Aron, not Abra, on whom Cal is focusing the intensity of his feelings, even as Abra acts on her conflicted desires. "Girls follow you around, don't they?" she says, hopefully, trapping Cal in an open field. Cal couldn't look less interested. Several scenes later, she repeats the line verbatim, almost as a suggestion to him. Again, he has virtually no response. "Are you interested in hearing about me?" she asks after going on and on about her life. Clearly, he's not. "Why are you telling me all this?" he says. She ruffles his hair — like Lee Remick's Carol, she realizes that she's going to have to be the aggressor — and he looks almost alarmed.

That may be because his interests lie elsewhere. In a major sequence in the film in which Cal's ambisexuality makes as much of a leap from subtext to text as any movie of the 1950s could permit, he wanders into a crowded gymnasium in search of Gustav Albrecht (Harold Gordon), a man from whom he needs something. The gym is full of "real" men — they're burly, they're bigger than Cal, and they're all exercising — and he is immediately kicked out. "These boys are trying to get in shape, so beat it," he's warned. Not to be stopped, he sneaks in again; he wants to play with the big boys. He grabs a rope suspended from the ceiling, swings on it, and giddily, accidentally, flies into the arms of the much larger Albrecht. From there, he follows Albrecht into the locker room and talks to him as the older man strips and showers. Cal keeps peering over a ledge as Albrecht scrubs himself (and as he does more than once in the movie, Kazan makes Dean appear more boyish by putting an object in his way that he's not quite tall enough to see over). When Albrecht emerges from the shower nude, toweling himself, Cal can't stay away; he comes up behind him, giving him so little room that Albrecht has to say to him, "Don't get so near me! I don't want to get all hot again."

With encounters like that, the forbidden love that is officially meant to animate *East of Eden* — Abra's and Cal's — feels beside the point, and Kazan ultimately makes sure we know it is. Cal's journey toward manhood is blocked by a tortured relationship with his Bible-thumping father and an anguished one with his straight-arrow brother. In the movie's closing shot, Abra politely departs, leaving Cal to sort out those feelings without the distraction of romance. Shortly before that denouement, Aron says to Cal, "Don't touch her! You're mean and vicious and wild." It's a description that's almost completely at odds with the performance we've been watching.

Dean's Cal is never a persuasive sexual threat to his brother, and throughout the film has seemed more anguished than vicious. If Brando's Stanley Kowalski and Beatty's Bud Stamper are the masculine (albeit deeply compromised) ideals, men who are viewed lustfully through a lens that can feel, at different moments, female, homosexual, or inadequately heterosexual, then Clift's Chuck and Dean's Cal are the other side of that equation. They are Kazan's failed men — his "boys" — and their feelings of masculine insufficiency, their sexual indifference, and their deep sensitivity takes them as close to a sympathetic midcentury conception of homosexual protagonists as any American director of the time cared or dared to go. Today, it's easy to sneer at the dated and patronizing notion of homosexuality as an inadequacy, a failure of maleness, a blight — or a way station on the road to heteronormativity. It's cringe-making, to be sure. But the generosity of spirit and complicated empathy Kazan brings to these portrayals needs no such excuses made for it: It's modern, and, viewed within the context of 1950s studio moviemaking, it is unique.

NOTES

1. Richard Schickel, *Elia Kazan: A Biography* (New York: HarperCollins, 2005), 499.

2. Ibid., 3, 292.

3. Elia Kazan, *Elia Kazan: A Life* (New York: Knopf, 1988), 494–5.

4. Ibid., 27–28.

5. Ibid., 30.

6. Ibid., 41–42.

7. Ibid., 574, 597.

8. Ibid., 573–74.

9. Elia Kazan, *Kazan on Directing* (New York: Knopf, 2009), 186.

10. Schickel, *Kazan*, 164.

11. Tennessee Williams, *A Streetcar Named Desire*, reprinted in *Tennessee Williams: Plays 1937–1955* (New York: Library of America, 2000), 481.

12. Kazan, *Kazan on Directing*, 56–57.

13. Ibid., 212.

14. Warren Beatty quoted in Schickel, *Kazan*, 376.

15. Kazan, *Kazan*, 599.

16. Patricia Bosworth, *Montgomery Clift* (New York: Harcourt Brace Jovanovich, 1978), 344.

17. Michel Ciment, *Kazan on Kazan* (London: Secker and Warburg, 1973), 132.

SAVANNAH LEE

The Other Side of the Story
Elia Kazan as Director of Female Pain

Elia Kazan is best remembered as a director of male actors and teller of male stories — *On the Waterfront* (1954) being arguably the most famous example. But a second look reveals that there is another side to this story. Throughout his career he directed actresses in stories about women. Three of his films in particular can be reconstituted as examples of female pain if one sets aside the way we ordinarily assess them. Doing so sheds light on a different aspect of Kazan's legacy than is ordinarily considered.

Pinky (1949) is usually thought of as a movie about racial issues. *A Streetcar Named Desire* (1951) tends to be seen as a Marlon Brando film. *Splendor in the Grass* (1961) is remembered as the outstanding debut of Warren Beatty. But in fact, a case can be made that these films are equally about the pain of women. Kazan was every bit as interested in the characters of Blanche (Vivien Leigh) and Stella (Kim Hunter) as he was in the character of Stanley Kowalski (Brando). He was just as interested in the character of Deanie (Natalie Wood) as he was in the character of Bud (Beatty). And in the controversial and often-overlooked *Pinky*, the story is entirely that of the conflicted, racially stranded title heroine (Jeanne Crain). In bringing out this neglected side of these three Kazan films, we can reclaim him as a director of women in epic female stories and balance our sense of his true significance to film history.

Kazan's autobiography is studded with fascinating little moments of attention to women and female experience. Take his description of watching Arthur Miller make mean jokes at a party: "I felt sorry for his wife. It's the terrible fate of wives, I thought, to be helpless in a situation like this one."[1] Or interviewing Natalie Wood for the part of Deanie in *Splendor in the Grass*: "I wanted to find out what human material was there, what her inner life was."[2]

This interest in discovering the inner life of a woman, especially from a midcentury man, has to be considered remarkable in its own right. Even more so was the fact that he liked women to have inner lives that were "masculine" in depth, difficulty, and toughness. About his second wife, Barbara, he writes: "Something bold and out of the ordinary about her struck me. . . . There was a hardness there — she made her own rules — and with it, an honesty."[3] About Jeanne Crain's relentless goodness on the set of *Pinky*, he lamented: "There would be days when I'd long for a bitch!"[4] On location in Athens, he said, "I acquired a mini-harem," but he found himself unable to truly enjoy them because "none of the girls had anything difficult about them. Or challenging."[5]

Perhaps the most extraordinary passage is one about wives. Explaining why men inevitably start sleeping around, Kazan pauses to look sympathetically on those they leave at home:

> They [the wives] have the same needs — rejuvenation, entertainment, reassurance, hope — that men have. Most women have not been able to find relief and help [through extracurricular sex] as readily or as easily. I've noticed the faces of wives who, impelled by their notion of duty and even more by their fear of being abandoned . . . do their duty all their lives through, preserving their real thoughts in silence and their deepest desires unfulfilled. The faces of these good creatures acquire a wistful aspect, a dreamy look, as they fade back permanently from life and the hope of solution. They live in a fog of neglect and longing.[6]

Finally, there is this fascinating aside in his discussion of "people with mysterious gifts":[7] "I've found they have a strength that is extraordinary, and their strength is a gift to me. So it's been . . . with the actors and *particularly the actresses* [emphasis mine] I've worked with. Their precious gifts, for which they paid in pain, have made me successful when I was successful."[8]

No one will ever know why a twentieth-century American man from a distinctly patriarchal culture of origin developed such a curiously generous attitude toward women, such an appreciation for "boldness" and "difficulty" in them, such respect for their talents — "for which they paid in pain." He paid them back with films that did justice to their sacrifice.

Pinky was intended to strike a progressive blow against racism. It is the story of Patricia "Pinky" Johnson, a very light-skinned black woman who started "passing" (for white) when she went north to study nursing. Now a registered nurse, she has come home to the rural Deep South to deliver a message to her grandmother (Ethel Waters), who lives in profound poverty with the other African Americans of the town. While there, she reexperiences the bigotry and degradation of being an African American under segregation. She also becomes the nurse of an aging wealthy white woman, Miss Em (Ethel Barrymore). The two become friends, though Miss Em's relatives know that Pinky is black and are suspicious of her. When Miss Em dies and leaves her antebellum mansion to Pinky, the relatives contest the will. Pinky's friends and family advise her to run away for her own safety, but Pinky fights back in court — and wins. She puts the old mansion to use as a clinic and school for African Americans.

Pinky's heart is in the right place. Unfortunately, however, the film has dated badly. To begin with, there is the fact that a white actress plays the role of the eponymous African-American heroine. It should be noted that Elia Kazan himself did not make this choice. He came onto the project after the original director left, when shooting was already under way. Nonetheless, the casting of a white actress in a black role only effaces what it purports to represent, making the entire movie a tragic mockery of its own premise.

Furthermore, all of the active racists in *Pinky* are whites of the lower class. The policemen and drunks who humiliate Pinky are uneducated, unwashed, unshaven. The whites who end up persecuting her in court are social climbers who reveal their trashy origins by their inability to recognize a cheap imitation brooch when they see one. The educated and affluent white people who surround Pinky, by contrast, are good guys. They just need a little push to come through and do the right thing. This is a clear attempt by the script to absolve American society of systemic racism and blame it all on a few ignorant bad apples.

These flaws make the film deeply reactionary and offensive by today's standards. Kazan himself did not appear to take *Pinky* at all seriously, stating in his autobiography, "We all knew we were not making a masterpiece."[9] How ironic, then, that *Pinky* was something of a Waterloo for him, as the film that made him realize "I was inept at my profession."[10] This insight came about when he caught himself allowing his cameraman and editor to make all his pictorial decisions for him because he himself had no idea how to shoot the film. "After making four films and picking up an Academy Award for directing, I was still a stage director and in no way prepared to do . . . subjects that called for bold pictorial treatment."[11] (He obviously learned from the experience!)

Elia Kazan moves Jeanne Crain into position in a production still from *Pinky*.
Photo courtesy of the Wesleyan Cinema Archives.

I want to examine the film from a more abstract and symbolic standpoint. It *can* be seen purely as a metaphor for being stuck between two worlds — any two worlds, whether familial, national, racial, gender, even psychological, as in a tale of madness. *Pinky* can be seen as a kind of *Romeo and Juliet*, with Pinky as a Juliet pulled between two kinds of belonging.

But here's the significant fact for our purposes: there is no Romeo.

Or rather, the Romeo is Pinky herself. It's her dormant self-loyalty and self-identity, to which she finally commits herself at the cost of everything she has previously wanted. She rejects her man to marry her pride. "You can't live without pride," she declares — which is sadly a revolutionary statement for a female film hero in that or any other time.

For all its deep and serious flaws, therefore, *Pinky* is nonetheless an example of sustained cinematic attention to the subjectivity of a female character — a female character who has more on her mind than what dress to wear tomorrow, and more in her story than the traditional limits of female experience (i.e. figuring out which man to marry and/or what to do about her parents).

Pinky is not a man's story. But neither is it a woman's, in the sense that it does not conform to the familiar outlines of female concerns. It's not a white person's story either, and, as filmed, it certainly is not a black person's story! Instead, in more abstract and symbolic terms, it's an *outsider's* story. Everywhere Pinky goes, she knows she will be misunderstood, and she knows she will take the blame when the truth comes out. Perhaps this is why Kazan so often shows her walking alone beside fences — gates — borders — always on the outer side. No-man's-land. The visual symbolism is clear and striking: there is no safe place for her, nor is there any escape. (When her would-be rapists go after her, for example, they trap her against one of these fences.) Unrecognized in her community, lionized by the enemy, she's a forced double agent in a war she never declared. In a way, *Pinky* is not even a story at all. It's an existential snapshot with a Hollywood arc jammed down on it like an ill-fitting hat.

How many female film heroes have functioned as existential symbols as they walk along in heels and a pencil skirt?

It only gets more remarkable when one considers how personal this symbolism must have been to Kazan himself — not in racial terms, but in abstract ones. This immigrant boy knew nothing of the black experience and never pretended to. But he certainly knew what it meant to look like one thing while really being another. He knew what it meant to stand forever outside the fence in the dust. He knew what it meant to hear the train everywhere he went, always being reminded of instability, transition, going-between. He knew what it meant to be welcomed on appearances and then rejected on essence.

Pinky, as played by Jeanne Crain, is not black. But she is female. Elia Kazan chose to lavish his most potent visual symbology of the outsider experience, *his* outsider experience, on a female character. He speaks through her. Maybe this is one reason the racial mimicry of *Pinky* didn't seem to bother him — because he was already doing a kind of gender mimicry or crossidentification through the character of Pinky. Through her, he, in a sense, recast himself as a woman.

The racial mimicry, which he did not initiate, was arrogant. But the gender identification achieves something like humility. Kazan walks with this character the whole way, even through the humiliation of men looking up her skirt in a judge's office and the terror of the highly realistic near-rape by the locals. Kazan's rueful understanding of exactly how such men would act, combined with his focus on Pinky's subjective experience of their assault and its aftermath, is actually quite moving to witness. Among other things, *he* grants Pinky her rage, in silent visual contrast to the script. (Often he speaks in his autobiography of the canny, survival-oriented friendliness put on as a false front by the refugee, while inside, rage and bitterness brew.)

Such commitment by a male director to the unvarnished, human female experience would be notable in any time, let alone 1949.

A Streetcar Named Desire is one of the most famous films of the twentieth century. Everyone knows the clichés. Everyone can say "I have always depended upon the kindness of strangers." Everyone can yell "Stell-lahhhh!" Everyone has a mental picture of the awe-inspiring Marlon Brando in his white T-shirt as Stanley Kowalski. This dominant male performance, however, has skewed people's views of this film. In fact, it is possible to position *A Streetcar Named Desire* as a tale of two sisters.

Stella DuBois Kowalski, pregnant with her first child, is torn between her fragile sister, Blanche, and her brutish husband, Stanley. Blanche has come to find refuge with Stella after being fired from her teaching job. She wants to locate a decent man to marry as a last resort in life.

Stella supports her sister. Stanley, however, instinctively mistrusts the woman, sensing her ambivalence, weakness, and sexual secrets. The resulting conflict between Stanley and Blanche becomes both a clash of worldviews and a human tragedy, as Blanche's increasing vulnerability only worsens Stanley's hostility.

Stella defends her sister and makes it clear she does not want Stanley to interfere with Blanche. At the same time, she resists Blanche's efforts to all but seduce her away from Stanley. ("Don't, don't hang back with the brutes!" Blanche cries.) Though Stella essentially agrees with Blanche's view that Stanley belongs in the Pleistocene era, she considers that more of a positive than a negative. When he "smashes all the lights," it's "a thrill."

Less of a thrill, however, is his refusal to honor her request to leave Blanche alone. He digs up dirt on Blanche's promiscuous past and proceeds to ruin her efforts to find love with Mitch (Karl Malden), one of Stanley's poker buddies.

When Stella finds out what Stanley has done, she is memorably livid. She tears his shirt and screams at him in rage. But any chance of resolution is cut short when she must go to the hospital to have her baby. Blanche, crushed, humiliated, and bereft of her only ally in the house, defiantly confesses her sins and pleads for understanding from Mitch. When this fails, Blanche begins to lose touch with reality. After Stanley rapes her in a final fit of contempt, she comes completely unglued.

Stella returns home to find Blanche irreversibly deranged. The joy Stella would otherwise take in her new motherhood is spoiled. While she looks on in anguish, Blanche is taken away to a mental institution as Mitch has to be restrained from beating up the unrepentant Stanley. After Blanche's exit, Stella declares that she will never return to the house she shares with Stanley (and where Stanley is calling to her). She runs upstairs to the neighbor's house.

Thematically, *A Streetcar Named Desire* is a duel between Blanche and Stanley. Structurally, however, *A Streetcar Named Desire* is about two *women* trying to negotiate their desires, loyalties, and destinies in the cruel strictures of pre-sexual-revolution America. Womanhood is their koan. In this dark story, madness and defeat are their answers.

What's remarkable is the importance placed on those answers by Elia Kazan. In *A Streetcar Named Desire*, Kazan has created a movie where the subjectivity, actions, and inner lives of these two women are treated with absolute profundity. Their layered, nuanced arcs are capable of withstanding the deepest investigation and analysis, the most numerous and broadranging interpretations. Kazan shows us every aspect of the sisters' journey

Stella Kowalski (Kim Hunter) walks down the stairs and back to her wailing husband in a publicity still from *A Streetcar Named Desire.* The next time she takes the stairs she runs away from him. Photo courtesy of the Wesleyan Cinema Archives.

to their tragic double terminus, including the legendary moment when Stanley cries for Stella.

It is said that in proper Hollywood screenplay structure, the midpoint of a film features either a false defeat or a false victory for the story's hero. Stanley's iconic bawling for Stella is such a moment—but what often goes unrecognized is that the moment belongs to Stella. When he calls for her, the entire movie stops for *her* reply. What seemed to be his moment turns into hers—and is revealed to have been hers all along, a setup for this signal event. In supreme and silent triumph, carrying her breasts like the spoils of war, Stella descends a spiral staircase to her husband. Like a prima ballerina, she sets the pace, making everyone wait. Stanley sinks to his knees.

Stella DuBois Kowalski is the pivotal character of *A Streetcar Named Desire.* She doesn't get the most screen time, but she's the one presented with the movie's central dilemma. Here is her husband; here is her sister. What, as the enmity between the two gets further and further out of hand, is Stella going to do about it? How will she resolve her loyalties to each party, including herself? In the end, it's up to her to balance the books.

Admittedly, she's the least interesting member of the Blanche-Stella-Stanley triumvirate. But she is the most crucial. The ending of the film actually belongs to her — the real ending, which is not Blanche DuBois giving herself over to "the kindness of strangers," but what happens next. If we've been paying attention to the right events, we've been explicitly prepared for it: it's the moment when Stella runs up the stairs. In keeping with ruthless screenwriting logic, this is a point-by-point reversal of Stella's earlier regal descent. In both cases, Stanley yells "Stella." Earlier, she came down to him in her own time and on her own terms. Now, she runs *up* the stairs, *away* from him, hunched over and fleeing like a refugee from what once seemed to be a plea but is now revealed as a command. And a petulant one at that. Stella's story, last and secretly most important of all, has resolved in tragedy.

It's Stella's sexuality that has done this to her. Seemingly the source of her power, it is actually the source of her shame and the conduit by which her own life and the lives of her sister and her sister's suitor are destroyed. This is the heart of *A Streetcar Named Desire*.

Coming from a time of strict sexual morality, *A Streetcar Named Desire* therefore explores one simple question: which sister is the true slut? Or, which sister is more sexually corrupt, given the insane rules of her society? Neither Tennessee Williams nor Kazan could bring themselves to condemn Blanche for her sexuality, even while recognizing that society could and would and did. So, given that Blanche is the one who has to take the heat, which sister really deserves it? The obviously dissipated one who has "had many meetings with strangers"? Or the legally married, monogamous sister who wanted only one man — but wanted him so badly that she was willing to ignore the fact that he was a lout?

Stanley Kowalski may not have intended any harm. He may sincerely believe that Blanche is "a calculating bitch with 'round heels.'"[12] But that's exactly how the outside world views Blanche as well. Stanley might as well have been one of the mob who chased her out of her prior hometown. He *is*, in fact, the mob who runs her out of New Orleans. He is an avatar of social convention. And it is Stella's marriage to him that leaves Blanche exposed and vulnerable. His personal hostility is bad enough, but then there is his destruction of Blanche's budding romance with Mitch, which amounts to a destruction of her entire future. (Despite the fact that Tennessee Williams wanted Stanley to be presented neutrally, it's worth noting that Mitch arrives at his own conclusion about the decency of Stanley's motives in coming between him and Blanche.) Blanche's sexuality never hurt anyone but herself. Stella's sexuality, by letting Stanley into her world, hurts everyone else, finally including herself. Her sister was right — and she knew it — but Stella failed to take action in time; now she has lost both her sister and her happiness.

This interpretation is contrary to Kazan's own. He believes Stella ends by declaring "fidelity to life. We go on with life . . . the best way we can. People get hurt, but you can't get through life without hurting people. The animal survives — at all costs."[13] Thus, Stella feels "grief and remorse but not an enduring alienation from her husband."[14]

Regardless of the specifics of Kazan's interpretation, however, *notice that he is describing the story in terms of Stella*. As a director, he very much recognizes that the final action of the work is hers. The final decision is hers. The only question is how we interpret it.

Thus another and more haunting question arises: which sister ends up more imprisoned? The one who is carted away to the asylum? Or the one who realizes she is in large part responsible for that tragedy, and trapped in the choices that created it?

In the end, that is the story of *A Streetcar Named Desire*. It's a portrait of the closeness and the distance between those two journeys.

And they are women's journeys.

Set in 1928, *Splendor in the Grass* should have been titled *Watch Out or Your Parents Will Ruin Your Life*. Take the mother of the doomed heroine Deanie (Wood). Deanie goes mad from the loss of her boyfriend Bud (Beatty). She also, however, goes mad from guilt over her sexual feelings for him, which is the fault of her mother (Audrey Christie). This woman's repression of Deanie's natural instincts is depicted by Kazan as the first step on Deanie's road to madness.

The movie opens with a frank portrait of Deanie's sexuality. After receiving Bud's kisses on a date, Deanie comes home and snuggles down on her living room couch (admittedly a bad choice of venue) in a manner which *could* be seen as just shifting around a bit to get comfy, but clearly isn't. Especially not given her subsequent look of panic and shame when her mother barges in.

Deanie flees from the interfering woman and busies herself getting ready for bed, not coincidentally taking off as many layers of clothing as the censors will allow. Kazan asks us to look seriously at her beautiful, ripe body.

In a publicity still from *Splendor in the Grass*, Deanie Loomis (Natalie Wood) yells at her mother after the boy she loves, Bud Stamper, has stopped seeing her. The loss will drive Deanie to attempt suicide. Photo courtesy of the Wesleyan Cinema Archives.

Isn't it ridiculous, he demands with his camera, that this girl is not getting what nature intended? Worse than ridiculous — isn't it morally wrong, even evil? There's no question of sleeping around here, if that even matters; she is completely devoted to Bud and he is likewise completely devoted to her. Why shouldn't she have him? Physically and even legally (she's a senior in high school), she's a woman. Her body and spirit are ready. Yet far from being liberated, Deanie is about to be even further repressed, setting the stage for her rapid decline.

Deanie asks her mother if it's normal for girls to have "feelings" about boys. Her mother says absolutely not. Women don't like that kind of thing. They only endure it so as to have children. Deanie, who has clear and un-ambivalent sexual feelings for Bud, has now been told that she is abnormal. The first tiny breach of her mental stability occurs, the first hint of the nervousness that, once amplified with the catastrophic loss of Bud himself, will bloom into psychosis.

After her mother leaves, Deanie defiantly settles down on her stomach in bed, but this time the intruding mother is inside her head. She gets up, sweetly kisses her pictures of Bud, and then prays rather than masturbates. Kazan wants us to understand that she would have been far better off doing the latter.

In the case of Deanie's boyfriend Bud, what is repressed in him is not sex but love. His father (Pat Hingle) is as worried about Bud's emotional feelings for Deanie as Deanie's mother is about the possibility of Deanie's sexual feelings for Bud. Bud's father does not want Bud falling in love, particularly not with Deanie, who is incapable of raising Bud's social status. He tells Bud to lay off Deanie for a while. If he needs to have sex, go find "another kind of girl." When Bud protests that he only wants Deanie, his father ignores him. He understands that his son needs sex, but cannot and will not understand that his son also needs love. With Deanie, as we have seen, it is the reverse. Her mother does not object to her being in love with Bud, but cannot and will not understand that she also needs sex. What should be whole within Bud and Deanie is sundered, and Bud and Deanie sunder too — from each other and within themselves.

As a result of this, Deanie undergoes a massive psychotic break and tries to drown herself in the falls. Kazan spares no detail of her helpless unraveling. Her repressed needs drown her reason just as she attempts to drown the body whose desires she could neither master nor fulfill.

Hers is the greater fall, so hers is the redemption. *Splendor in the Grass* starts out as Bud and Deanie's story, but ends as Deanie's.

She spends two and a half years in a mental hospital recovering from her breakdown. Certain events along the way help her out. She meets a young man in the hospital who makes her laugh, and she comes to terms with the poor judgment and well-meaning mistakes of her parents. But in the end, it is time that heals her, imperfectly, as time does. She simply outlives her youthful love of Bud, although nothing will ever equal it, or repair the tragedy of its pointless loss.

Her visit to Bud upon her release from the mental hospital illustrates this. Bud has married a woman who vaguely resembles Deanie (slim, dark hair, kind nature). Deanie is therefore confronted with the ghost of herself. In entering Bud's house, she crosses her own shadow. Bud has arranged for himself a facsimile of the life he could have had with Deanie. But Deanie, who is going to marry her fellow ex-patient, will not be able to arrange even this vague approximation of her life's former dream. When she embraces the young child Bud has had with his wife, the full extent of her loss is clear.

Sexual fulfillment was the least of it. She holds the life that should have come through her; she holds the future that should have been hers. Yet for the first time in a moment of crisis for Deanie, her response is interiorized, not visible to those around her; we only know of it because we know what she's been through and can see *into* her expression, not just the outside of it. In this moment, a viewer goes from *witnessing* Deanie's agony—her weeping, her breakdowns, her long struggle for recovery—to *feeling* it as if it were his or her own. The viewer becomes an active emotional participant in the scene. Kazan has made Deanie's pain into our own. Whether inwardly or outwardly, the viewer weeps.

But Deanie doesn't. She has gained enough distance from the situation to keep herself from being destroyed by it all over again. She will "take strength from what remains," according to the poem that gives the movie its title.

It has been said that, in a woman's film, womanhood is the "job" of the female hero. In *Splendor in the Grass*, Deanie's job—and it's revolutionary—is to be herself. Not in the clichéd sense of that term, but in a very deep, almost literary sense. Like Pinky, she ultimately marries herself, her own experience.

Instead of leading her outward into the world, however, as Pinky's self-allegiance did, Deanie's self-allegiance turns her (very quietly) inward. No longer will she listen to mothers or wait for boyfriends. No longer can she be shamed or swayed, or disappointed by any outward thing. Her locus of power and meaning is now entirely within herself.

She is the only figure in the film to make this transition. It is a transition of enormous subjectivity and interiority. It is also a very American transition, arriving at a place of complete (psychological, in this case) self-reliance. Deanie has a great deal of help in making that journey, but so does every hero, and the final test—going to see Bud again without falling apart—is on her own.

This is a journey that not every filmmaker, even in the more artistically liberal 1960s, would find it worthwhile to describe. But Elia Kazan did.

Pinky, Stella, and Deanie are three characters that, to my knowledge, have never been critically linked. But each of them undergoes an epic journey of self-inquiry and change, though the end result is very different. Pinky defines herself; Stella fails to; and Deanie earns a self-possession that the comparatively passive Bud will never have. (Indeed, *Splendor in the Grass* could *also* be titled *Witness the Horror Which Will Befall You If Your Boyfriend's Not Man Enough to Stand Up to His Father*.)

Part of the problem is that each of the three characters, and thus part of Elia Kazan's intentions as a director, has been hidden under various shadows. Pinky has generally not been seen as a woman but as an inept and dishonest presentation of an African American. Stella has been overshadowed by Stanley and Blanche, treated as little more than the device by which they are brought together. (To which one can only say — yes, exactly.) Marlon Brando casts a long shadow too — as does Warren Beatty in his spectacular debut in *Splendor in the Grass*. The character of Deanie, played by the more experienced and subtle Natalie Wood, has been taken for granted.

But to go ahead and state the obvious, each of these characters is more than that. They represent a heavy investment of time, effort, and understanding from Elia Kazan. He saw them as more than just "the girl." He saw their pain as more than a passive dilemma from which a male character ought to rescue them. He let them wrestle and struggle and triumph and fail. He made them matter. Their stories are there, waiting to be rescued from the "fog of neglect and longing" into which our understandable fascination with Kazan's fiery men have subjected them.

NOTES

1. Elia Kazan, *Elia Kazan: A Life* (New York: Knopf, 1988), 402.
2. Ibid., 603.
3. Ibid., 618–19.
4. Ibid., 375.
5. Ibid., 651.
6. Ibid., 369.
7. Ibid., 659.
8. Ibid.
9. Ibid., 375.
10. Ibid.
11. Ibid.
12. Ibid., 329, from a letter by Tennessee Williams.
13. Ibid., 351.
14. Ibid.

To watch Kazan's staging is a pleasure. He emanated vibrations you couldn't help catching. He knew how to use a location, including an accident. When Eva Marie Saint accidentally dropped her glove and Brando picked it up, this was the take we used. When a passing tugboat's whistle drowned out the dialogue (Brando's expression of guilt), Kazan let the expression of horror on Eva's face speak for itself. Few filmmakers have the ability to let the accident replace the preconception. All through *Waterfront*, *Baby Doll*, and *Splendor in the Grass*, I never saw a conventional or uninspired staging.

BORIS KAUFMAN

Documentary and Democracy in
Boomerang! and *Panic In the Streets*

*I*f one is searching for some term to describe the insistent yet curiously inchoate body of work produced by Elia Kazan in the 1940s (primarily under the aegis of Darryl Zanuck and Twentieth Century-Fox), "realist" is as good a tag as any. Undertaking his first five efforts as a film director during the last phase of true studio filmmaking, Kazan referred often to his desire in this period to go beyond the back lot. In his book-length interview with Michel Ciment, Kazan complains of the soundstage airlessness of his acclaimed debut *A Tree Grows in Brooklyn* (1945) — "the rooms were too clean, too nice, too much the work of the property man" — which became a "catastrophe" on his sophomore effort at MGM, the stock-footage epic *The Sea of Grass* (1947) with Spencer Tracy and Katharine Hepburn. "I could still make that story," said Kazan to Ciment, "but to do it right I would have to do it like Flaherty, to go out and spend a year with unknown actors [whose] faces are like leather, whereas Tracy's face by that time in his life looked like the inside of a melon."[1]

In these discussions, "reality" becomes an assumed, presumably self-explanatory virtue for both Ciment and Kazan. From his "first contact with reality on the screen"[2] in the location-shot semidocumentary procedural *Boomerang!* (1947) to his "personality really appear[ing] for the first time"[3] in the flavorful, New Orleans–set thriller *Panic in the Streets* (1950) — after the intervening retreat to the studio for the anti-Semitism exposé/Zanuck show-pony *Gentleman's Agreement* (1947) and its anti-racist companion piece *Pinky* (1949) — "reality" functions as shorthand for, and a gauge of, Kazan's auteurist development. Indeed, *Panic in the Streets*, with its memorably atmospheric evocation of tenements and docklands, has been duly singled out as the obvious precursor to *On the Waterfront* (1954), as per Thomas Pauly: "Kazan was left with the lingering impression that [*Panic in the Streets*] comprehended material from which another even better movie might be made . . . a more violent, more emotionally complex struggle could be created from conditions on the waterfront, the brutality of its way of life, the fearful, suspicious reserve of its residents."[4]

In all these readings the familiar auteurist teleology gets full play, a hindsight-derived narrative of a coherent, unique artistic personality emerging from previously impersonal or compromised material, and further, a transference of "reality" from the objective to the subjective. The story of Kazan's emergence as an artist has always been bound up with his increasingly intense expression — most prominently via Brando — of the psychic and emotional depth of the individual. "Direction finally consists of turning Psychology into Behavior," he had first written in his notebook for the stage production of *The Rose Tattoo* in 1947,[5] and this focus on interior realism, a turning away from the "objective" demands of the semidocumentary form, has consistently been associated with Kazan's cinematic maturation. As Brian Neve recounts, "Kazan felt that the cycle of Fox semidocumentary films, including his own *Boomerang!*, had become a 'formula,' of 'cold action against brick backgrounds.' Instead he wanted to dig deeper into reality and to handle the people with a 'WARMER FEELING'" — setting out once again the conflation of reality/emotionality/artistry that characterizes readings of Kazan's career, and thus the continued classification of *Boomerang!* and *Panic in the Streets* as formative preludes to the emerging auteur.[6]

It would of course be disingenuous to claim that Kazan's filmmaking skill does not develop considerably by the time of *Panic in the Streets*, or that his increasing freedom (both artistic and financial) after the success of *A Streetcar Named Desire* (1951) did not allow him to choose and develop projects in which he was particularly interested. Yet evolution aside, what is less remarked on is how much Kazan retained from this earlier period, both ideologically and stylistically. If *Boomerang!* and *Panic in the Streets*, as per the received narrative, did indeed offer openings onto reality within which Kazan's personality as an artist could express itself, those openings were part of a larger generic, stylistic, and ideological context. In the brief period lasting roughly from 1945 to 1948, the semidocumentary format became a prominent point of reference not only for a modular change in studio filmmaking, but for progressive hopes about the new, civic-educational role that Hollywood films could perform in postwar American society. Kazan, who by this time had migrated to the left-liberal center of the political spectrum and away from the collective ideals that had helped fuel his artistic and political formation with the Group Theatre, fit snugly into this model of institutional instruction.

As much as any self-directed evolution, the emergence of Kazan as auteur was facilitated by the disintegration of this earlier project and the progressive hopes invested in it, along with the rapid fragmentation of the intrinsically unstable semidocumentary format. However, that format's inclination toward instruction, and the concomitant belief that the ever more "fearful" and "suspicious" residents of postwar America required that instruction, did not entirely disappear, and Kazan's work of the early fifties — particularly *Viva Zapata!* (1952) and *On the Waterfront* — continues to bear its traces. Kazan's stylistic and artistic evolution comprised as well a strategic transformation of the instructional imperatives that had been integral to his cinematic apprenticeship, articulated now not in the declamatory fashion of the 1940s but absorbed more invisibly into the films' dramatic structure and their aura of heightened realism. The first stirrings of this transformation are evident in the passage from *Boomerang!* to *Panic in the Streets*, and an examination of these two earlier works may give evidence of those values that Kazan, well into his true heyday in the 1950s, continued to take for granted.

Though there were certainly precursors to the postwar semidocumentary cycle in such eve-of-war items as Anatole Litvak's *Confessions of a Nazi Spy* (1939), the format proper was inaugurated by the surprise success of Henry Hathaway's *The House on 92nd Street* (1945), detailing the (supposedly) true-life account of the FBI's infiltration and destruction of a Nazi spy ring attempting to smuggle atomic secrets out of the United States. As laid down by *The March of Time* newsreel producer Louis de Rochemont and an initially hesitant Darryl Zanuck, who "was clearly concerned that this innovatory form of film might place factual accuracy above drama,"[7] the emergent format would be characterized by the use of real-life stories (often drawn, as narration would remind the viewer, "from the files of government agencies"), typically framed as investigative narratives; location shooting, often with the employment of local people as extras or in small parts; a flat, reportorial style of narration and presentation that emphasized the drama of procedure rather than more flamboyant varieties of suspense; and a subordination of the individual particularities of protagonists to their institutional functions — often helped via the casting of dutiful journeymen such as Lloyd Nolan in *The House on 92nd Street*, though such stars as James Cagney and Jimmy Stewart, in Hathaway's semidocumentary follow-ups *13 Rue Madeleine* (1947) and *Call Northside 777* (1948), respectively, would also occasionally be recruited.

Elia Kazan and cinematographer Joe MacDonald shooting on
location in a petite New Orleans bar for *Panic in the Streets*. Kazan
employed actual locations and local people to provide the film with
a gritty, real-world atmosphere. Photo courtesy of the Wesleyan
Cinema Archives.

The enthusiastic public response to certain of these semidocumentary
thrillers was matched by far grander hopes from a more rarefied audience.
As Will Straw asserts in his excellent essay "Documentary Realism and the
Postwar Left," "It was an article of faith among progressive postwar think-
ers that the wartime collaboration between Hollywood and the institutions of wartime public education had produced a model of civic-minded
filmmaking appropriate to postwar life."[8] The initially warm reception of
the semidocumentary indicates the persistent hold the doctrine of realism
had over the Left, the broad spectrum of progressive opinion the format
satisfied, and the range of antecedents and projects to which it could be at-
tached. For the Communist or fellow-traveling Left, the semidocumentary's
provenance could be traced back to the Popular Front–era example of Pare
Lorentz and Frontier Films (on whose 1937 documentary *The People of the*

Cumberland Kazan had acted as assistant director). For liberal progressive writers and filmmakers, the format's deglamorized protagonists represented a healthy continuation of the collective heroes of the wartime combat films; and although Straw notes that "The emotionally flat heroes or male couples of institutional procedurals [are] weak inheritors of the battle film's dryly determined collectives," they still give evidence of "the mid-1940s suspicion of sentimental individualism."[9]

At the most ambitious end of the progressive spectrum, audience fascination with the meticulous, process-oriented narratives of the semidocumentaries, coupled with the format's institutional basis, singled it out as a potentially valuable vehicle of civic instruction: "A rationalist project for postwar cinema imagined fiction films engaged in an ongoing transfer of knowledge between the most innovative of midcentury intellectual disciplines (like psychiatry or sociology) and the moviegoing public."[10] Whatever form such hopes took, in this period the new strain of documentary realism became strongly linked to progressive, democratic values. As opposed to the "emotionalism" and sensation of thrillers such as *The Big Sleep* (1946),[11] the semidocumentary's mode of rational, institutionally sanctioned procedural investigation read as a veritable demonstration — to cite Kazan's thematic epigram for *Panic in the Streets* in his production notes — of "Democracy at Work"[12] — "democracy" in this formulation traveling under the guise of enlightened paternalism.

Along with *The House on 92nd Street, Call Northside 777*, and Jules Dassin's *The Naked City* (1948), Kazan's *Boomerang!* was one of the most celebrated and widely discussed specimens of the semidocumentary. Adapted by Richard Murphy from "The Perfect Case," a *Reader's Digest* story by Fulton Oursler, *Boomerang!* offers a pseudonymous account of how Homer Cummings — designated Henry Harvey in the film, and essayed by a dependably stolid Dana Andrews — a former Connecticut state's attorney and later attorney general under FDR, unraveled the seemingly watertight murder charge against a wrongly accused suspect in the inexplicable slaying of a beloved local clergyman. Opening with the murder and flashing back to establish the slain pastor's saintly credentials, the film tracks the increasingly frustrating manhunt for the killer, whose only identifying traits are that he wore a dark coat and light hat on the night of the murder. As political pressure mounts — courtesy of members of the city's precarious reform government and their electoral rival, a reptilian local newspaper editor — and public paranoia and indignation (fanned by the editor's yellow journalistic tactics) builds to a fever pitch, the police expand their net to bring in any-body even faintly resembling their vague description. This seems to hit pay dirt when the police finally pull in one John Waldron (Arthur Kennedy), an embittered, unemployed veteran with a dark coat, a light hat, and a .32 revolver that forensic tests establish as the murder weapon.

When he has been coerced into confession after forty-eight sleepless hours and positively identified by all eyewitnesses as the murderer, Wal-dron's fate appears sealed until his duly appointed prosecutor, Harvey, troubled by as yet undisclosed discrepancies in the case, announces that he intends to prove Waldron's innocence. Defying his political allies — including a threat of blackmail from one, the crooked real estate speculator Paul Harris (Ed Begley) — as well as outraged public opinion (which at one point manifests itself as a would-be lynch mob), Harvey systematically dis-mantles the police interrogation report, eyewitness testimony, and forensic evidence to win Waldron's freedom. And while this triumphal narrative of justice vindicated cannot, following its real-world model, conclude with the apprehension of the real killer, a noticeably sweaty fellow in the courtroom audience — previously seen in flashback confessing some unspecified, and apparently unmentionable, compulsion to the pastor — turns up dead in a car wreck shortly afterward. (Democracy, like other intangibles, apparently works in mysterious ways.)

What self-consciously elevates *Boomerang!* above the status of rote thriller or courtroom drama and into a treatise on democracy-at-work is its proudly proclaimed grounding in reality. Shot in Stamford, Connecticut, purportedly on many of the locations where the actual case transpired — a disingenuous claim, as the incident actually occurred in Bridgeport, which denied permission to shoot in its streets[13] — and featuring residents as extras and select nonprofessionals (including a local policeman and Kazan's uncle Joe Kazan) in small roles, *Boomerang!* plainly aims to capture more of its surroundings than the closed-off world of a "pure" procedural like *The House on 92nd Street*. As Straw notes, the enthusiasm for the film evinced by such commentators as Siegfried Kracauer and Parker Tyler turned on its move-ment beyond the somewhat sterile parameters of the semidocumentary's institutional starting point and out into the "social textures" (in Kracauer's wording) from which the story emerges. "As narratives got under way and characters followed their investigative paths into Kracauer's 'social textures,' the richness and diversity of those textures were always at odds with the solemn flatness of the institutional point of departure," writes Straw.[14]

Indeed, not only is *Boomerang!* "perhaps the least institutionally centered of films within the semidocumentary cycle,"[15] but it even appears to make something of an attack on some of the very institutions the format had been designed to celebrate. While the corruption of the city's reform government is localized in the person of Harris, the rank opportunism of the other city council members is not scanted by Kazan, particularly in a scene where Harris and the mayor loom over the skeptical Harvey at his desk, delightedly leering over the open-and-shut case against Waldron and the political dividends it will pay, and promising Harvey the state governorship if he successfully prosecutes the case. Though Lee J. Cobb's harried police chief is rendered sympathetically, the increasingly arbitrary exercise of police power in the hunt for the killer is certainly not looked on favorably — not least because, as against the rationalist exercise of professional prowess evinced by the institutional actors in other semidocumentaries, this investigation is hysterical, desperate, and thus profoundly irrational. Most interestingly, the film's embodiment of that specialized knowledge that certain sectors of progressive opinion hoped to impart to the public — a state-appointed psychiatrist (Dudley Sadler) working with the police — is depicted as a somewhat clueless accessory to the railroading of Waldron during his interrogation, and is later dressed down on the stand by Harvey.

In exemplifying the semidocumentary format, *Boomerang!* could thus simultaneously be seen as turning some of its fundamental premises on their heads, and carrying documentary realism into that sphere of social criticism that the Left continued to view as its highest calling. Yet while certain reflexes of Kazan's leftist past might be read into such elements, there is no sustained *systemic* critique of the forces that allow Waldron to be convicted, which is the crucial endpoint of the leftist documentary ideal. Apart from the familiar target of the venal editor (who plots strategy at his country club), the institutions that have colluded in this miscarriage of justice are eventually let off the hook. The police force and city government (Begley's desperate swindler aside) are finally shown, sympathetically, as being misled rather than ill-intentioned, and properly repentant: after Waldron is cleared, the same mayor whose fortunes were riding on Waldron's conviction stands supportively alongside Harvey, the very man who has cost him his crucial political victory.

If these institutional representatives are eventually returned to the side of the angels, tellingly, Harvey's greatest condescension during his courtroom performance is directed toward the eyewitnesses to the murder, each of whom is crucially mistaken in some detail of his or her original testimony. While these successive revelations could have been portrayed as the chilling ease with which fleeting impressions can be built into damning accusations, the authoritative air with which Harvey quashes each witness's statements cannot help but carry an overtone that these factual errors are personal failings on the part of these ordinary citizens — most obviously in the case of Waldron's vengeful ex-girlfriend, whose insistence that she saw Waldron just before the murder quite clearly tips the scale between mistaken impression and active malice.

In demonstrating the various follies of the eyewitnesses' testimony, Harvey is playing not only a legal but also a moral-educational role. Not only correcting error, Harvey gives a lesson in civic virtue via the rationalist pursuit of verifiable truth, as he minutely explains how he and his dedicated (and previously unseen) functionaries conducted a series of "experiments" (Harvey uses the word himself) to demonstrate how the various facets of eyewitness testimony could not possibly have been fully accurate.

Truth/reality and moral instruction are thus made coterminous — and in doing so, they reassert the inherently institutional basis of this "least institutionally centered" of semidocumentaries. The opening narration's purposeful omission of the name of the city in which these events took place, and its lyrical evocation of it as a veritable Anytown, USA, serves two purposes: to make the film's social texture familiar and comforting to the audience, the better to emphasize the drama of the radically unsettling events that beset it; and further, to make Harvey's ultimate victory, implicitly, the victory of the system and nation he represents. (After all, as the closing narration reminds us, the real-life Harvey did not receive the tainted reward of the governorship but was appointed attorney general of the United States, the highest recognition of the institutionalized democratic values he stands for.)

"Social texture" is thus ultimately contained within the universalizing impulses of institutional prerogative. While the location shooting constitutes a vital part of the film's contract with its viewers — the promise of bringing them closer to reality — the locations are fundamentally neutral until activated by the orchestrated spectacle of procedure that occurs within them. Rather than burrowing deeper inside those textures, the film's investigation only allows them to be catalogued. When a montage sequence shows dozens of men being rounded up and paraded through lineups, the film's tone fluctuates ambiguously between a certain reserved indigna-

Police chief Robinson (Lee J. Cobb, *front right*) and state's attorney Henry Harvey (Dana Andrews, *rear right*) present a lineup of possible murder suspects in a publicity still for *Boomerang!* Witnesses will falsely accuse John Waldron (Arthur Kennedy, suspect number 5). Photo courtesy of the Wesleyan Cinema Archives.

tion at the harassment of the innocent and a detached curiosity at these societal specimens that have been assembled under the institutional gaze. ("Angry men, indignant men, beaten men, and dazed men; men with long criminal records, and simple men snatched from peaceful pursuits, all to be shoved into the glare of the line-up platform," intones the narrator over this sequence, helpfully breaking down and classifying the human material before the audience.) Institutional process is the necessary completion of *Boomerang!*'s realist project, not only making reality legible to the viewer but becoming commensurate with it.

Just as this ability of the semidocumentary to harness realism to an institutionalized discourse — or rather a discourse of institutions — contributed to its vogue among progressive opinion in the early postwar period, that same ability soon caused it to fall from left-wing grace. Social-problem doyen Zanuck's application of the semidocumentary mode to William Wellman's *The Iron Curtain* (1948), a staunchly anticommunist account of the recent defection of Igor Gouzenko (played by *Boomerang!*'s Dana Andrews, no less), caused an uproar from many of the same voices that had formerly sung the format's praises. Yet while the susceptibility of the semidocumentary to use as a propagandistic affirmation of the Cold War state apparatus — thus betraying the paternalistic progressive faith in the format as a vehicle of enlightened civic instruction — seems a logical result of its institutional basis, the format was by no means monolithic enough to make this evolution inevitable.

Indeed, the semidocumentary mode had begun to fragment almost as soon as it had become established, disassembling itself into an assortment of appropriable, mutable techniques applicable to any number of ends — not only ideological, as in the rather isolated case of *The Iron Curtain*, but chiefly stylistic. "In many films in the late forties and early fifties," notes Foster Hirsch, citing Hathaway's *Kiss of Death* (1947), Dassin's *The Naked City*, Anthony Mann's *Side Street* (1950) and Kazan's *Panic in the Streets*, among others, "expressionist motifs invaded location shooting, transforming the real city into moody echoes of the claustrophobic studio-created urban landscapes."[16] Moreover, this transference or adaptation of studio effects to real locations was complemented by an increasing infusion of that "emotionalism" that the semidocumentary's studied dryness had previously guarded against. Whereas a film like *Boomerang!* had sought to contain hysteria and abnormality (such as the closet pervert "real" killer) within its stance of levelheaded rational inquiry, the sensational and the grotesque quickly staked their place within the format, whether through performance — as in Richard Widmark's immortal, giggling psycho turn as *Kiss of Death*'s Tommy Udo — or such memorable sequences, courtesy of Mann and cinematographer John Alton, as the steam-room murder in *T-Men* (1947) or the gruesome death-by-harvester in *Border Incident* (1949).

From being an end in itself, documentary realism was being steadily subverted into a vehicle for more expressive or ostentatious stylistic endeavors, a development not lost on an ambitious director like Kazan. *Panic in the Streets*, Kazan's second collaboration with *Boomerang!* scribe Murphy, not only offers a far less overtly didactic representation of reality than its predecessor, but supplants the earlier film's voice-of-God, you-are-there assurances with an evocatively seedy, lived-in rendering of the New Orleans underbelly. Tracing the race-against-time quest of public health official Dr. Clinton Reed (Richard Widmark) as he and his initially unwilling police counterpart Captain Tom Warren (Paul Douglas) attempt to track down three killers who have been unknowingly infected with bubonic plague by their victim, the film evinces both a surprisingly brisk narrative drive and a remarkably fluid camera sense — as Kazan stated to Ciment, *Panic in the Streets* taught him for the first time that "the environment was not just something you played against, it was something you played inside of."[17] Kazan's atmospheric use of shadowy train yards, the crisscrossing diagonals of tenement fire escapes, and the memorable, multileveled final pursuit through a coffee warehouse and underneath the docks may be his most obvious achievements, but he also brings a naturalness and flow to domestic scenes between Reed and his affectionately tart-tongued wife (Barbara Bel Geddes) and an expressionistic grotesquerie to the villainous side of the cast, getting much useful mileage out of a sweaty, hysterical Zero Mostel and the hulking yet strangely feline menace of Jack Palance.

Furthermore, this loosening of the strict semidocumentary mode allows for a far greater exploration of the setting's uniquely rich "social textures." Lacking *Boomerang!*'s omnipresent voice-over narration, which aligned itself with the surveilling, classifying, and controlling gaze of the film's institutional actors, *Panic in the Streets* places those actors in far greater proximity to, and interaction with, a wide array of social groups, each with their own distinctive habits and habitus: a seaman's hiring hall where the tight-lipped sailors inform Reed (who offers a cash reward for information about the dead man) that none of them is likely to talk to any authority figure out in the open; the captain of the ship that smuggled the dead man into the United States, who resents the intrusion of government representatives on his sovereign vessel; a Greek restaurant owner and his unknowingly infected wife whose decision to keep mum reflects the tendency of members of ethnic communities to stay "out of trouble" — that is, out of any kind of contact with the hegemonic mainstream of American society.

However, while *Panic in the Streets* thus offers a far richer social portrait than *Boomerang!* its dramatic engine is similarly predicated on the assorted fallacies of its societal specimens and the need for professionalized expertise to set them aright. Reed's search is complicated not only by the difficulty inherent in locating the associates of an undocumented, recently arrived immigrant in a teeming city, but in the obstinacy and obstreperousness of all those he encounters. As Pauly notes, "Dr. Reed's quest [becomes] an unnerving lesson in the public's opposition to what it does not want to hear and its ingrained suspicion of governmental agents. . . . Widmark's effectiveness derives largely from the circumstances of these scenes and their

In a publicity still for *Panic in the Streets*, public health official Dr. Clinton Reed (Richard Widmark) questions New Orleans longshoremen about suspicious passengers disembarking in the city. Kazan surrounded Widmark with real dockworkers and shot in the local union hall. Photo courtesy of the Wesleyan Cinema Archives.

vivid illustration of a lonely individual battling an immovable community that refuses to act on its own behalf."[18] While Pauly correctly identifies the drama's chief source of conflict, what his reading crucially omits is that the community has precious little opportunity to act on its own behalf. Reed, fearing that a general alert about the plague threat will spark a mass exodus from the city and an exponential spread of the virus, insists on keeping the reason for the citywide manhunt from the public—which later leads the now-compliant Warren to incarcerate a snooping reporter who upbraids Reed for this enforced secrecy and loudly proclaims the public's right to know.

Reed's frustration in the face of this "immovable community" is thus at least partially a result of his own actions, springing from his distrust of ordinary citizens and a disbelief in their ability to act for their own welfare. That this does not scan as more ideologically damning during the course of the film is due to Kazan's adeptness at weaving it into character and situation. Reed and Warren's characterizations, in Kazan's words, as "ordinary guys in ordinary spots, coping with outside threats,"[19] may make them akin to the purely functional protagonists of the semidocumentary, but they are far more prickly and individuated than the institutional standard-bearers who preceded them. Not simply the face of professionalized, paternalistic expertise, Reed's self-righteousness is linked to his own bruised self-esteem as an overworked, underpaid government functionary, unable to give his wife and son the life he wants for them and, most woundingly, unable to afford the second child he yearns for. Furthermore, the fact that Reed is proven emphatically right in keeping the plague a secret also robs him of public recognition and acclaim for his ultimate victory, such as that accorded Harvey at the conclusion of *Boomerang!* Unlike the object lesson in democracy afforded by *Boomerang!*'s courtroom setting, "democracy" in *Panic in the Streets* is something anonymous, ingrained, and those who exemplify it are ignorant of their own virtue. As Kazan quoted his friend and first producer at Fox, Bud Lighton, in notes he took during the shooting of *A Tree Grows in Brooklyn*: "At the end [of a film], a person should say to the hero: 'Gee! You did a great job' and the hero shouldn't know what the hell the other man is talking about."[20]

If Lighton's views were considerably shaped by his profoundly anticommunist, antiliberal "frontiersman" ethos — against which, as Kazan recounts tellingly in his autobiography, "my left-wing positions seemed provincial, my convictions shallow"[21] — his maxim applies with equal aptness to the functionalist cogs of the semidocumentary. While Widmark's harried doctor can be read as creating a bridge between the objective, rationalist world of the semidocumentary's institutionally sanctioned professionals and the subjective, emotional worlds Kazan would be drawn to in his fifties work, that quality of unawareness would become the key transformational agent in the ideological dimension of Kazan's future work. While *Panic in the Streets*, despite its more vivid characterizations and infusion of that much-sought-after "warmer feeling," still belongs to the declarative world of the semidocumentary and its insistent demonstration of how its principles are put into practice — at one point having Reed angrily enunciate the film's one-world thesis when defying the city councilors' claim to represent the best interests of the community ("we're all in a community, the same one!") — Kazan's two overtly political collaborations with Brando in the 1950s, *Viva Zapata!* and *On the Waterfront*, do not represent an abandonment of this didactic, instructional imperative, but a reversal in its mode of address.

Whereas *Boomerang!* and *Panic in the Streets* convey their messages via protagonists who speak with the voice of instructional authority, lecturing the ordinary citizens who linger on the edges of the frame (and thus by extension the film audience), Brando's Emiliano Zapata and Terry Malloy conversely assume the position of students in this tutelary dynamic, occupying the center of the films rather than being relegated to the wings. Zapata's and Terry's emotional awakenings are innately tied to their gradual ideological education — Zapata in the corruption of power and the amorality of Bolshevik-style professional revolution, Terry in the moral imperative of informing — educations now received from Kazan's limning of the characters' geographical and dramatic environments rather than from the semidocumentary's podium lectures, and confirmed by their grim fates — fates that are duly dictated by the films' emphatic tone of social and political realism. Reality itself, that sense of reality that Kazan so studiedly and skillfully cultivated, here supplants the personified mouthpieces of the earlier films, a disembodied, enveloping, and hence even more persuasive pedagogue.

Kazan's artistic maturation in the 1950s can thus be read not simply as a progressive escape from the formulaic material he shouldered during his formative cinematic years but as a gradually changing emphasis in the stylistic and ideological reflexes bequeathed to him by the increasingly fissiparous semidocumentary format. Just as the semidocumentary promised audiences a greater contact with reality on film, so the acting revolution Brando and Kazan helped usher into Hollywood cinema from the theatrical stage was founded on the imperative of a deeper penetration into the reality of the human personality. What allowed Kazan to assume the purpled auteurist mantle was his skillful combination of these two realist projects, as well as the lingering, and increasingly vague, aura of political import invested in the earlier of the two. Not simply a movement toward a greater degree of truth, Kazan's increasing contact with reality bore with it the residual codes and associations invested in the realist project during the years of his cinematic apprenticeship. How this affected Kazan's apprehension of realism's accompanying hypothetical — democracy — must for (thankful) reasons of space be left to others to gauge.

NOTES
With thanks to Bart Testa
1. Michel Ciment, *Kazan on Kazan* (London: Secker and Warburg, 1973), 50–53.
2. Ibid., 55.

3. Ibid., 62.

4. Thomas H. Pauly, *An American Odyssey: Elia Kazan and American Culture* (Philadelphia: Temple University Press, 1983), 129.

5. Brian Neve, *Elia Kazan: The Cinema of an American Outsider* (London: I.B. Tauris, 2009), 34.

6. Ibid., 28.

7. Brian Neve, *Film and Politics in America: A Social Tradition* (New York: Routledge, 1992), 105.

8. Will Straw, "Documentary Realism and the Postwar Left," in *"Un-American" Hollywood: Politics and Film in the Blacklist Era*, ed. Frank Krutnik et al. (New Brunswick: Rutgers University Press, 2007), 138.

9. Ibid., 139–40.

10. Ibid., 139.

11. Ibid.

12. Neve, *Kazan*, 28.

13. Richard Schickel, *Elia Kazan: A Biography* (New York: HarperCollins, 2005), 142.

14. Straw, "Documentary Realism," 141.

15. Ibid., 141.

16. Foster Hirsch, *Film Noir: The Dark Side of the Screen* (New York: Da Capo Press, 1981), 67.

17. Ciment, *Kazan on Kazan*, 64–65.

18. Pauly, *American Odyssey*, 129.

19. Ciment, *Kazan on Kazan*, 64.

20. Ibid., 50.

21. Elia Kazan, *Elia Kazan: A Life* (New York: Knopf, 1988), 251.

PATRICK KEATING

Elia Kazan and the Semidocumentary
Composing Urban Space

*D*uring the production of his 1950 film *Panic in the Streets*, Elia Kazan spent several weeks agonizing about the title. He considered a variety of options, only to reject them because they sounded like they could be titles for all the "pseudo-documentaries" being produced by "cheap companies."[1] In one note to Twentieth Century-Fox producer Darryl F. Zanuck, Kazan wrote, "If there is anything staler at the moment than just another documentary I don't know what it is."[2] The production notes are revealing, not just because they name some of the rejected options (*Port of Entry, Outbreak, Ring Waterfront Three*) but also because they show us how anxious Kazan was to escape the limits of a genre that had become one of Fox's specialties: the semidocumentary. In 1947, Kazan had directed one of the most celebrated examples of the genre, *Boomerang!* Even in that film, Kazan had begun to push the boundaries of the format, taking advantage of the genre's preference for real-world locations to compose remarkably original images of urban space. In *Panic in the Streets* (1950), Kazan would go even farther, abandoning the genre's tired clichés while taking full advantage of the semidocumentary's primary strength: the ability to reproduce the modern city in dynamic visual terms. Together, these films represent a major advance, reconceiving the limits and possibilities of the semidocumentary. Under Kazan's direction, what had started as a curious mixture of documentary and Hollywood conventions had become a new vocabulary for commenting on the complexity of urban space.

The typical semidocumentary is a fiction film loosely based on a true story and filmed on location — sometimes the very location where the original events took place. The plot often takes the form of a procedural, showing us how an institutional group, such as the police, tackles a particular problem. Some of the semidocumentary films feature a stern narrator explaining the events for us, a convention drawn from the documentary proper. Since the plots often contain an element of crime, some semidocumentaries are occasionally classified as film noirs, but most semidocs lack the mood of pessimism that characterizes the noir cycle.[3] For instance, Henry Hathaway's *The House on 92nd Street* (1945), often considered the first semidocumentary, tells the story of a well-adjusted protagonist doing good work for a smoothly functioning bureaucracy, all in the service of patriotic ideals. Aside from a few shadowy images, the film lacks many of the defining noir conventions. Instead, the film's most proximate inspiration is the wartime newsreel, which is no surprise, given the fact that the film was produced by *The March of Time* veteran Louis de Rochemont.

We might expect the semidocumentary, with its focus on institutions, to make a significant departure from the classical Hollywood film, which emphasizes individuals. As David Bordwell has argued, the classical Hollywood film is unified by a particular sort of character-driven causality. The characters are "goal-oriented" — in almost every scene, characters advance the plot by pursuing specific goals.[4] Although semidocumentary films occasionally stray from these norms by offering long montages detailing the intricacies of institutional procedures, the films never fully abandon goal-orientation. *The House on 92nd Street* opens with documentary footage of anonymous German spies, but it gradually focuses our attention on the battle between the goal-oriented FBI heroes and the equally determined Nazi villains.

Frank Krutnik describes the semidocumentary as a "hybrid of fiction film and documentary conventions."[5] This hybrid quality also characterizes the visual style of the semidocumentary. On the one hand, semidocumentaries usually observed classical principles of composition, using style to call attention to the most important story points. On the other hand, the films could also offer style as spectacle, encouraging audiences to appreciate the location shooting as an attraction in its own right. Kazan's Fox colleague Henry Hathaway was particularly good at creating this balance between story and spectacle. For instance, Hathaway's *Call Northside 777* (1948) has a thoroughly classical story to tell, with Jimmy Stewart playing a reporter who grows increasingly determined to learn the truth about a wrongly decided murder case. Fittingly, Hathaway's compositions are designed to draw our attention to the goal-oriented individual driving the story. Figure 1 shows McNeal (Stewart) interviewing Tillie (Kasia Orzazewski), the hardworking mother who wants someone to help her clear her son's name.

With the aid of centering and lighting, McNeal dominates the composition, towering above everything else in the frame. At the same time,

I

Reporter Jim McNeal (Jimmy Stewart) questions a mother (Kasia Orzazewski) whose son has been found guilty of murder in Henry Hathaway's *Call Northside 777*. This frame enlargement depicts the use of location for both narrative and spectacular purposes that was common to the semidocumentary.

Hathaway does not ignore the rest of the space. Location shooting was one of the film's selling points, and Hathaway knows how to use realism as spectacle. The deeply perspectival image draws our eyes to the lower left corner of the frame — not to add some extra narrative significance, but to prove to us that this scene was, in fact, shot in a real hallway.

These are the conventions Kazan was working with — and, to some extent, against — when he directed *Boomerang!* and *Panic in the Streets*. *Boomerang!* with its true story exposing police interrogation procedures, filmed in a small Connecticut city, was a clear example of the semidocumentary trend. Photographed by semidoc specialist Norbert Brodine, the film was produced by de Rochemont, who produced two of Hathaway's films at Fox. Made three years later, *Panic in the Streets* is a more purely fictionalized work, but it also draws extensive resources from the trend, using carefully selected New Orleans locations to tell a story with strong procedural elements. As in *Boomerang!* Kazan worked with a cinematographer who had experience in the semidocumentary — in this case, Joe MacDonald, who photographed *Call Northside 777*.

At first glance, both Kazan films appear to adopt the familiar visual strategies of the semidocumentary style, with crisply focused images imbuing the story with the atmospheric authenticity of the real-life locations. However, a closer look will reveal that Kazan was thinking very deeply about the semidocumentary's unique challenges and opportunities. Whereas Hathaway often uses his real locations as a striking backdrop for a story playing out in the foreground of the shot, Kazan creates compositions that comment on the nature of urban space — its connectedness, complexity, and unpredictability.

To better appreciate the originality of Kazan's contribution, we can start by examining the narratives of the two films. It would be an overstatement to call *Boomerang!* and *Panic in the Streets* nonclassical films, but they do introduce significant variations on classical cinema's norms of narrative construction, variations Kazan will emphasize with his careful use of composition. Both films start with an initial causal event and examine how that cause produces ripple effects throughout the city. On the one hand, both films walk a well-worn path by becoming goal-oriented narratives, following a protagonist who is attempting to understand the initial cause and control its effects. On the other hand, both films consistently raise questions about the extent to which we can understand the events in traditional causal terms — questions that are magnified by the fact that institutional procedures can amplify or redirect the causal chain in unexpected ways.

The initial cause in *Boomerang!* is an intentional action — the murder of a priest — but the fact that the murder is committed by a mentally unstable man suggests that the action's intentionality is mixed with a sense of irrational uncontrollability. (By the end of the film, the identity of the murderer is quite clear, though the film technically leaves the mystery unresolved.) This initial cause produces rippling effects throughout the city, in part because the city in question is quite small: most of the citizens know each other. The film also examines the role of institutions in amplifying the cause's effects. Early in the film, one montage shows us the reporter Dave Woods (Sam Levene) typing a series of columns. Images of the reporter are intercut with scenes of various citizens responding to the news, often swayed by the reporter's cynical stance. A few minutes later, the film shows us another montage, cutting between a police sergeant on the radio and various attempts to round up the criminal. While this concern for institutions is typical of the semidocumentary, which often examines the role of the press and the police, *Boomerang!* is unusually skeptical of the institutions it represents. In most semidocs, institutional procedures are dull but necessary exercises that gradually bring the protagonist closer to the truth. Here, institutional procedures lead to outcomes that are marked as trivial (an increase in gossip) or absurd (rising paranoia among men who happen to wear dark coats and light hats). Institutions amplify the effects of the initial cause, but in a way that is neither beneficial nor rational. The film eventually advances a compelling critique of the police's tough interrogation tactics — a critique that stands in sharp contrast to the uncritical celebration of state power in canonical semidocs like *The House on 92nd Street*.

Most of *Boomerang!* is photographed in a straightforward classical style, using clearly lit compositions to direct the spectator's eye to the most important story point. However, within this classical context, there are a few images that suggest that Kazan was attempting to translate the film's thematic concerns into visual terms. Both of the montages mentioned above follow a certain pattern, cutting back and forth between an individual (the reporter or the policeman) and a group (people responding to the news, or the police rounding up suspects). One image (figure 2) shows several women reacting to the latest news of the murder. The composition itself is striking, with all the crisp lines and sharp angles of a Charles Sheeler painting, but the most daring thing about the shot is the fact that Kazan refuses to dissect the scene with editing. Instead of cutting back and forth between the women as they speak their lines, Kazan holds on this group composition, forcing us to shift our attention from one woman to the next — not always an easy task, since the women are spread all over the frame. In this way, Kazan emphasizes the themes of connectedness and unpredictability: connectedness because we can see at a glance how one person's actions will affect multiple other people; unpredictability because we can never be completely sure how the connections will play out. We can never quite guess who will speak next, and we can never be sure who will agree or disagree with whom. A more conventionally filmed scene would have provided us with enough redundant cues to let us predict the flow of the conversation; here, the act of shifting our eyes from one corner to the next is a physical reminder that this conversation is governed by unpredictable connections.

Elsewhere in the film, Kazan uses offscreen space to emphasize the theme of unpredictability. The opening murder scene shows a gun appearing suddenly from offscreen. Here, the use of offscreen space is hardly unusual, given the need to keep the murderer's identity a secret, but Kazan will later turn this image of abrupt intrusion into a minor motif, suggesting that suddenness and randomness are a defining feature of the film's small-

2

Neighbors discuss the latest news about a murder case in a frame enlargement from *Boomerang!* Kazan holds on the distant, wide framing to highlight the film's themes of connectedness and unpredictability.

city world. One scene shows a group of firemen discussing the reporter's stories. The scene ends as they are called to an emergency, and several other firemen slide down the poles to enter the shot. This sliding-down action is an amusing bit of business to top off a lighthearted scene, but Kazan stages the action to maximize the unforeseen quality of the event: most of the scene is played out in the midground, and it is quite astonishing when a man falls into the immediate foreground from above. A few minutes later, as the police are rounding up all the men with light hats and dark coats, we see a shot of a man running along the train tracks. Again Kazan surprises us with an abrupt entrance, as a police car rapidly pulls into the immediate foreground, cutting off the man's escape. The shot itself would not look out of place in a semidoc by Hathaway or Anthony Mann, but the fact that Kazan is repeating the intrusion motif established in the opening murder gives the image an added significance. The initial killing was a disorderly action intruding on the orderly town. Institutional procedures are supposed to contain this disorder, but here they only serve to spread it, producing the kind of spatial surprises that Kazan is underlining with his use of the sudden intrusion from offscreen space.

By the ending, *Boomerang!* has returned to a more classical stylistic vocabulary, using a fairly conventional style to show us a lone individual pursuing his goal against obstacles both institutional and personal. Produced three years later, *Panic in the Streets* is more consistently original, using narrative and stylistic techniques to take the semidocumentary in a new direction. Both Kazan and screenwriter Richard Murphy (who also wrote *Boomerang!*) were anxious to distinguish *Panic* from the increasingly predictable semidocumentary trend. Murphy prefaced his screenplay with some pointed comments on the genre:

> There's no use making one more in the line of "documentary" stories, and there's no use repeating BOOMERANG. The style that's grown up in these documentaries is cold action against brick backgrounds. It's a formula. . . . There are no big heroes in this story. And there are no big villains, except the germ of the plague. . . . It has to do with the basic philosophy of democracy: ordinary guys in ordinary spots can cope with real outsized threats to the people's lives.[6]

Murphy follows through on these goals by crafting a story with an unusually dispersed narrative structure. As in *Boomerang!* the initial cause is a murder, but here the murder itself is far less important than the fact that the victim was suffering from a form of plague at the time of his death. In other words, the initial cause is no longer an intentional action; it is a force of nature. As a member of the Public Health Service, the protagonist, Clint Reed (Richard Widmark), has a clear goal, to stop the spread of the plague, but he faces a very powerful obstacle — the connectedness of the city (and, more broadly, the city's connectedness with the rest of the world). New Orleans is much larger than the small city of *Boomerang!* so the connectedness is not the result of the fact that everyone knows each other. Rather, it is the simple result of contiguity — our lives are affected by the people next to us, whether we know them or not. The problem of urban anonymity greatly increases the unpredictability of events — Reed is trying to stop a plague, but he has barely any idea where to begin. Reed succeeds in the end, but the film continually stresses the fact that he is not an omnipotent hero. He must rely on the help of others, including people he loves, notably his wife Nancy (Barbara Bel Geddes); people he dislikes, including Captain Tom Warren (Paul Douglas); and people he does not even know, such as the Chinese workers on the boat. Even with all this help, chance plays a large role in Reed's ultimate success. He happens to find the culprits just as they are leaving their hideout; arriving a few minutes later, he would have failed.

As we have seen, Kazan was sympathetic to Murphy's desire to create something different from the standard semidoc thriller. Kazan also embraced the theme of democracy, while interpreting that theme in a very particular way: for Kazan, democracy is synonymous with conflict. One draft of the shooting script contains several notes that were handwritten by Kazan. One note reads: "This will become a cops and robbers picture unless it becomes something else!! This is something else — the Spectacle and the Technique of Democracy at Work! Its virtues . . . its faults." Kazan's goal is "to show how the conflict is fruitful and that only thru conflict do the men arrive at understanding & esteem and only thru conflict do they surpass themselves."[7] Brian Neve points out that Kazan's ideas about democracy-as-conflict reflect his turn toward liberal anticommunist thinking — specifically, the ideas found in Arthur Schlesinger Jr.'s 1949 book *The Vital Center*.[8] As an actor-oriented director, trained to build a scene around conflict, Kazan had no trouble translating these political ideas into dramatic terms. Instead of showing a powerful hero taking charge of the situation and directing the city's efforts to stop the plague, the film presents a series of power struggles and shifting alliances. Reed's Public Health Service conflicts with Warren's police force, but then the mayor forces them to work together. Later, Warren sides with Reed against a reporter, winning Reed's admiration just before the mayor decides to throw his support to the press. Kazan wants us to sympathize with Reed (even in his rather disturbing plan to silence the press), but Kazan is careful not to demonize any of the other institutions. Whenever other characters object to Reed's plans, they do so for good reasons, not because they are one-dimensional villains.[9] Peter Biskind describes Kazan's attitude toward institutions as one of "corporate liberalism," celebrating the wisdom of federal institutions while expressing skepticism about more local institutions like the police and the local press.[10] Biskind is right to point out that Kazan's sympathies lie with Reed (the representative of the federal government), but Kazan's dramatic instincts stress the balance between opposing sides, maximizing the theme of productive conflict.

While allowing him to develop this theme of democracy-as-conflict, *Panic in the Streets* also gave Kazan the opportunity to craft a distinctive vision of urban space — a space that is connected but nearly uncontrollable, with small causes triggering large effects all over the map. Here, the film joins an important tradition of films commenting on the changing nature of cities in postwar America. In a landmark work on space in film noir, Edward Dimendberg attempts to understand these shifts by proposing a useful distinction between centripetal and centrifugal space. Dimendberg writes:

> We may define centrifugal space historically as the set of consequences resulting from the tendency, already evident by the middle of the nineteenth century in the United States, toward movement from the urban center to its boundaries. . . . If centripetal space is characterized by fascination with urban density and the visible — the skyline, monuments, recognizable public spaces, and inner-city neighborhoods — its centrifugal variant can be located in a shift toward immateriality, invisibility, and speed.[11]

Films about centripetal space are films about the density of the urban downtown, a space that draws crowds of people toward a city center. Films about centrifugal space are about downtown decay, with technological developments like the automobile and social developments like "white flight" combining to produce a movement away from the center. Like many film noirs, *Panic in the Streets* expresses complex anxieties about the changing nature of urban space. At first glance, the film would appear to be about centripetal space, given its close examination of several inner-city locations. However, the film is ultimately an expression of anxiety about the transition to centrifugal space. Reed is worried that the plague will incite a "panic," forcing masses of people to evacuate the city. The plague itself is an immaterial, invisible force that threatens to escape the confines of the city, moving at a speed that no institution can stop. On a more abstract level, we might say that Kazan's vision of democracy is itself centrifugal — there is no centralized authority, just different groups struggling for control.

How does Kazan translate these spatial themes into cinematic terms? Here, it is tempting to suppose that Kazan might rely on "centrifugal" compositions, which disperse the attention across the frame, as in figure 2 from *Boomerang!* However, there are good reasons to resist this temptation. First, we should be careful about using Dimendberg's spatial terms too loosely; they are designed primarily to help us understand the cultural significance of urban spaces represented on film; they are ultimately not terms about cinematic composition. Second, we must remember that Kazan is, after all, a Hollywood filmmaker charged foremost with the task of telling a story. A thoroughly decentered composition would lack the narrative clarity that any classical film would require. Instead of offering a series of chaotic frames, Kazan choreographs some remarkably complicated shots, commenting on urban space by emphasizing the themes of connectedness, anonymity, and unpredictability.

The morgue scene is particularly complex. Kazan stages the scene in two long takes, and he uses camera movement to explore the real-world location (figures 3–5).[12] First, we see two men chatting in the foreground, as the body is wheeled in on a gurney in the background. Because the opening scene has already hinted to the audience that the body might be more dangerous than it appears, the fact that the two men are having an upbeat conversation while facing away from the body emphasizes the obliviousness of their attitude. The camera dollies back and pans to the left as one of the men, Jerry, walks forward and greets Kleber (George Ehmig), the technician who will examine the body. Here, Kazan introduces a strategy he will employ throughout the scene — a strategy of concealment and revelation. The police have wheeled the body into another hallway, so we focus our attention on the conversation in the foreground. However, the conversation takes place in front of a doorway, which opens up a space for us to see the body being wheeled by in the background. Kazan's decision to stage the scene in this manner places extra emphasis on the doorway as a means of connecting the two spaces — emphasizing the theme of contiguity and producing a small spatial surprise.

The next moment proves even more surprising: Jerry walks into another room and stands against a dark background, but then the dark background lights up and we realize that he is standing next to a glass window revealing an examination room. As in the beginning of the scene, Jerry is shown constantly moving away from the body — only to have the body reappear in the background of the shot. A less subtle filmmaker might have given us low-angle shots with the body looming ominously in the foreground, but Kazan's approach only hints at the importance of the body, while placing special emphasis on the contiguity of the spaces. Ultimately, this particular body will be cremated to limit further contamination, but that alone will not stop the plague, since it will have already affected all the other bodies it has come into contact with. The problem is not the threat of this particular body — the problem is a spatial problem, since this one cause can produce an effect in so many contiguous spaces. Instead of giving us ominous shots of the body, Kazan gives us more subtle — and more relevant — shots of these connected areas.

3

4

A dead body infected with the bubonic plague enters a morgue
unbeknownst to its inhabitants in these frame enlargements
(figures 3–5) from *Panic in the Streets*. In the two long takes that
form the scene, Kazan emphasizes the potentially dangerous effects
of urban connectedness by staging the action in contiguous spaces.

5

As if to underscore the point that these two spaces are connected, regardless of the glass barrier between them, Kazan then cuts inside the examination room. As Kleber examines the body and comes to understand its significance, Jerry tries to engage him in a lighthearted conversation. At one point, an anonymous woman appears in the background and identifies another body. On one level, the woman in the background is just a redundant story cue, reminding us that this is, in fact, a morgue. On another level, the staging continues to develop the film's themes. As we gradually realize the true danger of the body just offscreen in the foreground, we come to understand that it could end up infecting anyone, including this woman in the background. This is why Kazan places so much emphasis on contiguity — contiguity has become causality.

At the end of the scene, Kleber asks everyone to leave the room, and he shuts the door. When he steps to the right, the camera pans to follow him, revealing the two men from the beginning of the scene standing behind the glass window. This final image contrasts with the opening of the scene. The men who had been in the foreground are now in the background, just as their lighthearted tone has been replaced by Kleber's stern sense of determination. The image also hints at the challenges ahead: Kleber may have closed the door, but the presence of the glass window suggests that the outside world is already connected to this locked-in space, no matter how many doors he closes.

What this description cannot convey is the scene's unpredictable quality.

We know that the body is important, but we cannot keep our eyes locked on the body because it keeps getting wheeled offscreen, onscreen, then off-screen again. In the second shot, we can barely see the body at all, as it rests below the frame line. The body cannot be the center of our attention, so we must look to the other characters—but we have not met any of them before, and we cannot be sure whom to look at. The first shot misleads us into thinking that Jerry will be the focus. The second shot places more emphasis on Kleber, the most important character in the scene, but even here Kazan's staging encourages us to split our attention between Kleber and the background characters. Here, the story is introducing the theme of centrifugal space, introducing a cause that threatens to spread outward. But Kazan does not just use a disorganized, "centrifugal" composition to evoke this theme. Instead, he gives us a pair of precisely choreographed shots that force us to skip from one area of the frame to another, vigilantly looking for causally significant details, without slipping into confusion.

A comparison with *Call Northside 777* is instructive. In contrast to Hathaway, Kazan is less interested in locking our eyes on a single goal-oriented individual, and he is more fully committed to the task of narrativizing the entire space. We pay attention to every person in the frame, because we know that each person might be affected by the disease. The point here is not to criticize Hathaway—his compositions are well suited for the goal-driven story he is trying to tell. In *Panic in the Streets*, the story is more unusual, with a goal-oriented protagonist who can barely keep up with a causal chain that threatens to escalate beyond his control. Kazan's more complex visual style does justice to this complex narrative causality.

As a final example, we can consider a scene featuring the protagonist, Reed, to see how Kazan asks us to keep our attention on the goal-oriented hero without losing our awareness of the causally charged space around him. Later in the film, Reed and Warren go to a Greek restaurant looking for someone who has seen the original victim, Kochak, when he was still alive. Kazan's composition narrativizes the entire space, encouraging us to notice the fact that this location brings together several links in the causal chain. First, Reed shows a picture of Kochak to Mefaris (Alex Minotis), the owner of the restaurant. Because Reed's back is turned, we cannot see his face—a compositional strategy that shifts our attention away from Reed and toward Warren and Mefaris on the edges of the frame. Next, Warren walks to the left, and the camera follows him, momentarily placing Reed offscreen. A moment later, the camera follows Warren again as he walks back to Reed, creating a new composition with Warren on the left, Reed on the right. In the background is Fitch (Zero Mostel), one of the men they are searching for. Fitch's appearance is another surprising moment, but Kazan offers this revelation as subtly as possible: there is no big close-up of Fitch, and no sudden musical cue announcing his presence. Instead, Fitch appears small and out of focus. Kazan can afford to be this understated with the revelation because he has already trained us how to watch the film. We know that Reed is not the only important causal force, so we have learned to scan the frame for other details. The composition itself is not necessarily centrifugal. Fitch is almost perfectly centered; if he were not so central, we might not notice him at all. Instead, we can say that anxieties about the changing nature of urban space have been expressed in a narrative that places a great deal of emphasis on unpredictable causality, and Kazan has managed to tell that story by crafting a multilayered composition with shifting areas of interest.

Although Kazan is best known as an actor's director, these early films show a director with a remarkably thoughtful approach to visual style. The semidocumentary trend encouraged audiences to notice real spaces in a way they never had before. Kazan took advantage of the opportunity to comment on the changing nature of those spaces. In postwar American society, with the increasing tension between the centripetal and the centrifugal, urban spaces were becoming more complex and unpredictable. *Panic in the Streets* — expanding on ideas introduced in *Boomerang!* — offers a narrative of competing social institutions, chance intersections, and the threat of an invisible pandemic, displayed with a visual vocabulary of unpredictability that rejects the neat hierarchies of a conventional Hollywood style. Judiciously drawing on the resources of the semidocumentary trend, while eliminating its more clichéd conventions, Kazan tells the story of these spaces.

NOTES

I would like to thank Lisa Jasinski, Joan Miller, and Lisa Dombrowski for providing me with materials drawn from the Elia Kazan Collection at the Wesleyan Cinema Archives.

1. Elia Kazan, telegram to Darryl F. Zanuck, November 28, 1949, box 21, *Panic in the Streets*, Elia Kazan Collection, Wesleyan Cinema Archives, Wesleyan University.

2. Elia Kazan, telegram to Darryl F. Zanuck, October 28, 1949, box 21, *Panic in the Streets*, Kazan Collection.

3. Thomas Schatz offers a useful summary of the semidocumentary trend, explaining how the trend both draws on and departs from the film noir style. See Thomas Schatz, *Boom and Bust: The American Cinema in the 1940s* (New York: Scribner's, 1997), 378–392. J. P. Telotte offers nuanced interpretations of several major semidocumentary films in *Voices in the Dark: The Narrative Patterns of Film Noir* (Urbana: University of Illinois Press, 1989), 134–178.

4. David Bordwell, *Narration in the Fiction Film* (Madison: University of Wisconsin Press, 1985), 157.

5. Frank Krutnik, *In a Lonely Street: Film Noir, Genre, Masculinity* (New York: Routledge, 1991), 202.

6. Richard Murphy, screenplay for *Port of Entry*, box 21, *Panic in the Streets*, Kazan Collection. *Port of Entry* was the film's working title.

7. Elia Kazan, notes on the screenplay for *Port of Entry*, box 21, *Panic in the Streets*, Kazan Collection.

8. Brian Neve, *Elia Kazan: The Cinema of an American Outsider* (London: I. B. Tauris, 2009), 27.

9. By contrast, *On the Waterfront* offers a much simpler take on institutional conflict, with the corrupt union bosses representing a bad institution and the government crime investigation representing a good one. Here, Kazan's corporate liberalism has turned into a one-sided endorsement of state power.

10. Peter Biskind, *Seeing Is Believing: How Hollywood Taught Us to Stop Worrying and Love the Fifties* (New York: Pantheon Books, 1983), 26.

11. Edward Dimendberg, *Film Noir and the Spaces of Modernity* (Cambridge, Mass.: Harvard University Press, 2004), 177.

12. Kazan later stated that *Panic in the Streets* was the first film where he felt confident enough to dictate the visual style, taking the opportunity to experiment with longer takes and more complex staging. See Michel Ciment, *Kazan on Kazan* (New York: Viking Press, 1974), 61–65.

LISA DOMBROWSKI

Choreographing Emotions
Kazan's CinemaScope Staging

Elia Kazan's philosophy of directing was quite simple: the director's job is to arouse emotion in the viewer by "rendering psychology into behavior, into action."[1] Most critics and historians have focused primarily on one method through which he achieved this goal: his knowing, manipulative, and inspired work with actors. It is not surprising that Kazan is lauded more as an actor's director than as a visual stylist. His early years as an actor; his long career as a director in the Group Theatre and on Broadway; his central involvement with the Actors Studio and the teaching of the Method; and the impressive list of actors whose stars were launched via their work with Kazan — Marlon Brando, James Dean, Warren Beatty, Karl Malden, Eli Wallach, Lee Remick, among others — all testify to his tremendous ability to understand how best to elicit the desired emotion from a performance. On the other hand, Kazan's visual style was less consistently vibrant, as he himself admitted; his films can appear more a series of individual experiments than a unified body of work marked by recurring stylistic traits.

Nevertheless, sustained attention to Kazan's visual style — particularly his excellent work on location — is long overdue. Beginning sporadically in *Boomerang!* (1947) and progressing through *Panic in the Streets* (1950), *Viva Zapata!* (1952), and *On the Waterfront* (1954), we see Kazan embracing the tools of cinematic staging beyond conventional scene coverage and cuts into close-ups. Twentieth Century-Fox launched CinemaScope in 1953, and the new widescreen system enabled Kazan to expand on his early staging experiments in a more systematic way. His two CinemaScope films, *East of Eden* (1955) and *Wild River* (1960) — both shot in rural locations — demonstrate the range of visual strategies Kazan utilized to express character conflict and emotion through widescreen staging and editing. Precise staging in depth, aperture framing, and dynamic movement between the foreground and background appear in both intricately choreographed long takes and more conventionally edited sequences, boldly highlighting relationships between characters and their environments. This careful organization of spatial and graphic relationships within the frame links Kazan to a long line of visual stylists intent on crafting a cinema based in images rather than words.

Kazan first internalized the role of staging in visual storytelling when he was at Yale University School of Drama. In his autobiography, Kazan describes an important lesson he learned from Alexander Dean, the professor of directing: "Dean taught directing as an art of position, picture, and movement. The stage positions and movements told the story of the scene and the relationship of the characters; in this way, behavior, feeling, and dramatic conflict were suggested. . . . The director's job was to contrive a kinetic pattern that told what was happening. The actor, as a vehicle of expression, was not to be relied upon. The stage picture, as it developed, told the event."[2] Position, picture, and movement—beyond simply dialogue and the actor's performance, these were tools the director could use to clarify character relationships and emphasize dramatic conflict. When Kazan began directing at the Group Theatre, he felt Dean's example gave him a leg up on his peers, who considered the job simply a matter of coaching actors. He vowed to achieve what Dean taught him: "the shaping of scenes and the manipulation of the positions and movements of actors so that the stage pictures revealed, at every moment, what happened, . . . My work would be to turn the inner events of the psyche into a choreography of external life."[3]

This was a goal Kazan brought with him when he started to direct films. But he quickly found himself falling into a pattern whereby he blocked actors "moving in and out of dramatic arrangements just as I might have done on stage, with the camera photographing them mostly in medium shot," and occasionally cutting into a close-up for emphasis. "In every difficulty, I'd rely on the spoken word rather than a revealing image."[4] Kazan approached *Panic in the Streets* as his opportunity to place a new emphasis on crafting a pictorial cinema, one in which stories are told through pictures and editing rather than through dialogue. In particular, he begins to stage action across multiple planes during extended takes, using precise movement and compositional cues to direct the viewer's gaze. It is a visual strategy he adopts again in *Viva Zapata!* and *On the Waterfront* and extends in new directions in *East of Eden*.

East of Eden was shot less than two years after the rollout of Cinema-Scope, one of the widescreen technologies that major studios adopted during the 1950s in order to differentiate films from television and combat declining attendance. CinemaScope challenged filmmakers used to relying on close-ups and editing; all of a sudden, these techniques were called into question, given the nature of the 'Scope frame—2.35 times as wide as it was high, more than double the size of the preexisting Academy frame. The increase in frame size forced filmmakers to consider how to activate the extra width (particularly during close-ups) and how to direct the viewer's attention when more than one element dominated the frame. At the same time, technical limitations associated with 'Scope's anamorphic lenses, the current film stocks, and available light restricted most CinemaScope films from simultaneously presenting objects in focus on multiple planes, as one might find in a 1940s Orson Welles or William Wyler movie. Film critics and professionals engaged in an ongoing debate throughout widescreen's first decade regarding how CinemaScope might impact classical aesthetic norms. Many anticipated reductions in the use of close-ups, camera movement, editing, and dynamic staging along with a greater incidence of extended shot lengths and more distant framings.[5] In practice, however, rather than merely adopting proscenium staging and spreading characters across the frame at a distance from the camera, most Hollywood filmmakers after 1955 integrated conventional scene construction and close-ups with some form of depth staging, thereby highlighting character emotions while emphasizing their position in the environment. In *East of Eden* and *Wild River*, Kazan's imaginative combinations of axial and lateral depth staging—organizing objects not just into depth but across the widescreen—and the means he uses to guide the audience's attention at any given moment through blocking, composition, and movement vividly illustrate his application of Alexander Dean's staging and his innovative exploitation of the CinemaScope frame.

Adapted from a portion of John Steinbeck's novel of the same name, *East of Eden* is a Cain and Abel story set against the backdrop of World War I in California farm country. It concerns the two Trask brothers, here called Cal (James Dean) and Aron (Richard Davalos). While Aron is a "good boy" and much loved by his father, Adam (Raymond Massey), Cal is considered a disappointment. In his preproduction notes on Steinbeck's novel, Kazan records his decision that "Cal is the character . . . that the audience has got to get to know and understand. He is the focus of the audience's emotion."[6] As such, Kazan and screenwriter Paul Osborn structured the narrative around Cal's pain and failed attempts to win his father's affection. Kazan ultimately came to see the narrative as a love story between a black-sheep son and his father: "Like all love stories, this starts with antagonism and a conflict. Cal feels rejected, not wanted, slighted, second."[7] During shooting, Kazan's goal was to visually highlight Cal's emotions and point of view through staging, editing, and Dean's performance.

The first time we see Cal and his brother interact with their father is in the second scene of the film. After failing to come home the night before, Cal finds Adam and his good friend Will (Albert Dekker) at an icehouse discussing Adam's scheme to create a refrigeration system for railroad cars. Soon Aron and his girlfriend, Abra (Julie Harris), arrive, leading Adam to reveal to Will his preference for Aron. In Kazan's script, opposite the dialogue lines for this scene, he jotted down a reminder of what he wanted to accomplish: "This scene dramatizes the life story of Cal — his history of rejection and the anger that builds up from it."[8] The twenty-two-shot scene in the completed film illustrates how Kazan emphasizes Cal's feelings of isolation through classical principles of staging and composition that direct the viewer's gaze while creatively activating the lateral and axial depth of the CinemaScope frame.

In the first seven shots of the scene, the editing and compositions highlight Adam's disapproval of his son's late-night carousing and Cal's hurt, establishing the basic emotional dynamic between father and son. The sequence begins with a medium-long shot of Adam and Will standing under the beams of the icehouse discussing refrigeration. The two men face each other in profile, standing in the left and right thirds of the frame in the foreground with a brown corridor between them emptying onto a green field in the background. Adam continually gestures into the open space in the central third of the frame; his hand movement, the empty corridor, and the color contrast between the icehouse and the field direct the viewer's gaze toward the center of the screen rather than at the two men talking, thereby priming the viewer for Cal's entrance. Once Cal walks into the corridor, a series of shot-reverse-shots emphasize Cal's alienation from his family by juxtaposing Cal, isolated in a tight shot, and wider two-shots of Adam and Will sharing the frame together. Each cut is prompted by Adam's commentary regarding Cal's poor behavior or a glance by Cal, silently shamed but still yearning for his father's approval. The editing pattern, difference in shot scale, and Dean's performance draw our attention to Cal's reactions and elicit sympathy for the young outcast.

The subsequent shot in the scene lasts five times as long as the average, as sets, camera movement, and blocking subtly shift viewer attention between multiple planes of action in different areas of the frame in order to further develop Cal's alienation. As Adam and Will walk left across the foreground of the frame from the icehouse to the shed, the camera tracks back and to the left; meanwhile, Cal, abandoned by his father under the icehouse, walks left in the background under the building's wooden beams and ice chute. While the camera is ostensibly following Adam and Will in the foreground, we are still able to see Cal in the background, framed between the two older men throughout the entire camera move. The unusual aperture framing of Cal, as well as his position under the wooden beams of the icehouse, fasten the viewer's gaze on his slowly diminishing figure despite the fact that he is out of focus and in the rear plane. The viewer scans the width and depth of the image, glancing between the dominant figures in the frame—the men talking in the left foreground—and Cal, on the periphery of the image in the rear. Kazan thereby activates the diagonal depth of the CinemaScope frame to visually illustrate the emotional tension and distance between father and son. While Adam introduces Will to the refrigeration idea in the foreground, the action more central to the narrative is taking place in the background—a subtle but clearly marked picture of Cal's yearning for the acceptance of his father.[9] Finally, Cal settles behind a wooden beam and a barrel on the extreme right of the frame, now barely visible; in moving to the right, he opens the central space under the ice chute in the background for the entrance of Aron and Abra. The viewer's gaze is thus diverted from Cal to Aron and Abra as they occupy the central third of the frame and stroll into the foreground, hand in hand, to greet Adam and introduce another line of conflict.

The next six shots of the sequence return to the editing pattern utilized at the beginning, in which Cal is isolated in the frame and separated from the interactions of others. Here, however, the effect is more poignant, as Cal watches his brother receive the affections of his father and the warm-hearted Abra. Kazan's notes on this script page highlight his intention: "Here strongly dramatize Cal's exclusion. This exclusion, rejection is the plot."[10] (He underlines each word two times.) Accordingly, we see Cal in tight shots, framed on all sides by crisscrossing girders that suggest entrapment. His glances across the yard motivate the cuts, as Cal winces at his father's warm embrace of his brother. Kazan returns to depth staging when Aron and Abra leave the yard; Aron takes Abra's hand and turns her around in the frame away from Cal as the couple walks into depth behind him. The blocking and exchange of glances across the screen suggest the romantic triangle that will be activated later in the film, while the presence of the ice chute in the center background is yet another instance in which Kazan primes the viewer to remember a significant setting before action occurs there.

After Aron and Abra disappear behind Cal, Adam's offscreen voice barks at his prodigal son, redirecting the viewer's attention to their fractured relationship. Cal walks forward and to the left while the camera tracks back to frame him in a low-angle three-shot with his father and Will. Although Cal is finally engaging with his father, he nevertheless remains diminished in the frame. Adam is centered and looking down on Cal, who stands on the right side of the frame in a slightly more distanced plane, while Will sits in the foreground left, responding with enthusiasm to Cal's idea to make money growing beans. Adam witheringly replies, "But I'm not particularly interested in making a profit, Cal." The compositions in this final section of the scene emphasize Adam as the central and dominant figure, highlighting his displeasure even as Cal, initially the most frontal and animated of the three men, makes his impassioned pitch. By framing all three characters in the same shot, Kazan is able simultaneously to illustrate Cal's eager pitch, his father's deflating response, and Will's defense of Cal's scheme, juxtaposing the actions of the older men and initiating a question regarding which of the two is more encouraging and "fatherly" toward Cal.

The last shots of the sequence punctuate the seemingly impossible distance between father and son by finally incorporating the ice chute the viewer has been staring at in the background for so long. After Adam and Will exit offscreen left and go into the shed, Cal is left alone in the frame, the ice chute looming behind him; the score swells, emphasizing his isolation. As Adam's voice continues offscreen, Cal retreats into the midground and runs up the ice chute to the top, the camera tilting to follow his climb. While Cal remains out of focus and small in the frame, the camera movement, his figure movement, the lines of perspective created by the ice chute, and the door that frames him direct the viewer's gaze to the top of the chute as he lights a cigarette. Adam suddenly emerges out of the shed in the foreground left and yells at Cal in the extreme background right to extinguish his cigarette; visually connecting the two is the ice chute, creating a leading line from father to son that doubles their glances across the screen and into depth. Like the earlier shots in this sequence that utilize lateral and axial depth, this final shot could not have been achieved except in widescreen. It simultaneously

In these frame enlargements from *East of Eden*, Cal Trask (James Dean) shadows his father, Adam (Raymond Massey, in dark hat), and seeks his approval, only to be discouraged; Adam's friend Will Hamilton (Albert Dekker, light hat) is more encouraging. Kazan carefully choreographs the scene using depth staging, aperture framing, and leading lines to highlight Cal's diminishment and feelings of rejection.

activates the full expanse of the screen, while also providing conventional classical cues, such as camera movement, figure movement, aperture framing, lines of perspective, and balance within the frame, to direct the viewer's gaze and visually depict the unrequited love at the heart of the scene.

The icehouse scene is a virtuosic example of how Kazan utilized staging possibilities provided by the wide CinemaScope frame to punctuate character emotion across a scene, and many of the strategies illustrated here appear throughout the film. A number of individual shots also stand out for their bold 'Scope staging. In his 1971 interview with Michel Ciment, Kazan notes that CinemaScope encouraged him to compose laterally across the frame and to create frames within the frame.[11] The introduction of the Trask family home immediately following the icehouse scene notably contains shots composed with both strategies, further accentuating the gloom and distance dividing Cal and Adam. The first interior shot presents the Trask house as rigid, dark, and claustrophobic. In the foreground is a darkened living room; in the midground, a perfectly centered archway covered in shadow; and in the background, three figures sitting around a table lit from above: Adam on the right, Aron in the middle, and Cal on the left, each separated by window panels and symmetrical in the frame. The living room floor, walls, and archway frame the men, with the contrast between the darkened foreground and lighted rear plane further lending an air of entrapment. And Cal *is* trapped: divided from his father, forced to endure Bible reading and interrogations. The shot visually explains why Cal stays out all night (to escape this scary, repressive house) and where Adam's disapproval originates (in an inflexible sense of morality). Later in the scene, after Aron leaves and Kazan juxtaposes Adam and Cal in canted close-ups, he returns to a wider framing. With the camera now positioned in the archway, we see the father and son sitting at the far ends of the table, divided by the entire expanse of the widescreen, an overhead lamp and Aron's empty chair bisecting the frame. Here the composition dramatically illustrates the gulf that separates father and son in a more overt manner than would be possible with the smaller Academy frame.

In these examples, Kazan's decision to spread out Cal and Aron laterally within the composition follows logically from the shape of the CinemaScope frame and enables him to depict the father-son conflict in a pictorial fashion. Later in the film, we see Kazan make a more counterintuitive choice in order to punctuate a highly emotional turning point: after his father brutally rejects his hard-won birthday present, Cal retreats under a large willow tree, Abra consoles him, Aron castigates him, and Cal decides to reveal the bitter truth about their debauched mother. Kazan diagrammed detailed camera setups for this sequence in his script, carefully noting the blocking of Cal, Abra, and Aron at each narrative beat in relation to the tree and the Trask back porch. These notes lay the groundwork for what we see in the finished film — remarkably, rather than positioning the characters across the frame or into depth, as in our prior examples, Kazan does the opposite. In a wide framing, Cal cowers in the far background center behind the trunk of the willow tree; only his feet and legs are visible under the tree's voluminous branches. (In his script, Kazan drew a picture of Cal's figure engulfed by the willow tree, describing him hiding "like a wounded fearful animal.")[12] We hear what sounds like Cal's sobbing, but unlike the diagrams in Kazan's script, the completed film provides no close-up to punctuate this; instead, we are left to imagine the depth of Cal's anguish. Abra runs to join Cal under the willow tree and comfort him, her skirt pressed up against his legs, everything above her waist, as with Cal, obscured. With a reduction of visual cues to explain what is going on — the bulk of what we see across the whole frame is the giant willow tree — we focus on what *is* revealed: the two pairs of entwined legs, and the muffled sounds coming from behind the tree. Is Abra giving Cal a hug? Stroking his face? Kissing him? Again, Kazan leaves it to our imagination — a bold but arguably more powerful choice than clarity, as the lovemaking now takes place in viewers' heads. By obscuring his protagonists at such a heightened emotional moment, when they finally (seemingly) give in to their attraction, Kazan makes a staging choice one might expect more from Kenji Mizoguchi — lover of distant framings, dorsal staging, and obscured faces — than a classically trained Hollywood filmmaker.

Once Aron enters the foreground of the shot, the hidden romance is over; he calls to Abra, and she walks into a new foreground. Now Kazan stacks Cal, the tree, Aron, and Abra in compressed depth in the center of the frame — again, a highly unusual choice that counters classical norms and refuses the advantages of CinemaScope. Cal's feet are barely visible in the far background; Aron faces away from the camera in midground, hidden in darkness and obscuring the trunk of the tree; and Abra stands in front of him, facing the camera and lit most brightly. As Aron warns Cal never to touch Abra again, calling him no good, mean, vicious, and wild, our eyes are drawn to Abra — the only character whose face is visible — and the divided anguish she feels. Aron's tight, controlled voice tells us all we need to know about him — he sounds exactly like his father — but we wait for Cal's response, as we neither see nor hear him. When he emerges from behind the tree branches, cloaked in darkness, we know the table is about to be turned on Aron. This is truly imaginative staging, a challenge both to dominant Hollywood norms and to the wide CinemaScope frame, but nevertheless completely emotionally evocative — an obscured picture that the viewer is encouraged to complete.

Wild River was Kazan's second CinemaScope film and features what the director described as a more "laconic" visual style.[13] Inspired by Kazan's experiences shooting People of the Cumberland (1937), the story is about a 1930s Tennessee Valley Authority (TVA) administrator, Chuck Glover (Montgomery Clift), who travels to a rural river town in order to convince an elderly woman, Mrs. Garth (Jo Van Fleet), that she, her family, and her African-American tenants must move off of their soon-to-be-flooded island. While trying to convince Mrs. Garth to accept the inevitable, Chuck becomes romantically involved with Carol (Lee Remick), Mrs. Garth's widowed daughter-in-law. The central conflict in the film is between the differing values and goals of Chuck, the idealistic, forward-thinking TVA administrator, and Mrs. Garth, the powerful and stubborn matriarch who is deeply rooted to her land. In his story development notebook, Kazan worked out the central point of the film: "A man in the right, sure of being in the right, and out to do right, discovers that people can be wrong from his viewpoint. And still be right. And awesomely right from a moral and human angle. . . . And he reverses his course, sets out to salvage the human pieces. And make peace with his conscience."[14] While Chuck is the central protagonist and the means through which the narrative is organized, Kazan crafts the film to provide equal weight to the person and arguments of Mrs. Garth — indisputably the stronger of the two characters. As a result, the viewer is left, like Chuck, with a deep ambivalence about the TVA administrator's ultimate success: he wins the battle, but at what cost? Kazan consciously adopted a new visual approach to depict the protagonists' conflict and its relation to the land. He told Michel Ciment, "Wild River was the first picture where I said to myself: I'm going to be as lyric as I can — I'm going to stop the action." He continued, "I thought a film can be both true — realistic — and completely poetic. And that became the ideal of my aesthetic."[15] The wide CinemaScope frame became Kazan's ally, enabling him to visualize emotions and conflict in a pictorial yet organic fashion by highlighting characters within their environment.

In this frame enlargement from *Wild River*, Chuck Glover
(Montgomery Clift) arrives at the Garth homestead to speak with
its matriarch, Ella Garth (Jo Van Fleet, *center of porch*); Carol Garth
(Lee Remick, *far left*) watches. Kazan activates the full width of the
frame as the women, one by one, turn away from Glover.

The authority of Mrs. Garth and her power on the island are vividly
illustrated through Kazan's staging of her initial encounters with Chuck.
The first time he visits her house to plead with her to leave, the shot is
composed to emphasize her influence, intractability, and silent contempt.
While Chuck stands in the foreground right of center and faces away from
the camera, the front porch of the Garth family house is spread across the
rear plane, with Carol standing against a beam on the left, Mrs. Garth sitting dead center on her chair with a child at her feet, and an older woman
flanking Chuck on the right side of the frame. Staring Chuck down and
ignoring his entreaties to talk, Mrs. Garth gets up without a word and goes
into the door behind her, followed initially by Carol and then by the older
woman. Chuck is left to make his case to a five-year-old. The departure of
Mrs. Garth, the acquiescence of Carol, and the emptying of the frame create
a picture of exactly what Chuck has been forewarned: he is an intruder on
the Garth land, and the family will not listen to anything he has to say.

Chuck's second visit to the island presents the same conflict but in a
different way: here we see Kazan utilizing the wide 'Scope frame to position Mrs. Garth within the context of her environs while still allowing her
dominance in the frame. In the scene, Mrs. Garth is providing her black
workers with a parable to explain why it is unjust that the government
should force her to sell her land: she may want to buy her tenant Ben's dog,
but he has the right to refuse, as his dog means more to him than money.
Mrs. Garth is centered in the foreground of the frame facing the camera

Chuck Glover (Montgomery Clift) walks into the aperture produced by Ella Garth (Jo Van Fleet) opening the door in this frame enlargement from *Wild River*. Kazan uses a series of frames within the frame to direct the viewer's attention across space and into depth during the scene.

in a medium shot, the prominent locus of attention; Chuck watches from behind her in the midground left, with Carol in the background and other island residents crowding the edges of the frame on either side. Two tall poles stand in an inverted V-shape in the center midground of the image, creating leading lines that frame either side of Mrs. Garth; these poles, as well as the juxtaposition of her face against the sky, separate her from the characters surrounding her and make her stand out in the composition. Once again, Kazan creates an image that illustrates who's in command: Mrs. Garth. Chuck, Carol, and the tenants function merely as witnesses to the exchange between Ben and Mrs. Garth, and as testaments to Mrs. Garth's moral authority — we are watching them absorb her lesson.

These two examples highlight how Kazan organizes the wide Cinema-Scope frame through classical compositional principles to visualize narrative conflict in a relatively straightforward fashion. A later scene operates much more self-consciously, drawing attention to Kazan's careful staging. When Chuck arrives to tell Mrs. Garth that her sons have agreed to sell her property and she has no choice but to get out, Kazan utilizes aperture framing, character movement, and point-of-view editing to overtly highlight the divide between the characters, Chuck's canny, patient appeal, and Mrs. Garth's stubborn refusal to leave. The scene opens with Mrs. Garth peering through a window next to her door, her face centered and boxed in by the square panes that graphically subdivide the image, the first in a series of aperture framings that dominate the compositions in the sequence.

Then Kazan provides us with what she sees: Chuck walking toward her in an extreme long shot, photographed through the porch from her point of view, an interloper among her land and horses with the river behind him. We already know the news he brings; Kazan builds suspense by allowing us to imagine how Mrs. Garth will react to it and him. We learn the answer in the next shot, composed over Mrs. Garth's shoulder as she looks out the window; the door masks the left half of the frame and the wall the right third, directing the viewer's gaze toward Mrs. Garth and the windows in the center. As Mrs. Garth pulls the curtains back, Chuck is revealed outside in the opening; the windowpane creates an aperture framing that centers him on the screen and redirects our attention.

Mrs. Garth stubbornly remains hiding behind the house's barriers, but still Chuck advances. He may not be the strongest of men, but he will not stop. After Chuck and Mrs. Garth twice exchange glances and Chuck begins to call to her, Mrs. Garth leans in to open the front door, creating yet another aperture in the center of the screen that Chuck walks into in extreme long shot. In the absence of deep focus, Kazan utilizes other compositional tools to direct the viewer's gaze into depth. The masking of the door and wall, precise aperture framing, Mrs. Garth's glance, and the leading line of her arm concentrate viewer attention on Chuck's small, out-of-focus figure in the background of the image. But even as Chuck tells her of the sale of her island, Mrs. Garth again turns her back on him and closes the door.

Though Kazan fully adheres to classical staging conventions in this scene, the multiple apertures and the amount of compositional space that is utilized solely to direct our gaze add a very self-conscious aspect to the action. The viewer is unusually aware of the act of looking — we are looking at Mrs. Garth looking at Chuck walking up to her house, perhaps for the last time. Our attention is focused first on one character and then on the other, encouraging us to recognize that what Mrs. Garth is looking at — Chuck — is no longer just a persistent intruder, or a threat to her island, but really the end of her island. And still she cannot accept the truth — for the end of her island will be the end of her, too. So she closes the door. Here we see Kazan attacking the challenges of staging in CinemaScope with creativity and rigor, producing a wonderful example of how positions, pictures, and movement can highlight character relationships and conflict. The last time I watched this scene with an audience, someone actually gasped when Chuck walked into the aperture produced by the open door — Kazan's command of the medium is just that striking.

By the early 1950s, Kazan's films begin to experiment with the expressive potential of visual style in a manner that is much bolder than his earlier work. In *East of Eden* and *Wild River*, we see him embracing the pictorial opportunities provided by the new CinemaScope technology. Along with other innovators of widescreen style such as Otto Preminger and Vincente Minnelli, Kazan adapted CinemaScope to preexisting classical norms, integrating conventional editing patterns with lateral and axial depth staging to produce "intimacy" within the confines of the wider frame. In doing so, Kazan advanced his attempts to create a visual cinema, one in which character emotions and conflict are externalized not only through an actor's performance but also through the visual choreography of a scene. Admittedly, not all of Kazan's films are as beautifully composed as these two—his notebooks are full of self-criticism and acknowledgments of his slow learning curve when it came to the creation of fully cinematic films. But *East of Eden* and *Wild River* link Kazan to a long line of directors— going back to Yevgeni Bauer and up through Hou Hsiao-hsien—who are masters of pictorial staging, and they are vivid rebukes to critics and historians who consider Kazan primarily a director of actors rather than a visual stylist.

NOTES

Thanks to David Bordwell for his comments on an early version of the first scene analysis from East of Eden.

1. Elia Kazan, "The Pleasures of Directing," in *Kazan On Directing* (New York: Knopf, 2009), 254–255.

2. Elia Kazan, *Elia Kazan: A Life* (New York: Knopf, 1988), 49.

3. Ibid., 90.

4. Kazan, "Pleasures," 259, 267.

5. See Andre Bazin, "The End of Montage," reprinted in *The Velvet Light Trap* 21 (summer 1985), 14–15; Richard Kohler, "The Big Screens," *Sight and Sound* 24, no. 3 (January/February 1955), 120–126; Charles G. Clarke, "CinemaScope Photographic Techniques," *American Cinematographer*, June 1955, 336–337, 362–363; R. L. Hoult, "Approach to Wide-angle Motion Picture Photography," *American Cinematographer*, July 1957, 442–444, 458–460; M. K. Shinde, *Shinde's Dictionary of Cine Art and Film Craft* (Bombay: Popular Prakashan, 1962); Charles G. Clarke, *Professional Cinematography* (Hollywood: American Society of Cinematographers, 1964).

6. Kazan, preproduction notes on *East of Eden* novel, December 15, 1952, Elia Kazan Collection, Wesleyan Cinema Archives, Wesleyan University.

7. Kazan, preproduction notes on *East of Eden* novel, April 3, 1953.

8. Kazan, note on *East of Eden* script, Kazan Collection.

9. V. F. Perkins discusses how Otto Preminger exploits the wide CinemaScope frame to develop a similar tension between foreground/background action during the raft scene in *River of No Return* (1954), an early 'Scope film frequently championed for its role in developing widescreen aesthetics. See V. F. Perkins, "*River of No Return,*" *Movie* 2 (September 1962), 18.

10. Kazan, note on *East of Eden* script.

11. Michel Ciment, *Kazan on Kazan* (London: Secker and Warburg, 1973), 122–123.

12. Kazan, note on *East of Eden* script.

13. Elia Kazan, quoted in Richard Schickel, *Elia Kazan: A Biography* (New York: HarperCollins, 2009), 372.

14. Elia Kazan, story development notebook, *Wild River*, 1957, Kazan Collection.

15. Elia Kazan, quoted in Ciment, *Kazan on Kazan*, 137.

I am a mediocre director except when
a play or a film touches a part of my life's
experiences.

ELIA KAZAN

Lost *River*

*I*n the summer of 2005 I received an urgent phone call from a woman producing the supplemental material for a proposed DVD release of Elia Kazan's *Wild River* (1960). Could I provide the audio commentary for it? And could I do so within the next two or three days? The studio, Twentieth Century-Fox, was planning to put the film out in February 2006. I was in New York at the moment, without access to my research material, but I had recently completed my biography of Kazan, so the film, and his (and my) thoughts about it were fresh in my mind. Besides, it is one of my favorites among his pictures, and I was eager to talk about it. So, two or three days later, I found myself on a recording stage at 1600 Broadway, offering my thoughts about *Wild River*. A couple of months later someone else from Fox was on the phone, asking my production company to make a short film about the Kazan picture, also for inclusion on the DVD. We, of course, owned an extensive interview I had done with the director — it had served as the basis of a television film I had written and directed about him. So we made that little film, too.

After which, total and mysterious silence. February 2006 came and went — no DVD. The silence persisted until fall 2010, when at last divine intervention (in the form of the always passionate Martin Scorsese) occurred. Kazan was Scorsese's beloved master, a huge shaping force on the latter's sensibility and career. Scorsese made a highly personal film about Kazan and pressed Fox to release a boxed set of DVDs containing his documentary as well as the many films he made at the studio. So, 101 years after Kazan's birth and 7 years after his death, all of Kazan's features have at last been re-introduced to the public via home video.

This is obviously a good thing. But somehow it does not entirely erase the long years of silence and frustration that have surrounded *Wild River*. From its conception, through its troubled development — which required almost two decades — through its limited, desultory release in 1960 and its entombed half-century aftermath, the picture was among the most enigmatic and deeply buried failures by a distinguished director in movie

Elia Kazan (*center*) and Ralph Steiner (*left, behind camera*) in a production still from the 1937 documentary *People of the Cumberland*. Kazan's experiences in Tennessee while making the film informed his development of the story for *Wild River*. Photograph by Marion Post Wolcott. Photo courtesy of the Wesleyan Cinema Archives.

history. This is particularly so since it is, quite obviously, a very good film that, in some respects, flirts persuasively with greatness.

Its roots lie deep in Elia Kazan's past. In 1937, he was an actor, stage manager, and aspiring director in the Group Theatre; but it was summertime, the Group was on hiatus, and a new entity specializing in documentaries, Frontier Films, was preparing to make its first short film, eventually entitled *People of the Cumberland* (1937). Kazan's lifelong friend, the photographer Ralph Steiner, was one of Frontier's founders, and Kazan signed on to work as an assistant on the picture, which showed the hard lives of backcountry people in Tennessee — and the hopeful effect building a new school had on them. It's hard to say, exactly, what Kazan contributed to the movie, but he was later voluble on the effect these sly, hard, deeply traditional people had on him. Put simply, he adored them. They had about them a hard-shelled authenticity that he had been looking for most of his life. They were as far as it was possible to be from the twitterings of the New York artistic and intellectual communities, in which he had been caught up since graduating from college. Moreover, he saw that it was possible for the cameras to penetrate their lives and give an honest accounting of them. Much of his latter-day preference for casting nonactors wherever possible stems from this experience.

In 1937 the major issue in the region was the intrusion of the Tennessee Valley Authority (TVA). Its purpose was to construct a series of dams, causing a rerouting of the Tennessee River, in order to bring electricity to the area. The larger social good of that project was obvious. Less obvious was its effect on the lives of the local population, who had been farming the area for centuries. Many of their farms would be flooded, and they would suffer forced relocation and, worse, the loss of a sustaining tradition. I'm not sure that this conflict, the central theme of *Wild River*, occurred to Kazan at the time. But the beauty of the country, and the integrity of its people, were firmly fixed in his mind as he attended his developing career as a theatrical director over the next six years.

Then in 1941 he was asked to direct a show entitled *It's Up to You*, a kind of agitprop revue—this time sponsored by the government rather than poised in opposition to it. It was designed to encourage public support for wartime food rationing. The piece was not in Kazan's accustomed realistic style. It was very much in the presentational manner of the Federal Theater's "Living Newspaper" productions (its writer had worked on those shows) and it was supervised by representatives of the U.S. Department of Agriculture, one of whom had worked in the Tennessee Valley. He and Kazan bonded over bourbon, folk music, and backcountry stories.

The man was a well-educated New Dealer and he seemed to Kazan a perfect protagonist for a story about the TVA —a political and cultural sophisticate full of idealism confronting mulish rural traditionalism, learning its virtues while yet clinging to his own more progressive values. Kazan went so far as to imagine Burl Ives in the role, and may have begun scratching notes about the film while he was still working with this Department of Agriculture role model.

Then, however, his mind shifted. He decided that his intruder should not be such an agreeable figure. Kazan thought he should be more abrasive, more the way he or his friend Clifford Odets had been in their younger days—cocksure, ideologically certain in their views, more than a little patronizing of anyone who stood in their way. He flashed on the attitudes he and Steiner had brought with them to their Tennessee filming. In his notebook he wrote: "YOU KNEW ALL ABOUT IT BEFORE YOU LEFT NEW YORK. Mighty dynamic you were . . . intense . . . 100 times surer of yourself than you are today."[1] He also thought this visitor from another planet should be a Jew, stirring the inherent prejudices of the backcountry folks. Though he was born in Greece, Kazan had looked like a "kike" (his word) to the locals, and he correctly surmised that prejudice would wind the dramatic tension of his film more tightly.

So he set to intermittent work on his screenplay, never producing anything that satisfied him. Over the years, he hired Ben Maddow (a Frontier Films colleague and an experienced screenwriter) and Calder Willingham, the novelist, to write drafts of the script, none of which pleased him. Kazan was distracted. These were the years of his ascendancy, when he established himself as America's leading stage and screen director, and they were years of political turmoil as well, when he was embroiled in bitter controversy over his "naming names" testimony before the House Un-American Activities Committee (HUAC). It has always seemed to me that had he made his film during the Truman presidency, when the New Deal was still a living legacy, it might have had more relevancy for audiences. By the time it was released it seemed to be ancient history.

Still, he persisted, eventually hiring the playwright Paul Osborne, who had served him well as the adapter of *East of Eden* (1955), to write what became the more or less final draft of *Wild River*. He owed Fox one last film on a multipicture deal, and even though Darryl F. Zanuck, his chief supporter, was no longer in charge of production at the studio, its new boss, Buddy Adler, remained patient and sympathetic with the project, though he confessed he could see nothing in it that would compel audience interest.

The movie Kazan put into production in 1959 was in important aspects different from his original idea. In particular, his idealistic New Dealer lost his Jewishness — he was now Chuck Glover, a Wasp — and his aggressiveness: in Montgomery Clift's portrayal he is almost puppyish in his desire to ingratiate himself with the people whose land he must acquire for the TVA. His chief antagonist is Ella Garth, matriarch of a family whose farm occupies an entire island in the middle of the river. Played by a stonily magnificent Jo Van Fleet, she yet develops an ironic affection for Chuck. In turn, his cause is not aided by his developing love for Ella's widowed daughter-in-law. Carol, luminously played by the lovely Lee Remick, is shy and tentative in manner, yet also determined to reclaim a life of her own.

Kazan had an aesthetic agenda in addition to his more obvious political and psychological ones. He had been drawn to the movies because of their epic potential. He had loved the great Russian directors (Sergei Eisenstein et al.) and wanted to emulate the scale of their work. Yet he felt that by and large, he had mostly been photographing stage plays. He saw in *Wild River* the possibility of a grand-scale pastoral, something he had tried to attain in *East of Eden*, but with fewer words and less complexity in its characters. This, I think, he accomplished, thanks in great degree to the limpid cinematography of Ellsworth Fredericks.

Not that this desire overrode the moral of the story, which was the great theme of Kazan's later years. Simply put, it was: Actions imply choices that, in turn, have consequences. He often put that point in personal terms: If you marry this woman, it means you don't marry that one; if you choose to direct this script, it means you can't make that other one. Most of his life this man had guided himself by politics and by his devotion to a realistic aesthetic. Now he was acknowledging an existential component — an existential mystery, if you will — as *the* determinative matter in our lives.

As it happened, the production of *Wild River* — much more than its text — proved his point. The problem was Clift. Kazan had known him for years — he had been in the cast of his Broadway production of *The Skin of Our Teeth* and he had, for a time, been a familiar in the Kazan household, drawn especially to Kazan's wife, Molly, as a sort of surrogate mother. Kazan had not particularly liked him — not in comparison to his rivals among the other revolutionizing actors of the postwar era, Marlon Brando and James Dean. "He was a dutiful kid, Monty," he once said to me, "But he was still some way or other a cripple. Some way, some subtle way, he wasn't entirely healthy."[2]

That was literally so by 1959. His perfectly beautiful face had been permanently marred in an auto accident a couple of years earlier and he had taken to drink and drugs, which rendered him an unreliable presence on the set. He was, it must be said, the anti–Chuck Glover, as Kazan originally conceived him. Under Kazan's orders ("I can't stand drunken actors") he remained sober as Kazan rebalanced his film. In particular, Remick's character takes him in charge; when the time comes, it is she who seduces him, which was the opposite of Kazan's original intention. It is her strength that adds sufficient steel to his spine so that he accomplishes his mission, though the end of the Garth's island fiefdom is more Chekhovian (complete with axes chopping down trees, à la *The Cherry Orchard*), more regretful than triumphant. Cannily, Kazan revised his thinking about Chuck: "I exaggerated his weakness, I made him less strong." Always "trembling on the brink

Montgomery Clift and Elia Kazan consult during the production of *Wild River*. Kazan used Clift's shaky health and fragile self-confidence to highlight his character's weaknesses and add ambiguity to the story. Photo courtesy of the Wesleyan Cinema Archives.

of collapse," Clift was kept in the game by Van Fleet and Remick. "They liked him. They supported him. They kept the thing going for his sake. Jo and Lee both were goddesses."[3]

I think Clift, in his way, gives quite a good performance; he is ever the fish flopping, sometimes comically, outside this river's water. Yet he was also an important factor in dooming whatever chances the film had for critical and commercial success. It was not just that he was weak and distractible in himself; it was that Kazan always had a problem with stardom — if Clift, indeed, was still a star. In general, the director thought stars were overpriced and overprivileged. And, of course, they challenged his authority on the set. If you look over his filmography, you see that his leads tended to be either movie stars of the second rank or solid Broadway types. The great exception to this rule was Brando, who was his discovery, thus someone over whom he had — for a time — dominance.

Remick fit that category; she made her movie debut in Kazan's *A Face in the Crowd* (1957). But she was not then, if she ever was, a performer who could carry a picture commercially. Van Fleet, too, had a history with Kazan; she had won the supporting actress Oscar for *East of Eden*. She was a fierce and commanding presence, but she was a famous nutcase whose reputation for difficulty made it impossible for her to establish herself as a supporting player audiences cared about.

In a sense, that was all right with Kazan. He always believed that a film's theme was what the audience responded to, though his own movie track record was mixed in that regard. In any case, this was, for him, a very personal film, despite the fact that the largest of his ideas, the hidden price we pay for our choices, is hidden from viewers. What those few people who actually saw the movie focused on was the story of a principled progressive in conflict with people clinging to their roots, the eventual loss of which was virtually foreordained.

Yet Kazan thought his film was, in the end, successful. "It was a different version from what my script was," he said, but he clung to the belief that Clift fitted its revised form "beautifully."[4] I think he was largely correct about that. You could even argue that it was perhaps a more subtle film than originally intended. But it did lack the kind of melodramatic conflict that might have allowed audiences to forget its historical circumstances and concentrate on a more ferociously staged drama. The picture begins with a newsreel montage of the river in full, terrifying flood — sweeping man and all his works away. It ends with shots of a small plane, carrying Chuck, Carol, and her children away from the serene valley, its waters controlled by a huge, gleaming dam — "mission accomplished," as one might put it.

The question recurs: Suppose Kazan had been able to make *Wild River* in the late forties or early fifties, before Eisenhower had imposed his quietus on the nation, at a point where the defense of the New Deal's legacy was still lively and the TVA, in particular, was regarded as one of its great, unambivalent successes? Might people then have seen the film as a source, at least, for passionate discussion? As important, might they have seen that it was a powerfully personal film, in which its prime creator tried to express his feelings about the political matters that had for so long preoccupied him? For Kazan, despite his HUAC testimony, remained a passionate, if anticommunist, liberal — almost a radical. For him now to question the cost of grand government schemes, to sympathize affectionately with the people standing helplessly in their path, was no small thing. Indeed, it was a very good thing, a measure, if you will, of the "humanism" (hateful word) that always lay just beneath the bustle of his showmanship.

There was, of course, nothing showy in this grave film. And a price was paid for that. Twentieth Century-Fox did not so much release *Wild River* as let it escape into the world. It was given an "art film" release in a relatively few places. The hope, presumably, was that a few good reviews might kick-start interest in the thing. They weren't bad, but they were more dutiful than anything else—they had none of the heat that had greeted his previous films (*Baby Doll*, 1956; *A Face in the Crowd*)—and there was a sense in them that Kazan was past his time—even though his very next film, *Splendor in the Grass* (1961) would be a success. (It had sexual energy and an appeal to the youth market that *Wild River* lacked.) Kazan had to beg Fox to release *Wild River* in foreign territories, where the reviews were better but the business just as bad. He tried to buy the picture back from the studio, but its price ($300,000) was beyond his means. So, without stars we want to nostalgize, taking up an ostensible subject that most people today have never heard of, it long languished in the land of Nod, on the far side of Eden (or *East of Eden*). It is a particular pleasure to welcome it back to another land—the land of the living—this clear-eyed, finely judged and deeply humane story about the costs and consequences of the choices we make in pursuit of the principles we cannot help but embrace.

NOTES

1. Elia Kazan, notes on the production of *Wild River*, Elia Kazan Collection, Wesleyan Cinema Archives, Wesleyan University.

2. Elia Kazan, interview with author.

3. Ibid.

4. Ibid.

Late Kazan, or The Ambiguities

*E*lia Kazan remains a difficult icon of auteurist cinema. During the formative years of auteurist criticism, Kazan's commercially and critically acclaimed major works of the 1940s, 1950s, and early 1960s — *A Tree Grows in Brooklyn* (1945), *A Streetcar Named Desire* (1951), *On the Waterfront* (1954), *East of Eden* (1955), *Baby Doll* (1956), *Splendor in the Grass* (1961) among them — offered bold, irrefutable examples of a powerful artistic vision exerted in spite, and almost in defiance, of the commercial exigencies of the studio system. Yet notwithstanding Kazan's canonization as one of the more influential and original American filmmakers of the postwar era, the autobiographical tendency in auteurist criticism has to this day continued to exert a heavy influence on readings of his work. With few exceptions Kazan's films continue to be considered first and foremost as expressions of his contentious political beliefs and especially his notorious shift from ardent New Deal liberal in the 1930s — and, briefly, Communist Party member — to willing testifier before the House Un-American Activities Committee (HUAC) in 1952. Indeed, a consideration of Kazan's politics has today become an almost mandatory point of departure for any discussion of his work and legacy.

Ironically what remains largely ignored — despite the dominant thrust of Kazan criticism — is the strong and crucial autobiographical direction taken by the neglected films that together constitute the final major phase in Kazan's long career: *America America* (1963), *The Arrangement* (1969), *The Visitors* (1972), and *The Last Tycoon* (1976). These four films all center around characters whose identities have suddenly become unmoored and unstable, male protagonists who were once firmly defined by their place and professions and who suddenly find themselves grappling with life and career decisions that often directly echo those infamously made by Kazan himself — and that he discussed at length in his own long-awaited memoir, *Elia Kazan: A Life*, finally published in 1988. More than simply dominant motifs, the often openly autobiographically inspired instability of self in the flawed but fascinating late films points toward a major thematic and structural pattern that can be traced, retrospectively, back across Kazan's entire oeuvre. Largely ignored by scholars and critics, the final films together offer an important vantage point from which to reconsider his body of work and the shaping, unifying forces within it. Frequently dismissed as aberrant and overripe, the late films represent a major reorientation of Kazan's work away from the high-strung classicism of his emotionally intense yet stylistically understated earlier work. Most important, the more radical and experimental styles alternately embraced by the last four films bring into sharp relief the mode of narrative ambiguity underlying and structuring Kazan's work across its different periods.

Of Kazan's last four films, *America America* and *The Arrangement* in particular invite, even demand, an autobiographical reading as adaptations, respectively, of his first two eponymous and highly personal novels. The often harrowing story of *America America* depicts Stavros, a young Greek villager struggling to work and wrangle his way toward the United States via Istanbul, based in both the novel and the film on the life of Kazan's paternal uncle and childhood hero, Joe Kazan. The original novel and film of *The Arrangement*, meanwhile, draw their story from Kazan's own life, with the director a clear model for the hero, Eddie "Evangelos" Anderson (played in the film by Kirk Douglas), a highly successful first-generation Greek struggling through a turbulent midlife crisis. Significantly, both films feature decidedly unsympathetic and difficult protagonists, self-made and endlessly self-absorbed men who seem prepared to do anything not only to survive but also to succeed. As if in response to the criticism continuously hurled at Kazan's post-HUAC work and career — despite the many awards and accolades — these ruthlessly driven and ultimately selfish characters openly embody and enact the very same negative qualities often ascribed to Kazan himself. Thus, while young Stavros in *America America* literally ·prostitutes himself to obtain passage aboard a United States–bound steamer, Eddie Anderson's ruthless ambition as a slick advertising executive in *The Arrangement* — which could almost be imagined as a sequel of sorts to *America America* — is similarly cast as a destructive and morally compromised act of "selling out."

The voice-over narration that opens *America America* is spoken off-screen by Kazan himself ("My name is Elia Kazan," it begins), quite literally announcing the autobiographical turn in his work while also exemplifying the "outspoken" and, at times, quite aggressive style his late films explored. Working with two innovative artists who would each play major

In this frame enlargement from *America America*, the protagonist Stavros (Stathis Giallelis) waits for scraps of food from the sultan's table as a voice-over describes how he will make his parents proud. Kazan repeatedly juxtaposes contrasting images and sounds in the film to emphasize the disjunction between Stavros's reality and his dreams.

roles within the New American Cinema of the 1970s—cinematographer Haskell Wexler and editor Dede Allen—*America America* makes prominent use of Wexler's edgy, handheld camera work and Allen's nouvelle vague montage with its abrupt jump cuts and nervous, instinctual rhythm. *The Arrangement*, meanwhile, goes even further to distance itself from the more classical and stylistically understated mode of Kazan's previous studio films by expressing Eddie Anderson's protracted mental and emotional breakdown via a wide range of often audacious and unexpected visual flourishes: rapid jump cuts, cartoon graphics to depict a fantasy fistfight, and comic "fast-forwarding" of both image and dialogue. If Kazan's earlier films are closely inspired by his training and continued work in the theater (he directed almost a play a year during his studio tenure), starting with *America America* his films instead begin to embrace a more overt style and narrative complexity, in keeping with Kazan's reinvention of himself as a novelist. Indeed, if his earlier works use their relative stylistic restraint to frame the intense Method Acting performances for which they are justly famous, in the late work the opposite is true: as the acting grows increasingly subdued, reaching a muted and almost somnambulistic extreme in Kazan's enigmatic final film, *The Last Tycoon*, the narrative and visual style grow more unpredictable and intense, almost as if the films themselves are trying deliberately to outperform the actors.

The bold stylization of Kazan's last four films is also a direct and important expression of their fractured and spatiotemporally ambiguous narrative and stylistic structures. *America America* inaugurates and exemplifies the new formal complexity of Kazan's last films with its use of expressive, often ironic jump cuts and Soviet-style "intellectual" montage, such as the sudden midsentence jump cut, toward the beginning of the film, from a soft-spoken Turkish provincial governor in his office reading aloud an edict from the sultan to a blustery army general in his headquarters who continues the very same sentence, suggesting the ultimate indistinguishability of the repressive institutions each represent. Allen's editing is used to especially powerful effect in the sharp cuts that follow Stavros's letters home by juxtaposing his reassuring lies to his family with the harsh indignities of his hardscrabble life. This editing strategy reaches a tragic extreme in the film's memorable last sequence, which cuts from Stavros, at last in New York City, frantically working as a shoeshine boy and imploring his customers to "Hurry up, people are waiting!" to his family back in Anatolia anxiously watching and waiting as the restive Turkish soldiers round up fellow Greek villagers.

The coexistence of completely parallel and irreconcilable realms suggested by *America America*'s sharp juxtaposition of Old and New World is extended throughout the late films and heightened into an unstable and ambiguous temporal and moral condition. For *America America*'s parallel of the United States and Turkey, more than simply contrasting two very different cultures, also describes the coexistence of two alternate temporal modes. This concept is beautifully evoked in the poetic monologue spoken by Stavros's would-be father-in-law, who rhapsodizes about the pleasures of extended postprandial repose, affectionately describing a life of ritualized and seamlessly intertwined familial and professional obligations, a life in sharp contrast to the accelerated time-clock-driven world of the New York that beckons and eventually engulfs the restless Stavros. In much the same way, *The Arrangement* posits a simultaneity of ultimately dissonant worlds and similarly uses temporal markers to distinguish them. Eddie Anderson's familial home — and the presence of his elderly immigrant parents — exacts a fierce talismanic hold that pulls him back into dizzying extended flashback

In a publicity still from *The Arrangement*, Eddie Anderson (Kirk Douglas) looks into a mirror and remembers the glory days of his father (Richard Boone). Kazan utilized a range of expressive visual techniques to suggest Eddie's inner subjectivity. Photograph by Frank D. Dandridge. Photo courtesy of the Wesleyan Cinema Archives.

sequences that vividly reenact scenes with the older man standing alongside Eddie's former childhood self, reliving the guilt and recriminations forced on him, principally by his father.

Throughout *The Arrangement* and the late films the past resurfaces within the present as a rebuking and frequently menacing force. This is given particularly disturbing form in *The Visitors*, an ominous study of masculinity and violence in which two revenge-seeking Vietnam veterans track down and brutally punish the former fellow soldier who reported their war crimes. The stinging flashback of one of the convicted soldiers to the original battlefield crime — the rape of a young Vietnamese villager — reveals the toxic presence of the past as a damaging influence on the present. In Kazan's eponymous adaptation of F. Scott Fitzgerald's unfinished 1941 novel *The Last Tycoon*, meanwhile, dark conflict wells from the disharmony between Old and New Hollywood, represented by the aging studio executives on the one hand and the "Boy Wonder" Monroe Stahr on the other. The existence on the studio lot of the mausoleum to the deceased wife whom Stahr still mourns and yearns for further underscores the uneasy and unhealthy coexistence within the film of historical past and present.

Studio executive Monroe Stahr (Robert De Niro) enjoys a rare moment of happiness as he dances with the young actress Kathleen Moore (Ingrid Boulting) in a publicity still from *The Last Tycoon*. Photo courtesy of the Wesleyan Cinema Archives.

A certain disorientation of time and space recurs throughout Kazan's late films as a major theme and structural device. In all four films the protagonists—and, to a certain extent, the films themselves—try in vain to reconcile and bridge irreparably separate worlds, drifting uneasily and ambiguously between them. This dilemma, or in-between condition, takes on almost schematic dimensions in the late work—for example, in the figure of the ocean liner that occupies a literal central place in *America America* and whose slow passage between the Old and New World is a figure for Stavros's own limbo state and the crucial decision that awaits him. Equally overt are the two architecturally similar and almost adjoining houses that are the primary location in *The Visitors* and that were in fact the real-life Connecticut homes of Kazan and his son. In contrast to the houses' deceptively similar facades are the radically different lives lived within them: the father, an ardently patriotic World War II veteran, stays up all night working on his Western adventure novels; the disillusioned Vietnam veteran who has married his "peacenik" daughter works a day job at a nearby helicopter factory. The depiction of alternate worlds in *The Last Tycoon* seems especially schematic, if not overdetermined, with Monroe Stahr constantly escaping from his dark and luxuriously appointed studio office to his unfinished shell of a beach house whose empty frame carries overtly symbolic weight, both clearly resembling a cage and, even more significant for Kazan's cinema, a theatrical stage.

The troubled simultaneity of alternate and irreconcilable worlds that is such a defining feature of Kazan's late work also possesses a strong moral dimension, as overt expressions of the grave life decisions made at great cost by the films' central characters. Thus, in *The Arrangement* Eddie's struggle with past and present is also intertwined with his selfish desire to live with both mistress and wife, despite the intense emotional trauma suffered by the two women as a result. The radically different personalities, presences, and ways of life represented by Eddie's dowdy Beverly Hills wife (played with strained dignity by Deborah Kerr) and his Greenwich Village mistress (Faye Dunaway) only heighten the ambiguity of his indecision and inability to make a choice until the very end. One of the more disturbing and problematic aspects of *The Visitors*, certainly one of Kazan's darkest films, is precisely the film's refusal to offer any clear moral judgment or resolution by presenting all of the characters as deeply indecisive and wavering between opposite, extreme emotional states — anger and remorse, violence and self-peace. In the end the film avoids privileging any individual character by suggesting instead that everyone, from the convicted rapist-soldiers to the antiwar couple and the World War II veteran, is somehow responsible, indeed, guilty, for the violent morass of Vietnam.

On one level the recurrent attempts by Kazan's late films to somehow bridge or coexist within two separate and at times conflicting worlds — equally defined as actual, geographical, and moral regions — seem to mark a striking contrast with his earlier work. For the most part Kazan's canonical studio films carefully restrict themselves to a single or only a few evocative locations. This is most famously the case with the Deep South, to which Kazan's work repeatedly returned during the 1950s — from the New Orleans of *Panic in the Streets* (1950) and *A Streetcar Named Desire* to the Mississippi, Tennessee, and Arkansas of *Baby Doll*, *Wild River* (1960), and *A Face in the Crowd* (1957), respectively. With the exception of *A Streetcar Named Desire*, all of these films were shot on actual Southern locations carefully chosen for their authenticity and expressive landscapes. Making judicious use of extended long takes and carefully researched local and period detail, films such as *Wild River* and *Splendor in the Grass* go to great lengths to evoke a depth of feeling for the small town communities that play such a major role within them.

Yet for all of the richly evocative specificity of place that Kazan's classic films so dramatically capture, the same vividly conjured locations also share a deep instability as profoundly emotional sites rich with a sense of imminent loss. Think, for example, of the island community in *Wild River* whose scheduled and irreversible inundation is announced at the very start of the film, or the small midwestern town in *Splendor in the Grass* that quickly comes to stand for the lost love and youth of Deanie and Bud, or even the plague-threatened city in *Panic in the Streets*. Throughout Kazan's films the studio and non-studio locations used so effectively to evoke place represent the home and community that characters are forced either to betray or leave—from the tenement neighborhood in *A Tree Grows in Brooklyn* and the Hoboken docks in *On the Waterfront* to the small towns of *Splendor in the Grass* and *Wild River*. Kazan's canonical films are, above all, dramas hinged upon difficult, almost impossible, choices. In this way the films are haunted by the lingering presence of roads not taken; the places and people left behind lie at the heart of the rich ambiguity nourished by these films.

While Kazan's films of the forties and fifties are clearly, even quintessentially, products of the Hollywood studios, they nevertheless also resist certain aspects of the studio-era narrative cinema, pushing most especially against any type of quick or easy denouement and favoring richly ambiguous endings. Narrative resolution in Kazan's films is instead most often hard won and, in the end, deeply unstable. Indeed, Kazan's most successful films often seem, paradoxically, to be animated by a will to irresolution, an attempt to delay the inevitable decision between two worlds—the choice between the father, the artistic dreamer, and the mother, the steely realist, in *A Tree Grows in Brooklyn*, for example, or the mobsters on the one hand and on the other the alternate family life represented by the young Edie in *On the Waterfront*. In both of these films, of course, the difficult choice is made *for* the characters, decided in each case by the sudden death of the family member who essentially served as an obstacle to change: the father in *A Tree Grows in Brooklyn* and Terry Malloy's brother Charley in *On the Waterfront*. Progressively in Kazan's films, however, such choices are elaborately delayed and then made even more ambiguous once finally decided—as in *Wild River* and *Splendor in the Grass*, where the worlds of the island and the pre-Depression small town are so irreparably lost that any sense of total closure is ultimately denied. In the minds of the characters as well as the audience, the bittersweet endings of these films evoke a haunting commingling of the vanished, extinguished world of the past and the now impoverished present.

Paradoxically, the deepest thematic unity of Kazan's oeuvre lies in the recurrence of disunity and disjunction as dominant motifs and as the underlying structural logic that extends from the very earliest through the last works. The seemingly inevitable corrosion and destruction of familial, amorous, and political bonds is quite striking across Kazan's nineteen features, in which family and community seem always to be sown with the seeds of their own imminent and irreparable destruction. By offering an alternate, reiterative yet increasingly ambiguous variation of the disarray and dissolution so central to Kazan's canonical films, his last four features reveal an important thematic unity within his larger oeuvre. While often overly mannered and not entirely successful, *America America*, *The Arrangement*, *The Visitors*, and *The Last Tycoon* also provocatively address the autobiographical conundrum that is still central to writing on Kazan. Scholars and critics typically search Kazan's films for immediately resonant metaphors of his controversial personal and professional choices, inevitably returning to the same selective iconic moments, such as the final scene in *On the Waterfront*, to alternately find expressions either of Kazan's remorse or stubborn refusal to repent. Yet the late films expose a richer pattern at work within the pained, protracted character decisions that recur throughout Kazan's films, revealing these troubled decisions as a type of intensive narrative motor that furiously propels the films forward while also generating their complex thematic, narrative, and spatiotemporal ambiguities.

Previous page: Photograph by Frank D. Dandridge.
Photo courtesy of the Wesleyan Cinema Archives.

People of the Cumberland
   1937. Documentary. Frontier Films. Directors: Sidney Meyers, Jay Leyda.
   Assistant Director: Elia Kazan. Cinematography: Ralph Steiner.
It's Up to You
   1941. Stage play with film material. U.S. Department of Agriculture.
   Screenplay: Arthur Arent. Music: Earl Robinson. Cast: Helen Tamiris.
A Tree Grows in Brooklyn
   1945. Twentieth Century-Fox. Producer: Louis D. Lighton. Screenplay: Tess
   Slesinger, Frank Davis, Anita Loos. Story: Betty Smith. Cinematography:
   Leon Shamroy. Editing: Dorothy Spencer. Art Direction: Lyle Wheeler.
   Music: Alfred Newman. Cast: Dorothy McGuire (Katie Nolan), Joan Blondell
   (Sissy Edwards), James Dunn (Johnny Nolan), Lloyd Nolan (Officer McShane),
   James Gleason (McGarrity), Ted Donaldson (Neeley Nolan), Peggy Ann Garner
   (Francie Nolan).
The Sea of Grass
   1947. Metro-Goldwyn-Mayer. Producer: Pandro S. Berman. Screenplay:
   Marguerite Roberts, Vincent Lawrence. Story: Conrad Richter. Cinematography:
   Harry Stradling. Editing: Robert J. Kern. Art Direction: Cedric Gibbons, Paul
   Groesse. Music: Herbert Stothart. Cast: Spencer Tracy (Col. James B. Brewton),
   Katharine Hepburn (Lutie Cameron Brewton), Robert Walker (Brock Brewton),
   Melvyn Douglas (Brice Chamberlain).
Boomerang!
   1947. Twentieth Century-Fox. Producer: Louis de Rochemont. Screenplay:
   Richard Murphy. Story: Fulton Ourster. Cinematography: Norbert Brodine.
   Editing: Harmon Jones. Art Direction: Richard Day, Chester Gore. Music: David
   Buttolph. Cast: Dana Andrews (Henry L. Harvey), Jane Wyatt (Madge Harvey),
   Lee J. Cobb (Chief Harold F. Robinson), Cara Williams (Irene Nelson), Arthur
   Kennedy (John Waldron), Sam Levene (Dave Woods), Karl Malden (Detective
   Lieutenant White), Arthur Miller (lineup suspect).
Gentleman's Agreement
   1947. Twentieth Century-Fox. Producer: Darryl F. Zanuck. Screenplay: Moss
   Hart. Story: Laura Z. Hobson. Cinematography: Arthur Miller. Editing:
   Harmon Jones. Art Direction: Lyle Wheeler, Mark-Lee Kirk. Music: Alfred

Newman. Cast: Gregory Peck (Philip Green), Dorothy McGuire (Kathy Lacy), John Garfield (Dave Goldman), Celeste Holm (Anne Dettrey), Anne Revere (Mrs. Green), June Havoc (Elaine Wales), Albert Dekker (John Minify).

Pinky

1949. Twentieth Century-Fox. Producer: Darryl F. Zanuck. Screenplay: Philip Dunne, Dudley Nichols. Story: Cid Ricketts Sumner. Cinematography: Joe MacDonald. Editing: Harmon Jones. Art Direction: Lyle Wheeler, J. Russell Spencer. Music: Alfred Newman. Cast: Jeanne Crain (Patricia "Pinky" Johnson), Ethel Barrymore (Miss Em), Ethel Waters (Pinky's Granny), William Lundigan (Dr. Thomas Adams), Basil Ruysdael (Judge Walker).

Panic in the Streets

1950. Twentieth Century-Fox. Producer: Sol C. Siegel. Screenplay: Richard Murphy, Daniel Fuchs. Story: Edna and Edward Anhalt. Cinematography: Joe MacDonald. Editing: Harmon Jones. Art Direction: Lyle Wheeler, Maurice Ransford. Music: Alfred Newman. Cast: Richard Widmark (Dr. Clinton Reed), Paul Douglas (Police Captain Tom Warren), Barbara Bel Geddes (Nancy Reed), Walter Jack Palance (Blackie), Zero Mostel (Raymond Fitch).

A Streetcar Named Desire

1951. Group Productions/Warner Bros. Producer: Charles K. Feldman. Screenplay: Tennessee Williams, Oscar Saul. Story: Tennessee Williams. Cinematography: Harry Stradling. Editing: David Weisbart. Art Direction: Richard Day. Music: Alex North. Cast: Vivien Leigh (Blanche DuBois), Marlon Brando (Stanley Kowalski), Kim Hunter (Stella Kowalski), Karl Malden (Mitch).

Viva Zapata!

1952. Twentieth Century-Fox. Producer: Darryl F. Zanuck. Screenplay: John Steinbeck. Cinematography: Joe MacDonald. Editing: Barbara McLean. Art Direction: Lyle Wheeler, Leland Fuller. Music: Alex North. Cast: Marlon Brando (Emiliano Zapata), Jean Peters (Josefa Zapata), Anthony Quinn (Eufemio Zapata), Joseph Wiseman (Fernando Aguirre), Arnold Moss (Don Nacio), Alan Reed (Pancho Villa).

Man on a Tightrope

1953. Twentieth Century-Fox. Producer: Robert L. Jacks. Screenplay: Robert E. Sherwood. Story: Neil Paterson. Cinematography: Georg Krause. Editing: Dorothy Spencer. Art Direction: Hans H. Kuhnert, Theo Zwirsky. Music: Franz Waxman. Cast: Fredric March (Karel Cernik), Terry Moore (Tereza Cernik), Gloria Grahame (Zama Cernik), Cameron Mitchell (Joe Vosdek), Adolphe Menjou (Commissioner of Police Fesker).

On the Waterfront

1954. Horizon Pictures/Columbia Pictures. Producer: Sam Spiegel. Screenplay: Budd Schulberg. Story: Budd Schulberg, Malcolm Johnson.

Cinematography: Boris Kaufman. Editing: Gene Milford. Art Direction: Richard Day. Music: Leonard Bernstein. Cast: Marlon Brando (Terry Malloy), Karl Malden (Father Barry), Lee J. Cobb (Johnny Friendly), Rod Steiger (Charley Malloy), Eva Marie Saint (Edie Doyle).

East of Eden

1955. Warner Bros. Producer: Elia Kazan. Screenplay: Paul Osborn. Story: John Steinbeck. Cinematography: Ted McCord. Editing: Owen Marks. Art Direction: James Basevi, Malcolm Bert. Music: Leonard Rosenman. Cast: Julie Harris (Abra), James Dean (Cal Trask), Raymond Massey (Adam Trask), Burl Ives (Sam, the Sheriff), Richard Davalos (Aron Trask), Jo Van Fleet (Kate), Albert Dekker (Will Hamilton).

Baby Doll

1956. Newtown Productions/Warner Bros. Producer: Elia Kazan. Screenplay: Tennessee Williams. Story: Tennessee Williams. Cinematography: Boris Kaufman. Editing: Gene Milford. Art Direction: Richard Sylbert, Paul Sylbert. Music: Kenyon Hopkins. Cast: Karl Malden (Archie Lee Meighan), Carroll Baker (Baby Doll Meighan), Eli Wallach (Silva Vacarro), Mildred Dunnock (Aunt Rose Comfort).

A Face in the Crowd

1957. Newtown Productions/Warner Bros. Producer: Elia Kazan. Screenplay: Budd Schulberg. Story: Budd Schulberg. Cinematography: Harry Stradling, Gayne Rescher. Editing: Gene Milford. Art Direction: Richard Sylbert, Paul Sylbert. Music: Tom Glazer. Cast: Andy Griffith (Lonesome Rhodes), Patricia Neal (Marcia Jeffries), Anthony Franciosa (Joey DePalma), Walter Matthau (Mel Miller), Lee Remick (Betty Lou Fleckum).

Wild River

1960. Twentieth Century-Fox. Producer: Elia Kazan. Screenplay: Paul Osborn. Story: William Bradford Huie, Borden Deal. Cinematography: Ellsworth Fredericks. Editing: William Reynolds. Art Direction: Lyle Wheeler, Herman A. Blumenthal. Music: Kenyon Hopkins. Cast: Montgomery Clift (Chuck Glover), Lee Remick (Carol Garth), Jo Van Fleet (Ella Garth).

Splendor in the Grass

1961. Newtown Productions/NBI/Warner Bros. Producer: Elia Kazan. Screenplay: William Inge. Cinematography: Boris Kaufman. Editing: Gene Milford. Production Design: Richard Sylbert. Music: David Amram. Cast: Natalie Wood (Deanie Loomis), Warren Beatty (Bud Stamper), Pat Hingle (Ace Stamper), Audrey Christie (Mrs. Loomis), Barbara Loden (Ginny Stamper), Zohra Lampert (Angelina).

America America

1963. Athena Enterprises/Warner Bros. Producer: Elia Kazan. Screenplay: Elia Kazan. Story: Elia Kazan. Cinematography: Haskell Wexler. Editing:

Dede Allen. Production Design: Gene Callahan. Music: Manos Hadjidakis. Cast: Stathis Giallelis (Stavros Topouzoglou), Frank Wolff (Vartan Damadian), Elena Karam (Vasso Topouzoglou), Harry Davis (Isaac Topouzoglou).

The Arrangement

1969. Athena Enterprises/Warner Bros.-Seven Arts. Producer: Elia Kazan. Screenplay: Elia Kazan. Story: Elia Kazan. Cinematography: Robert Surtees. Editing: Stefan Arnsten. Production Design: Gene Callahan. Music: David Amram. Cast: Kirk Douglas (Eddie Anderson), Faye Dunaway (Gwen), Deborah Kerr (Florence Anderson), Richard Boone (Sam Anderson), Hume Cronyn (Arthur).

The Visitors

1972. Home Free/United Artists. Producer: Chris Kazan, Nicholas T. Proferes. Screenplay: Chris Kazan. Cinematography: Nicholas T. Proferes. Editing: Nicholas T. Proferes. Cast: Patrick McVey (Harry Wayne), Patricia Joyce (Martha Wayne), James Woods (Bill Schmidt), Steve Railsback (Mike Nickerson), Chico Martinez (Tony Rodrigues).

The Last Tycoon

1976. Paramount. Producer: Sam Spiegel. Screenplay: Harold Pinter. Story: F. Scott Fitzgerald. Cinematography: Victor Kemper. Editing: Richard Marks. Production Design: Gene Callahan. Music: Maurice Jarre. Cast: Robert De Niro (Monroe Stahr), Tony Curtis (Rodriguez), Robert Mitchum (Pat Brady), Jeanne Moreau (Didi), Jack Nicholson (Brimmer), Donald Pleasence (Boxley), Ray Milland (Fleishacker), Dana Andrews (Red Ridingwood), Ingrid Boulting (Kathleen Moore), Theresa Russell (Cecilia Brady).

Alpert, Hollis. "Fitzgerald, Hollywood, and *The Last Tycoon.*" *American Film* 1, 5 (March 1976), 8–13.

Anderson, Lindsay. "The Last Sequence of *On the Waterfront.*" *Sight and Sound* 24, 3 (1955), 127–130.

Baer, William, ed. *Elia Kazan Interviews.* Jackson: University Press of Mississippi, 2000.

Basinger, Jeanine, John Frazer, and Joseph W. Reed, Jr., eds. *Working with Kazan.* Middletown, Conn.: Wesleyan University, 1973.

Behlmer, Rudy, ed. *Memo from Darryl Zanuck.* New York: Grove, 1993.

Bosworth, Patricia. "Kazan's Choice." *Vanity Fair*, September 1999, 165–184.

Braudy, Leo. *On the Waterfront.* London: BFI, 2005.

Brook, Vincent. "Courting Controversy: The Making and Selling of *Baby Doll* and the Demise of the Production Code." *Quarterly Review of Film and Video* 18, 4 (2001), 347–360.

Butler, Jeremy G. "*Viva Zapata!*: HUAC and the Mexican Revolution." In Donald R. Noble, ed., *The Steinbeck Question: New Essays in Criticism* (Troy, N.Y.: Whitston, 1993), 239–250.

Butler, Terence. "Polonsky and Kazan." *Sight and Sound* 57, 4 (Autumn 1988), 262–267.

Changas, Estelle. "Elia Kazan's America." *Film Comment* 8, 2 (Summer 1972), 8–19.

Chase, Donald. "*Wild River.*" *Film Comment* 32, 6 (November/December 1996), 10–15.

Ciment, Michel. *Kazan on Kazan.* New York: Viking Press, 1974.

Collins, Gary. "Kazan in the Fifties." *The Velvet Light Trap* 11 (Winter 1974), 41–45.

Colombani, Florence. *Elia Kazan: Une Amérique du Chaos.* Paris: Philippe Rey, 2004.

Cuevas, Efrén. *Elia Kazan.* Madrid: Cátedra, 2000.

Delahaye, Michael. Interview with Elia Kazan. *Cahiers du Cinéma in English* (March 1967) 13–35.

Fitzgerald, F. Scott. *The Last Tycoon.* Edited by Edmund Wilson. New York: Scribner's, 1941.

Garfield, David. *A Player's Place: The Story of the Actors Studio.* New York: Macmillan, 1980.

Gavin, Arthur. "The Photography of *East of Eden.*" *American Photographer* (March 1955), 149, 169–172.

Georgakas, Dan. "Don't Call Him 'Gadget': A Reconsideration of Elia Kazan."
    Cineaste 11, 4 (1982), 7–15, 39.
Girgus, Sam B. *Hollywood Renaissance: The Cinema of Democracy in the Era of Ford,
    Capra, and Kazan.* Cambridge: Cambridge University Press, 1998.
Hirsch, Foster. *A Method to Their Madness: The History of the Actors Studio.* New
    York: Norton, 1984.
Ingersoll, Earl G. "Bringing the (Gender) War Home: Vietnam and Elia Kazan's
    The Visitors." Post Script 17, 3 (Summer 1998), 55–68.
Jones, David Richard. *Great Directors at Work: Stanislavsky, Brecht, Kazan, Brook.*
    Berkeley: University of California Press, 1986.
Kaufman, Boris. "Filming *Baby Doll." American Cinematographer* 38, 2 (February
    1957), 92–93, 106.
Kazan, Elia. *Acts of Love.* New York: Knopf, 1978.
Kazan, Elia. *America America.* New York: Stein and Day, 1961.
Kazan, Elia. *An American Odyssey.* Edited by Michel Ciment. London: Bloomsbury,
    1988.
Kazan, Elia. *The Anatolian.* New York: Knopf, 1982.
Kazan, Elia. *The Arrangement.* New York: Stein and Day, 1967.
Kazan, Elia. *The Assassins.* New York: Stein and Day, 1972.
Kazan, Elia. *Beyond the Aegean.* New York: Knopf, 1994.
Kazan, Elia. *Elia Kazan: A Life.* New York: Knopf, 1988.
Kazan, Elia. *Kazan on Directing.* New York: Knopf, 2009.
Kazan, Elia. *A Kazan Reader.* New York: Stein and Day, 1977.
Kazan, Elia. Letter to the editor. *Saturday Review,* 5 April 1952, 22–23.
Kazan, Elia. Letter to the editor. *Saturday Review,* 24 May 1952, 28.
Kazan, Elia. "Pressure Problem." *New York Times,* 21 October 1951, sec. 2, p. 5.
Kazan, Elia. *The Understudy.* New York: Stein and Day, 1975.
Kolin, Philip C. "Civil Rights and the Black Presence in *Baby Doll." Literature Film
    Quarterly* 24, 1 (1996), 2–11.
Krutnik, Frank, Steve Neale, Brian Neve, and Peter Stanfield, eds. *"Un-American
    Hollywood": Politics and Film in the Blacklist Era.* New Brunswick, N.J.: Rutgers
    University Press, 2007.
Lafferty, William. "A Reappraisal of the Semi-documentary in Hollywood,
    1945–1948." *Velvet Light Trap* 20 (1983), 22–26.
Lightman, Herb A. "The Filming of *Viva Zapata!" American Cinematographer* 33, 4
    (April 1952), 154–155, 183.
Michaels, Lloyd. *Elia Kazan: A Guide to References and Resources.* Boston: Hall, 1985.
Morton, Frederic. "Gadg." *Esquire,* February 1957.
Movie, special issue on Elia Kazan, 19 (Winter 1971–72).
Murphy, Brenda. *Tennessee Williams and Elia Kazan: A Collaboration in the Theatre.*
    Cambridge: Cambridge University Press, 2003.

Navasky, Victor S. *Naming Names*. New York: Penguin, 1980.

Neal, Patricia. "What Kazan Did for Me." *Films and Filming* (October 1957), 9.

Neve, Brian. "Elia Kazan's First Testimony to the House Committee on Un-American Activities, Executive Session, 14 January 1952." *Historical Journal of Film, Radio, and Television* 25, 2 (June 2005), 251–272.

Neve, Brian. *Elia Kazan: The Cinema of an American Outsider*. London: I. B. Tauris, 2009.

Pauly, Thomas H. *An American Odyssey: Elia Kazan and American Culture*. Philadelphia: Temple University Press, 1983.

Pettit, Arthur. "*Viva Zapata!* A Tribute to Steinbeck, Kazan and Brando." *Film & History* (May 1977), 25–45.

Positif, Revue Mensuelle de Cinéma, articles on Elia Kazan, 241 (April 1981), 2–21.

Positif, Revue Mensuelle de Cinéma, "Dossier," Elia Kazan, 518 (April 2004), 78–104.

Rapf, Joanna E. "*The Last Tycoon* or 'A Nickel for the Movies.'" *Literature Film Quarterly* 16 (1988), 76–81.

Rapf, Joanna E., ed. *On the Waterfront*. Cambridge: Cambridge University Press, 2003.

Sarris, Andrew. *The American Cinema: Directors and Directions, 1929–1968*. New York: Dutton, 1968.

Schickel, Richard. *Elia Kazan: A Biography*. New York: HarperCollins, 2005.

Schulberg, Budd. *A Face in the Crowd: A Play for the Screen*. New York: Random House, 1957.

Schulberg, Budd. *On the Waterfront: A Screenplay*. Carbondale: Southern Illinois University Press, 1980.

Shelton, Lewis. "Elia Kazan and the American Tradition of Direction." *A & S: The Magazine of the College of Arts and Sciences* [Kansas State University], Spring 1983.

Silver, Charles. "Elia Kazan's *Wild River*." *Studies in Modern Art* 1 (1991), 165–181.

Smith, Wendy. *Real Life Drama: The Group Theatre and America, 1931–1940*. New York: Knopf, 1990.

Staggs, Sam. *When Blanche Met Brando: The Scandalous Story of "A Streetcar Named Desire."* New York: St. Martin's Press, 2005.

Steinbeck, John. *Zapata*. New York: Penguin, 1993.

Stevens, George, Jr., ed. *Conversations with the Great Moviemakers of Hollywood's Golden Age*. New York: Knopf, 2006.

Tailleur, Roger. *Elia Kazan*. Paris: Éditions Seghers, 1971.

Williams, Tennessee. *Baby Doll, The Script for the Film*. Harmondsworth, England: Penguin, 1957.

Williams, Tennessee. *A Streetcar Named Desire*. New York: New Directions, 2004.

Wood, Robin. "The Kazan Problem." *Movie* 19 (Winter 1971–72), 29–31.

Young, Jeff. *Kazan: The Master Director Discusses His Films*. New York: Newmarket, 1999.

CONTRIBUTORS

JEANINE BASINGER is Corwin-Fuller Professor of Film Studies at Wesleyan University, the curator of the Elia Kazan papers, and the author of nine books, including *The Star Machine*.

LEO BRAUDY is University Professor and Bing Professor of English and American Literature at the University of Southern California. Among other books, he is the author of the British Film Institute *On the Waterfront* volume, *The World in a Frame: What We See in Films*, and the coeditor of the anthology *Film Theory and Criticism*, now in its seventh edition.

LISA DOMBROWSKI is associate professor of Film Studies at Wesleyan University and the author of *The Films of Samuel Fuller: If You Die, I'll Kill You!* She researches the art and industry of motion pictures.

HADEN GUEST is director of the Harvard Film Archive and lecturer in Film and Visual Culture at Harvard University. A film historian, with a Ph.D. from the University of California, Los Angeles, Guest is completing an anthology of unpublished and unwritten writings by Sam Fuller, a critical history of the American police procedural film between 1930 and 1960, and a study of Pedro Costa's cinema.

MARK HARRIS is the author of *Pictures at a Revolution: Five Movies and the Birth of the New Hollywood*. His next book, on Hollywood studios during World War II, will be published in 2012. He is a columnist for *Entertainment Weekly* and frequently writes for *New York*, the *New York Times*, and several other publications.

KENT JONES regularly contributes to *Film Comment* and other magazines and websites, and a collection of his writing, *Physical Evidence*, was published by Wesleyan University Press in 2007. He is the writer and director of the 2007 film *Val Lewton: The Man in the Shadows*. He has worked on several documentaries for Martin Scorsese, including a film about Elia Kazan, *A Letter toElia*, which they cowrote and directed. He is now the Executive Director of The World Cinema Foundation.

PATRICK KEATING is the author of *Hollywood Lighting from the Silent Era to Film Noir*. He is an assistant professor in the Department of Communication at Trinity University, where he teaches courses in film and media studies.

SAVANNAH LEE holds a Ph.D. in art history from the University of Wisconsin, Madison. Her fiction has appeared in *Blue Earth Review*, *Neo-opsis*, *Clean Sheets*, the *Mammoth Book of Best New Erotica 8*, and the forthcoming *Mammoth Book of Best New Erotica 9*, the latter two edited by Maxim Jakubowski.

BRENDA MURPHY is Board of Trustees Distinguished Professor of English at the University of Connecticut. She has written a number of articles about Elia Kazan, as well as *Tennessee Williams and Elia Kazan: A Collaboration in the Theatre*, and *Congressional Theatre: Dramatizing McCarthyism on Stage, Film, and Television*. Among her other books are *The Provincetown Players and the Culture of Modernity*, and *American Realism and American Drama, 1880–1940*.

VICTOR NAVASKY, the former editor and publisher of the *Nation*, is professor of journalism at Columbia University, chairman of the *Columbia Journalism Review*, and author of *Naming Names*, which won a National Book Award.

BRIAN NEVE teaches film and politics at the University of Bath. Among his publications are *Film and Politics in America: A Social Tradition*, and *Elia Kazan: The Cinema of an American Outsider*. He is also joint editor of *"Un-American" Hollywood: Politics and Film in the Blacklist Era*.

JONATHAN ROSENBAUM was principal film critic for the *Chicago Reader* from 1987 through early 2007. His most recent books include *Goodbye Cinema, Hello Cinephilia*, *Discovering Orson Welles*, and *Essential Cinema*, and his website is jonathanrosenbaum.com.

RICHARD SCHICKEL is the author of more than thirty books, the latest of which is *Clint: A Retrospective*, and producer-writer-director of a similar number of documentary films, mainly about films and filmmaking. He was for over four decades a movie reviewer for major magazines.

ANDREW TRACY is the managing editor of *Cinema Scope* and a contributor to *Cineaste*, *Film Comment*, *Reverse Shot*, *Moving Image Source*, and other publications. He is currently pursuing a Ph.D. in history at the University of Toronto.

SAM WASSON is the author of *A Splurch in the Kisser: The Movies of Blake Edwards* and *Fifth Avenue, 5 AM: Audrey Hepburn, Breakfast at Tiffany's, and The Dawn of the Modern Woman*. His latest book, *Paul on Mazursky*, is to be published by Wesleyan University Press in 2011. He lives in Los Angeles.

Page numbers in italics refer to illustrations.

Bordwell, David, 149, 176n
Bosworth, Patricia, 111
Boulting, Ingrid, 21, *194*
Boyle, Peter, ix
Brando, Marlon, ix, 3, 8, 18, 20, 105, 112, 134, 145–46, 163, 185; in *On the Waterfront*, 13, 30–31, 38, 51, 130; in *A Streetcar Named Desire*, 103, *104*, 107–8, 115–16, 121, 129; in *Viva Zapata!* *39*, *40*, 42
Brecht, Bertolt, 44
Brodine, Norbert, 150
Brooks, Richard, 29
Bus Stop, 26

Cabinet of Dr. Caligari, 17, 30
Cagney, James, 135
Cahiers du Cinéma, 37
Callahan, Gene, 21
Call Northside 777, 135, 137, 149, *150*, 160
Camino Real, 70
Capra, Frank, 1
Carey, Timothy, 30
Casablanca, 62, 64
Cassavetes, John, 88
Cat on a Hot Tin Roof, ix, 25, 28
Cesar, 81
Chapman, Lonny, 83
Chekhov, Anton, 185
Cherry Orchard, The, 185
Christie, Audrey, 125
Ciment, Michel, 50, 111, 133, 143, 170, 172
CinemaScope, xiii, 30, 34–35, 163–76
Cirkus Brumbach, 59, 60, 62, 67–68
Clift, Montgomery, ix, xiv, 8, 13, 15, 21, 22, 23, *34*, 35, 103, 107, 110–12, 115, 172, 173, *174*, 184–85, *186*, 187
Cobb, Lee J., 14, 20, 32, 51, 139, *141*
Columbia Pictures, 76
comedy in Kazan's films, xii, 32, 81, 83–84, 89–98

Communist Party of the United States (CPUSA): Kazan's membership in, x, 20, 56, 189; Kazan's opinion of, 49–55, 57–59
compositions in Kazan's films, 30, 152–53, 157–61, 166–69, 170–75
Confessions of a Nazi Spy, 135
Cornfield, Robert, 26–27
Crain, Jeanne, 33, 116–17, *119*, 121
Crawford, Cheryl, 42
Crowther, Bosley, 81
Curtis, Tony, 26

Dark at the Top of the Stairs, The, 26, 28
Dassin, Jules, 19, 137, 142
Davalos, Richard, 112, 165
Day of the Locust, The, 26
Dean, Alexander, 164–65
Dean, James, ix, 3, 8, 13–14, 28, 29–30, *101*, 103, 107, 110, 112, 113, 115, 163, 165–66, *168*, 185
Dean, John, 49
Death of a Salesman, ix, 28, 57, 83
Dehner, John, 65
Dekker, Albert, 166, *168*
Demme, Jonathan, 1
De Niro, Robert, 21, 26, *194*
de Rochemont, Louis, 18, 135, 149–50
Dimendberg, Edward, 156
Douglas, Kirk, 19, *190*, *193*
Douglas, Paul, 16, 20, 142, 154
Dudley, John S., 84
Dunaway, Faye, 195
Dunn, James, 8
Dunnock, Mildred, 83

East of Eden, ii, ix, xiii, 28, 31, 33–35, 43, 73, 75–76, 99n, *101*, 113, *168*, 184, 188–89; characters, 28, 110, 112–15, 165–67; performances, 14, 107, 186; queer reading of, 112–15; story, 112,

men in Kazan's films, xiii–xiv, 7–8,
20–21, 23, 34, 64, 103–15, 124–25,
143–45, 165–67, 183–85, 189–90
Menjou, Adolphe, 62, 64, 65, 71n
method acting, ix, 6, 17–18, 27, 88, 90–91,
163, 191
Metro-Goldwyn-Mayer (MGM), 18, 26,
77, 133
Metty, Russell, 16
Miller, Arthur, ix, 38, 51, 100, 116
Minnelli, Vincente, xiii, 17–18, 77, 176
Minotis, Alex, 160
Mitchell, Cameron, 62
Mitchum, Robert, 17, 25
Mizoguchi, Kenji, 171
Moon Is Blue, The, 77
Moore, Terry, 62
Morton, Frederic, 79
Mostel, Zero, 15, 20, 143, 161
Mulligan, Robert, 29
Murphy, Brenda, 38
Murphy, Richard, 137, 142, 154–55

Naked City, The, 19, 137, 142
Neal, Patricia, 95, 96, 105
Neve, Brian, 134, 155
Newtown Productions, xii, 76–78, 80,
84–85
Nolan, Lloyd, 135
North, Alex, 75

Odets, Clifford, 46, 183
On Dangerous Ground, 17
On the Waterfront, ix, xi–xii, 13, 17, 20, 33,
56, 77, 84, 94, 116, 133, 145, 189; characters, 146; performances, 14, 30–31,
38; production, 76; reception, 89–90;
relation to Kazan's HUAC testimony,
51, 70; story, 135; style, 32, 130, 163–64;
themes, 13, 30–32, 162n, 196–97
Orzazewski, Kasia, 149, 150

Osborn, Paul, 30, 35, 75, 112, 165, 184
Oursler, Fulton, 137
Outbreak. See *Panic in the Streets*

Pagnol, Marcel, 43, 81
Palance, Jack, 15, 20, 29, 143
Panic in the Streets, xi–xiii, 5, 15, 29, 32,
43, 47, 56, 63, 67, 136, 144, 148, 158–59;
characters, 143–45; narrative struc-
ture, 151, 154–55, 160; story, 142–43;
style, 18–20, 133–34, 142–43, 150–51,
155–61, 163–64, 195; themes, 143–46,
154–55, 157–61, 196–97
Parker, Wyman, 1
Parks, Rosa, 82
Pauly, Thomas, 56, 133, 143–44
Peck, Gregory, 33
People of the Cumberland, 27, 136, 172, 182
performances in Kazan's films, 13–14,
22–23, 26–27, 29–32, 38–39, 88, 93, 97,
100, 107–8, 111, 184–86
Perkins, Osgood, 17
Perkins, V. F., 177n
Peters, Jean, 41
Peyton Place, 109
Phenix City Story, The, 29
Picnic, 26
Pie in the Sky, 27
Pinky, xiii, 20, 29, 33, 57, 116, 119, 133; cast-
ing, 118; characters, 117–21, 128–29;
story, 117–18; style, 118; themes, 120–21
Pinter, Harold, 21, 26, 81
Plumer, Rose, 28
Pollack, Sydney, 29
Port of Entry. See *Panic in the Streets*
Preminger, Otto, xiii, 77, 176–77
Production Code Administration
(PCA), 75, 77, 82, 103

Queen of Sheba, 60, 70n
Quinn, Anthony, 38

WESLEYAN FILM

A series from Wesleyan University Press
Edited by Lisa Dombrowski and Scott Higgins
Originating editor: Jeanine Basinger